7⁵ℓ

THE SOUTHERN EXPANSION OF THE CHINESE PEOPLE
"Southern Fields and Southern Ocean"

By the same author:
CHINA: A SHORT CULTURAL HISTORY
THE TOWER OF FIVE GLORIES
THE EMPRESS WU
FLOOD TIDE IN CHINA
THE BIRTH OF COMMUNIST CHINA
BARBARIAN BEDS

THE SOUTHERN EXPANSION
OF THE CHINESE PEOPLE

"Southern Fields and Southern Ocean"

by

C. P. FitzGerald

AUSTRALIAN NATIONAL UNIVERSITY PRESS
CANBERRA

1972

First published in Australia by
Australian National University Press
Canberra

National Library of Australia Card no. and
ISBN 0 7081 0220 4

*Printed in Great Britain by Richard Clay (The Chaucer Press) Ltd,
Bungay, Suffolk*

For millions of years
Our skies have been joined by the same
   clouds,
Our fields nurtured by the same rain;
Now, you have broken through the vast
   south western ocean
And come to China.

Poem by Ch'eng Tsu recorded
in the *Ming Shih*, Chap. 225, p. 66
Po-Na Edition.

CONTENTS

CONTENTS

LIST OF ILLUSTRATIONS

ACKNOWLEDGEMENTS

The research on which this work is based was done in the Department of Far Eastern History, and for the later chapters in the Department of International Relations, in the Institute of Advanced Studies, Australian National University. My thanks are due to colleagues in these departments for their suggestions and criticisms when some of the themes of this book were subjected to analysis in seminars. I owe valuable indications of available source material to Dr I. de Rachewiltz and to Professor Wang Gungwu in respect of the overseas Chinese communities in South East Asia. I have drawn largely upon Dr Stephen FitzGerald's work on Chinese Communist policy towards the overseas Chinese for the interpretation of the most recent phase of this relationship.

Dr Wang Ling has most kindly supplied the Chinese calligraphy for the poem by Ch'eng Tsu of the Ming Dynasty. The Cartography Section of the Department of Geography, Research School of Pacific Studies, Australian National University, have my thanks for the preparation of the maps. The plans of Chinese cities and Khmer temples were drawn from the source materials by Miss M. A. C. FitzGerald. For the typing of the manuscript I have to thank Mrs Nicola Dawson.

C. P. FitzGerald.

INTRODUCTION

Chinese influence, Chinese culture and Chinese power have always moved southward since the first age of which we have reliable historical evidence. When "China" meant the ancient confederacy of states acknowledging the overlordship of the Chou dynasty, Son of Heaven, and covered only the basin of the Yellow River, her influence, and soon her culture, began to penetrate the then alien peoples of the Yangtze valley. A few centuries later political power followed, and by the end of the first millennium B.C. the central provinces of what is now China were firmly attached to the new empire, even if their inhabitants were still very largely native peoples. By the end of the Han dynasty in 221 south China, the modern provinces of Kuangtung and Fukien, had also been incorporated and hegemony was exercised over what is now part of North Vietnam. The south-west of modern China remained beyond the frontier.

Throughout the centuries that followed down to modern times the southward spread of Chinese civilisation, followed by settlement and political control, continued. The Canton region was fully settled in the T'ang period, and its people still look back to that age (seventh to early tenth centuries A.D.) as the time of greatest colonisation and cultural advance. The Yangtze valley had long been annexed, but the provinces along the tributary rivers which flow northward to the Yangtze were not settled by Chinese of Han ethnic origin until the fourth to sixth centuries A.D. Consolidation of this new Chinese region was completed under the Southern Sung dynasty, when the capital itself was situated in the south China city of Hangchou. The Mongol invaders first conquered the south-west, Yünnan, and their Ming successors (1368–1644) settled that province. Kueichou, mountainous, poor and inaccessible was finally reduced to provincial status under the Manchu (Ch'ing) dynasty in the eighteenth century.

This brought the limits of the Chinese empire to the present frontiers of the Peoples' Republic, but the frontier, especially in the region south of Kuangtung province, was not established on its present alignment in earlier times. For long periods China ruled directly in the basin of the Red River, or Tongking, the heart of modern North Vietnam. On the other hand at those periods Yünnan, now Chinese, was then a foreign and often hostile kingdom. The frontier of today is the exact reverse of the frontier in T'ang and Sung times. Then Tongking was Chinese, and the border at Lao Kay faced the kingdom of Nanchao, ruled from Tali in Yünnan; today it is Yünnan which is Chinese, and Tongking is part of North Vietnam.

The purpose of this book is to examine the story of the southward expansion of China and her cultural influence both in the lands most directly affected by it (Vietnam, north and south, Yünnan, which ended within the empire) and the further countries of Laos, Cambodia, Thailand and Burma, which all to varying degrees came under this influence and acknowledged the power of China. Beyond these countries were others, Malaya, Java, Sumatra and Borneo, which experienced the influence of China and from time to time her political power also, but which did not until the modern inflow of Chinese settlers have such direct and intimate relations as those lands nearer to the frontiers of the empire. Yünnan is a special case, a kind of test to which the whole process of Chinese cultural and political expansion can be subjected. It could be seen as the model which further expansion would follow, if or when it becomes politically feasible; or it can be seen as the furthest probable limit of Chinese incorporation of a region formerly non-Chinese. Therefore the story of Yünnan will be given special attention, partly because of this intrinsic importance to the whole problem, and partly because it is very little known to Western readers.

Chinese expansion was not confined to the southern regions; Korea in the north-east was at various times directly ruled by China, and remained a sphere of strong Chinese influence, both cultural and political. China also won from the nomadic peoples of the far north, her age-old foes, the fertile and enormous provinces of Manchuria—the North-East as the Chinese call it. The borderlands beyond the Great Wall, the ancient meeting-place of the Desert and the Sown, now Inner Mongolia, an Autonomous Region of the Peoples' Republic, has been very heavily settled by immigrant Chinese from the near-by northern provinces. China, also, from Han times onward, exercised an intermittent sovereignty over the vast semi-desert territory of Sinkiang (Chinese Turkestan) in the north-west. This region, too, has been fully incorporated in the Peoples' Republic, and on account of its mineral resources, has received large-scale Chinese immigration. Tibet, for long a tenacious and dangerous enemy in the T'ang period, was conquered by the Manchus, lost under the early Republic, and reoccupied under the Peoples' Republic of China. Today it is firmly claimed as "part of China".

This book will not deal with the northern expansion, which in its cultural aspect has been treated very fully by scholars of Japanese history and those engaged in the study of the nomad peoples of Mongolia. Chinese relations with Korea and with the various peoples of Mongolia was the main theme of Chinese foreign policy throughout the centuries. These countries were close to the capital (almost always in the north), and their hostile power could strike at the heart of the empire, resulting in two total conquests and two which were confined to north China. The southern frontier was less dramatic. No power arose in the south capable of challenging the rulers of China, nor even of arresting for long the slow, steady spread of her southward drive. Yet it was in the south that Chinese civilisation came into direct contact with cultural influence emanating from another great centre of civilisation, India. The question in the north was more how far Chinese power could prevail over peoples who, although militant and fierce, had no rival ideology to proffer, and no artistic contribution strong enough to contend against the Chinese influence. In the south the Chinese met in the Hinduised kingdoms of Cambodia, Burma and Thailand such a rival force, and it has generally been assumed that Chinese culture did not in fact penetrate deeply into these countries. One purpose of this book is to test that assumption, especially in the less obvious fields of government and in some of the underlying aspects of art.

Modern circumstances such as the Russian colonisation of Siberia and the rise of Japan to the stature of a great power, even if one temporarily in military eclipse, have, it would seem, set a permanent limit to northward Chinese expansion and settlement. This is clearly not true of the southern borderlands. No local power, nor combination of powers, could unaided resist the authority of China today. The continuance of intervention or protection by great powers from beyond the seas must be regarded, historically, as uncertain, probably intermittent or temporary, and ultimately ineffective. It is not the main purpose of this book to examine present policies nor predict the immediate future; it is intended to seek to provide the background facts, the indications which the long course of history affords, to consider trends which have existed centuries before the present political configuration took shape, and which, it may be hazarded, will not easily be reversed or halted in the ages to come.

The phenomenon of Chinese cultural expansion and migratory settlement in new lands is not to be associated with particular policies or with contemporary régimes. It has proved to be one of the most enduring features of all Chinese history, beginning long before unity had been achieved within the future Chinese empire, independent of the nature of the government in power, and very often indifferent to the disapproval of that government. The action of the Chinese government, when it occurred at all, was the last event in a long series; the essential steps were taken by peasant farmers, merchants, pilgrims, refugees, pirates and adventurers.

The range of Chinese influence in her southern borderlands falls naturally into four categories. Yünnan, the region which was finally incorporated fully into the body of the Chinese empire; Vietnam, which received the culture but rejected the authority; Cambodia, Laos, Thailand and Burma, where the main features of Chinese culture are not apparent, but political influence was strong and pervasive; lastly Malaya and the Indonesian islands where in modern times massive Chinese immigration deeply affected the economy, the ethnic character and more recently the political life of countries which in earlier times had seemed only marginally concerned with China and only very occasionally affected by her power. Chinese influence itself also falls into differing categories. The direct influence of political power was rarely the most significant manifestation. It was in all these countries intermittent, dependent on the authority, greater or lesser, of the dynasty ruling in China and the ambitions of emperors, who were for the most part more preoccupied with the northern than with the southern borderlands, and very largely unconcerned either with the emigration of Chinese or with their activities when they had left the empire.

Artistic and cultural influence can more often be detected by examining works of art and literature, or by archaeological discovery, than by literary record. The great majority of those Chinese who voyaged south, either to settle or to trade were not men of higher education in their own culture. The Buddhist pilgrims, who were, did not continue to visit the southern lands after the decay of Buddhism in India and the rise of Islam in South-East Asia. Extant accounts by Chinese travellers after the end of the pilgrim era are late, or relatively late, mainly from the early Ming period. The nature and extent of Chinese trade with many of these countries is more easily disclosed by the quantity and character of the Chinese artifacts found in them than by any record remaining in literature or in official documents. Chinese imperial governments were not interested in trade unless it could be conveniently taxed. It may be surmised that the considerable volume which trade with the South-East Asian countries clearly attained at a fairly early period is evidence that such trade largely escaped the attentions of the imperial officials.

Much of the influence which China exercised thus remains anonymous. It is evident to any traveller that the Chinese culinary art has made a deep and beneficial impression on cooking in the whole southern region; but the adoption of these habits remains undated and unrecorded. Nor is it at all soundly established when and in what numbers Chinese migrants first settled in the countries of the south. There are some references to Chinese communities from a relatively early date, but no record of their growth or foundation. Those overseas Chinese who became educated and literate looked to the homeland and rarely, until modern times, concerned themselves with the countries in which they lived. It is by considering the situation in Yünnan that some light can be thrown, if only by the rather doubtful process of analogy, on what may have happened in other lands at an earlier, or even at a contemporary period. In Yünnan there are many indigenous or non-Han Chinese peoples in varying states of assimilation. It is possible to identify the stages through which assimilation has passed, or still proceeds. The penetration of the intrepid Chinese trader into tribes which are normally hostile to all strangers is well attested as probably the first step. He buys native products which have a rarity value in China; he sells Chinese products for which the tribesmen feel a need. Step by step he becomes more readily welcome and acceptable, he can establish a more permanent footing; his descendants settle.

The local language borrows from Chinese many terms which it did not use before, adds many new words for new artifacts and for ideas which it has now to express. Gradually it becomes a quasi-Chinese dialect, pronounced in a fashion almost unintelligible to Han Chinese, but none the less strongly marked by Chinese linguistic influence. It is not written, only spoken. As the wealthier members of the community begin to seek education, they turn to Chinese literature as the sole medium of expression open to them. They become bilingual, and later, perhaps, abandon the native language altogether. Those who have reached this stage are considered to be "Chinese". In this sense many millions of south Chinese are the descendants of peoples who were once quite alien both in speech and custom. In Yünnan, also, there is surviving evidence of the clash of cultures, for in this country there was originally a degree of Hindu influence exercised through Buddhism, which seems to have reached Yünnan by an overland route across Burma, and not either from the Chinese coast or from the northern route across central Asia. In this way Yünnan is akin to the countries of continental South-East Asia. Some surviving practices, and in the western border districts forms of Buddhism differing from those prevailing in China, attest this connection. There is also in Yünnan evidence of the tensions created by the adoption of Chinese social customs by peoples who traditionally had a differing pattern of culture. A sense of detachment from the rest of China is still manifest in habits of speech and thought.

One important influence in the spread of Chinese culture in the borderlands is missing from the countries which have remained beyond imperial jurisdiction. It was customary for many centuries to send political offenders, and also some criminals, into exile in remote parts of the empire.

Few of these ever returned to the north, and their descendants settled in the area to which the original exile had been consigned. In the T'ang period the region of Canton was a favourite place for such exiles, and many Cantonese families trace their origin to seventh-century officials who were sent away to what was then a raw frontier province. The practice continued in the Sung period (960–1278) but in Ming times Kuangtung and the far south were no longer considered fit places for exiles to go to. They were henceforth sent to the newly-acquired south-western province of Yünnan. The Manchu dynasty (occasionally varying the practice by sending political offenders to Sinkiang in the far north-west) also sent many exiles to Yünnan. In some parts of the province these were so numerous that they imposed the dialect of their native place upon their new enforced home, and it has continued to the present time.

There can be no doubt that the influence of these exiles was great. They came from the most educated and politically conscious class, they derived from provinces and cities of high culture and sophistication. They certainly tried to recapture some part of this way of life in their distant place of exile. In striking contrast to the mass of the immigrant Han Chinese, who were either ex-soldiers or peasant and small merchant pioneers, the exiles brought in a direct tradition from the mainstream of Chinese culture. It is never apparent that the exiles cherished feelings of hatred and revenge against the government which had banished them; they were, perhaps, for a time buoyed up with the hope that some change at Court would lead to their restitution to office and their homes. This sometimes happened. But for the greater number there was no such return. They had to settle, and their sons and descendants naturally accepted the new land as their native place, while retaining the proud memory that the family "came from" Nanking, Soochow, or some other centre of culture and wealth. These origins were still claimed by many long-established Yünnan families in the years before the last war.

No such system could exist in countries which were not under Chinese rule. In imperial times it was not considered right or desirable to exile men to a foreign land, or deport them from the empire. Some refugees undoubtedly did escape to the lands of the Nanyang, the Southern Ocean, as the Chinese call South-East Asia as a whole. At a later period, the nineteenth century, when foreign colonial rule was established in Malaya and in the East Indies (now Indonesia) there was a much larger flow of exiles escaping the oppression of the alien Manchu dynasty, but this had not been true at an earlier time. The Chinese empire usually demanded of its tributaries that their rulers should hand over such political refugees on pain of being considered as supporters of rebellion. These demands were too dangerous to ignore, and consequently the southern borderlands were no safe refuge for a political refugee. Colonial powers refused to comply with this system; the Manchu Court feared that in consequence anti-dynastic plots could be hatched with impunity among the growing communities of overseas Chinese, mainly drawn from the anti-Manchu southern provinces. They were quite right; it was in these places that the conspiracies which preceded the revolution of 1911 were hatched and from these communities that the funds of rebellion were raised.

The influence of exiles of stature as a cultural force among the overseas Chinese was slight; there were not very many of them, and by the age in which flight from Manchu persecution was possible, it was more likely to attract the refugee to Europe, Japan or America than to South-East Asia. Some of the more distinguished of these late exiles from China, who did settle or reside in the Nanyang, were themselves more conservative than the politically aroused classes of overseas Chinese. Men like K'ang Yu-wei, the monarchist reformer, who promoted Confucian learning in Singapore and Malaya, was in his later years a conservative, since he remained a loyal monarchist among a population increasingly republican in sentiment. Others, revolutionaries like Sun Yat-sen, who were not natives of the Nanyang, had their eyes and aspirations fixed on China itself. They came and went in Malaya, Java and other countries, raising money, organising rebellion, but taking no interest in nor in any way affecting the ordinary lives of resident Chinese, and still less of the non-Chinese population.

It was not until much more recent times, especially during and since the Second World War, that men of education originating in China, and taking refuge in the southern countries either from the Japanese invasion, the civil war or the new Communist régime, have made a distinct and perceptible contribution to the spread of higher Chinese education in these lands, particularly in Singapore and Malaya. The fact that universities were by this period established in these countries, where there had been no such institutions before the Second World War, has greatly added to the attractions of the south for families of education and scholars from China. It may be, therefore, that an influence tending to promote Chinese culture, hitherto lacking in the lands beyond Chinese rule, but formerly very potent in areas such as Yünnan, has taken root in those southern countries where a large Chinese population exists. In Yünnan and in the older centres of exile, these conditions also formerly prevailed. The Ming conquest of Yünnan had brought in a first wave of Chinese settlement, mainly ex-soldiers. The Manchu conquest brought in the large northern army of the General Wu San-kuei, a Chinese who had joined the new régime. His men settled around K'unming, the provincial capital, and imposed a dialect recognisably close to Peking speech upon that city. It was on the foundation of these considerable communities of Chinese settlers who themselves had little education that the later exiled scholars could establish the traditional educational system. Parts of South-East Asia have the large Chinese population, now economically prosperous, able to sustain universities and schools; they can now obtain the services of Chinese scholars, who are in effect exiles from China. An ancient situation may reappear in a new form.

Beyond the countries of direct Chinese influence, political and cultural, such as Yünnan and Vietnam, the most conspicuous evidence of Chinese civilisation is porcelain and pottery. Iconography and other forms of pictorial art in Cambodia, Thailand and Burma, as also in the Indonesian islands, remain under influences derived from India. But it is evident that at what now seems a very early period the export of Chinese ceramic wares had become an established trade—reaching indeed far beyond these countries—and that when, as in Thailand, local potteries were established, the products reflect very strong Chinese influence, leading some authorities to believe that they were the work of immigrant Chinese potters. The Chinese imports found a market not only among the civilised kingdoms of the south, but among tribes who were not at that time either literate or organised in large states. In Sarawak many examples of T'ang and Sung porcelain pots have been found cherished as sacred heirlooms by peoples of the interior tribes. Unacknowledged influences in architecture are also to be found in many of the cultures of the southern kingdoms, although in some cases the question arises whether these apparent affinities with Chinese forms do not in fact derive from the underlying pre-Hindu culture of continental South-East Asia, which in turn could well be related to the pre-Chinese (Han) culture of ancient south China.

Archaeological discovery in recent years in southern and south-western China has revealed the existence of art forms which have no continuity with later Chinese (Han) civilisation, but which do have a distinct and unmistakable affinity with forms which have centuries later penetrated into the southern Pacific cultures. The archaeology of south China, which will be of the first importance in the understanding of the spread and origin of the ancient art of southern Asia is as yet very little known. Until recent times it was wholly obscure. The few finds in the province of Hunan, at Ch'angsha, and in Yünnan, attest the existence in the first millennium b.c. of cultures which were quite unlike that of ancient north China, but were beginning to be affected by techniques which derived from the early Chinese bronze culture. In general these discoveries suggest some confirmation for the view, supported on historical evidence also, that Chinese culture was intrusive in this whole region of what is now south China which then constituted the southern borderlands of the Chinese world. The picture of Chinese southern expansion into the borderlands ancient or modern is not therefore one of a violent imperial conquest which brought in its train a new dominant culture. It is rather a pattern of seepage, of slow overspill from the great reservoir which was China, and which grew ever greater by the absorption of the former borderlands, and then spread still further into new regions. It was a combination of trading penetration, peasant and small urban settlement, enriched by the injection of exiles of higher education, and only finally, or at a late stage, consummated by political control and incorporation in the Chinese state. This last stage has never yet been reached in most of the later southern borderlands; in some cases, such as Vietnam, early political control was later renounced in favour of a more remote suzerainty; but whether direct or indirect in its operation Chinese influence and civilisation were deeply rooted in the countries nearest to the main territories of China proper, and radiated from these regions into lands which remained in the dominant aspect of their cultures non-Chinese. The original expansion was always by land; it is only at a comparatively recent period that communities formed in the Nanyang who had migrated across the seas. In modern times the dominant pattern has been the reverse. The adjacent countries, Vietnam and Burma, have received relatively few immigrants across the frontiers; the great Chinese communities of the Nanyang were established by migrants who came by sea, and in response to economic opportunities presented by the establishment of the large-scale colonial empires of the European powers. Chinese southward expansion had always more the character of a private pioneering venture than that of an imperial conquest and the formation of the present large communities in the Nanyang not only owed nothing to the policy of the reigning dynasty, but was actually strongly opposed by the imperial government of China.

CHAPTER ONE

EARLY CHINESE CONTACTS WITH SOUTH-EAST ASIA

In the reign of the Emperor Wu of the Han dynasty (140–86 B.C.) the kingdom called Nan Yüeh, or Southern Yüeh, which was centred on the city of Canton, was conquered and annexed to the Chinese empire. Nan Yüeh had been an outlying appendage of the previous short-lived Ch'in dynasty (221–209 B.C.), but had broken away when that régime collapsed. It was the conquest under Emperor Wu which finally joined this region to China and thereby opened the road of contact with the southern lands beyond the Chinese frontier. One of the provinces of Nan Yüeh was the region of the Red River plain and delta, or modern Tongking, the heartland of North Vietnam. This area also became part of the Han empire, and was known as the Commandery of Jihnan. The Yüeh people, from whom the old kingdom had taken its name, were in ancient times widespread along the coast of eastern Asia. They had formed kingdoms in the modern Chinese provinces of Fukien and Chekiang, and the chief of these, called simply Yüeh, had for a time contested with the major Chinese kingdoms of the north for supremacy over the whole of the Chinese world, in the fifth century B.C. Vietnam is the modern centre of the Yüeh, and the word *Viet* is simply the local pronunciation of the Chinese form Yüeh. The more northerly Yüeh were annexed to the Han empire and lost their separate national identity, although it is probable that a very large proportion of the present inhabitants of Fukien and Kuangtung are descendants of this people. The most southerly branch, established in the Red River basin, maintained their distinctive character, and even when incorporated in the Han empire, were restive subjects.

When the Han empire acquired the Red River basin it came into contact with peoples to the south who were not of Yüeh stock. The first of these to be mentioned are the Chams, who then occupied what is now South and Central Vietnam. Whereas the Yüeh and northern Chinese had some racial and linguistic affinity, the Chams were of a different race and the Han empire does not appear to have desired to annex their country. Relations with Linyi, which was the Chinese name for Champa, the kingdom of the Chams, existed, and were not always friendly, for the Chinese considered that the Chams had aided the Yüeh in a revolt in Jihnan Commandery in 190–2. It was in this period, towards the very end of the Later Han dynasty, that Chinese records first speak of the kingdoms of South-East Asia and give some account of them. These Chinese accounts of Champa, Cambodia and the small kingdoms then flourishing in the Malay peninsula are the first historical records of these countries, and even the names which they bore in their own languages are conjectural. The kingdom which the Chinese called Funan can be shown to have been the early, pre-Ankorian Cambodia. The Chinese name was pronounced at that time as *B'iu Nam*, which has been shown to be a rendering of old Khmer *Bnam*, equivalent to modern Khmer *Phnom*, which means a mountain. The contacts which are recorded are all official, envoys sent from China, and mention of return embassies from the southern kingdoms. It must be presumed that less formal contacts had been in existence for some time before relations on the high official level were established.

By the time that these official contacts, and the accounts they have left of the situation and character of the southern kingdoms were made, China itself was no longer a cohesive and powerful empire. The Han dynasty had fallen into confusion and civil war in the late second century A.D. and during the third century was divided between three rival states, known as the Three Kingdoms. The comparative weakness of the southern state of Wu, which had its capital at Nanking, may have been the reason why it sought knowledge and perhaps support from the non-Chinese kingdoms to the south. It was from Wu that two Chinese envoys went in 245–50 to Funan or Cambodia. It was also in the same period that a Cambodian (Funan) embassy to the Chinese Court is recorded, and that the Chinese first mention the states of the Malay peninsula. It would seem that the establishment of the capital of one of the Three Kingdoms in the relatively southern region of the lower Yangtze valley stimulated the exploration of the far south. It can be observed in later Chinese history that a period of confusion within the empire has been reflected in a stronger Chinese pressure on the southern borderlands, both by migration of displaced people fleeing from the north, and also because such periods usually involved the establishment of a separate régime in the southern provinces, which was too weak to recover the northern part of China, and instead tended to expand southwards against less formidable opponents. The fact that both in the Three Kingdoms period, and in the subsequent partition of China between the southern empire, ruled from Nanking, and Tatar invaders ruling the north from Loyang, the old capital, in the Yellow River valley (316–589), the southern empire expanded in this way and strengthened its contacts with the kingdoms of the far south seems to suggest that the connection between division in China and southern expansion is valid. When the empire was united, and always ruled from the north in such periods, the dynasty was preoccupied with the perennial problem of the northern frontier against the nomadic peoples of the Mongolian steppe.

At the time that the Chinese began to make close and continuing contacts with the kingdoms of South-East Asia, the main ethnic pattern now existing had already been established, probably more than one thousand years earlier. The peoples who were the ancestors of the Malays, the Khmer, and the various peoples of Indonesia had already moved into these countries, pushing the small earlier population into the deeper jungles and mountains. In Burma the Burmese themselves were not yet there, and the population of the lower Irrawaddy valley was Mon, a race akin to the Khmers of Cambodia. The Thais had not yet arrived in Thailand, and there, too, the original race would seem to have been Mon. The movement of the Burmese down from the Tibetan border occurred in the twelfth and thirteenth centuries A.D.; that of the Thais from Yünnan and south-west China at much the same period. Whether these considerable migrations are related to events in China will be considered later, but it would not seem probable that this connection can be shown in the case of the Burmese.

On the other hand the spread of the Vietnamese into what is now South Vietnam, but was earlier the kingdom of Champa, land of the Chams, is later and continued almost to modern times. It resulted in the virtual replacement of the original population by Vietnamese immigrants, but these came from what is now North Vietnam, or Tongking, and this region was not then any longer under direct Chinese rule. Overpopulation of the fertile Red River basin would seem to have been the driving force in the Vietnamese southward migration, for although the Chinese at an early date established contacts and relations with the southern countries, there was as yet no question of immigration. No early Han, or post-Han, Chinese account of the south mentions any Chinese resident population, and it is many centuries before such mention is first made in an official report. Northern Vietnam, when it was part of the empire, was no doubt ruled by officials drawn from other provinces, as was the Chinese custom, and some of these may have settled in the country on retirement. The seaport of Haiphong at the mouth of the Red River had probably some residents from Chinese provinces further north, such as Canton, but there is no record of any large-scale settlement or immigration. The Red River basin was perhaps already so fully settled that it was not attractive to immigrants seeking farm land; the necessities of a limited coastal trade would not bring large numbers of Chinese from the north or centre to the Vietnamese ports. Vietnam is thus an example of Chinese cultural penetration, but not of ethnic Chinese colonisation. In the further lands such as Cambodia, Burma, Thailand and beyond the seas the Chinese visitors would have found communities occupying the more fertile valleys who were of a different cultural influence, that of Hindu India. The Han envoys knew this, and refer to the Brahmans at the courts of these kingdoms. The Indian influence which formed the early civilisation of so much of South-East Asia was in fact brought peacefully, probably first by traders, and later refined and embellished by Brahman priests who came for the most part from south India. From the earliest period of which we have knowledge there already existed a cultural frontier along the fringes of the zones of influence of the two great centres of civilisation, India and China. It has remained in broad outline very much where we find it from the first. Vietnam is within the Chinese zone, and Yünnan was to become so. Burma, Cambodia, Thailand and Malaya were within the Indian zone. At a much later time Malaya and Indonesia, originally lands of Indian culture, were to be Islamised (with the exception of the island of Bali), but the other continental countries retained their culture of Indian origin, yielding neither to Chinese nor to Islamic pressures. Southern Vietnam, originally the Hinduised kingdom of Champa, was later to be overwhelmed by the southward movement of the Vietnamese and in this region culture of Chinese origin has driven out that of India. To some extent this happened also in Yünnan, but there, as in other remote regions, the question was rather more which culture would become established first, rather than whether one could replace another.

The influences which were later to come from China into the southern kingdoms of Hindu culture were therefore not religious, nor literary, but to some extent political, and also artistic. The main force of India's early cultural colonisation of South-East Asia certainly preceded any Chinese contact, and was on the wane before the Chinese pressure grew strong. After the decline of Buddhism in India, if not long before that, there seems to have been a steady decrease in contact between the mainland of India and the Hinduised kingdoms beyond the seas. This decline in the direct influences caused by Hindu and Brahman immigration coincided with the increasing southward movement of Chinese power, but was not caused by that movement. China's influence grew because the empire became stronger, more populous, and more involved in the southern provinces which had themselves been only Chinese colonies in the Han period. Contiguity or proximity helped; India was far away, China was relatively near by. The fact that the former Hindu kingdoms had adopted Buddhism, while that religion was declining in India and growing stronger in the Far East, was doubtless an intellectual influence separating them from contemporary India, and in some sense bringing a closer contact with China, even though the form of Buddhism practised in South-East Asia (other than Vietnam) was different from that followed in China and in Japan.

Up to the late Han and immediate post-Han period Chinese contacts with the southern kingdoms beyond Vietnam seem to have been wholly official; that is to say we have no record of any non-official contact, although by inference some can be suspected. Late in the Han dynasty an embassy from the Roman emperor Marcus Aurelius Antoninus arrived at the Chinese Court (166). Although the envoys, who were probably Roman subjects from the eastern provinces claimed to be ambassadors, the Chinese rather doubted this, and suspected that they might be merchants. In any case they certainly came by sea, and a few years later, in 222, an official envoy from the Roman Empire was received at the southern Court of Wu, one of the Three Kingdoms between which the Han empire had by then been divided. He too came by sea, and the Court of Wu proposed to send back with him, by the same route, their own envoy. Unfortunately this man died *en route*, and so no record of his voyage could reach the Chinese archives. These facts do testify that the sea route to the south, and to lands far beyond South-East Asia, was now frequented, and that trade was carried on. A number of objects of Roman manufacture, and coins, have been found along the route, from Vietnam to Thailand, northern Malaya and beyond. One reason why the Chinese doubted whether the "ambassadors" of Marcus Aurelius (An Tun to the Chinese) were genuine was the fact that they offered as presents objects which the Chinese recognised to be products of the southern borderlands. This fact alone proves that they were familiar with such products, and their knowledge of them must have come by trade.

The ancient Chinese historians are not interested in trade or records of commerce, unless these matters happen to impinge on some political or ritual concern. Archaeology may reveal the extent, or give some idea of the volume of this trade, but there is as yet very little evidence of what the Chinese sold in return for the things they bought. This may well be due to the nature of the goods. Silk was, as is well known, the great Chinese monopoly and export in the Han period, by the land route to central and western Asia. There is no reason why it should not also have been sent south by sea, but it is hardly to be hoped that such examples of Han textiles as have been found preserved in the dry sands of the north-western deserts will be matched by similar discoveries in the wet jungle lands of South-East Asia. Porcelain, which was to become the great export in later centuries, and testify to the range and volume of Chinese trade to the south, was not yet perfected in China itself. Other peoples could and did make pottery vessels, which served their needs; they had no reason to import Chinese vessels of the same material. When the Chinese had invented porcelain, its superior qualities over any pottery at once opened for it a world-wide market which ultimately reached to Europe.

It was the rise of Buddhism in China which was to provide not only the next powerful motive for the exploration of the sea route to the south, but also a literary record of such voyages, distinct from the official archives of diplomatic missions. Buddhism had been introduced to China by Indian missionary monks in the late first century B.C. It was officially recognised and received Court patronage early in the first century A.D. and thereafter slowly gained headway. It had reached China by the land route across central Asia, and the Hindu Kush, a route which had been opened up by the armies of the Chinese emperor Han Wu Ti, in the first century B.C. Chinese rule in central Asia was restored and extended, after a brief hiatus, in the first century A.D. and the security of travel now assured caused a considerable expansion of trade. The Indian missionaries, like their distant successors, the Christian missionaries of the fifteenth and sixteenth centuries, followed the new trade route. But communications remained difficult. The route was arduous, particularly the mountain zone between India and central Asia, which was not the route followed by the silk caravans. These kept to the north and descended into what is now Russian central Asia on their way to Black Sea ports, or to Persia.

The early Chinese pilgrims who set out for India to seek more Buddhist scriptures and learn the true doctrine in the great Buddhist monasteries which then flourished in what is now north-west Pakistan and Afghanistan, as well as in the Ganges valley, had braved the fearsome crossing of the great mountain barriers. In 399 one of these pilgrims, a north Chinese monk named Fa Hsien, set off on this journey and after great dangers and hardships arrived in India. There he sojourned for several years at various famous monasteries. He went south to Ceylon, already a centre of Buddhism, which was to hold that faith long after India had virtually abandoned it. Fa Hsien then learned that he could return to China by the sea route, and avoid the terrifying mountains of the north-west. In 412 he set out by ship, with his precious collection of scriptures and other religious treasures, and sailed to Sumatra. There he stayed two years, finding that in that country also Buddhism had been introduced and was flourishing. Finally he sailed—as it would seem in a Chinese ship—for Canton. The voyage was stormy; the captain lost his reckoning, and the ship made landfall on the coast of Shantung, hundreds of miles beyond its destination, after passing seventy days at sea without sight of land. Fa Hsien may not have been the first pilgrim to use the sea route, but he was the first to write a book about it, which has been preserved.

The first point which strikes the reader of Fa Hsien's account of his sea voyage is the size of the ship. He says that "he shipped on board another large merchant vessel which carried over two hundred persons with provisions for fifty days. . . . A north-east course was set in order to reach Canton; and over a month had elapsed when one night in the second watch a violent gale and tempestuous rain was encountered, at which the travelling merchants and traders going to their homes were much frightened." The other passengers were in favour of putting the religious man ashore on any island they could find—an interesting example of the abiding belief that priests are bearers of ill-luck to sea voyagers—but Fa Hsien was saved by the intervention of a passenger whom he calls a "religious protector" who threatened to report any such crime to the ruler of China, whom he said was an ardent Buddhist. The merchants spared him, and later when provisions were almost exhausted, decided to persuade the captain to steer north-west, convinced that as the ordinary voyage to Canton took only fifty days they must have gone off course. Twelve days later they sighted the coast of Shantung, where they obtained fresh water and vegetables. "And now, after having passed through much danger, difficulty, sorrow and fear, suddenly reaching this shore and seeing the old familiar vegetables, they knew it was their fatherland."

Clearly the passengers, or most of them, were Chinese; they were familiar with the route, and knew that the voyage should only last fifty days. This account thus gives the first certain knowledge that Chinese travelled to the island countries of the south and carried on their trade there. It is not clear how long they normally stayed in Sumatra, but it would seem probable that they made a seasonal journey, going down with one monsoon and returning with the next. Fa Hsien says he spent five months in Sumatra after coming from Ceylon. This was probably the interval between south-east monsoons which enabled ships to travel northwards. Seasonal sojourns by merchants are the pattern of much early intercourse between nations by sea, and were matched by the traders from Europe centuries later who came out to the Far East. Since the stay was often long, and chance, or sickness might prevent a man from returning home the next season, it is likely that a number became semi-permanent residents, and intermarried with the local people, who were not at that time inhibited from doing so by religious beliefs. It is also very improbable that the Chinese visiting merchants brought their own women with them, although the masters of the ships very probably did.

The special importance of Fa Hsien's travels and his account of them to any study of China's relations with the southern countries is that they are the first positive pieces of evidence of Chinese commercial as opposed to political and religious contacts with the region, and that his story more than suggests the presence in some of these countries of a seasonal trading community of some size. His ship carried two hundred or more passengers, who would seem to have been mainly, if not exclusively, Chinese. There is no suggestion that it was the only ship plying the route between Sumatra and Canton, and it is clear that the journey was familiar to many of these passengers, suggesting that they had made it frequently. That it had its perils is plain enough, but ocean travel was to be perilous for many centuries to come without deterring intrepid voyagers in all parts of the world. It is also of interest that the captain only lost his reckoning after the storm when "the sky was constantly darkened". He was not therefore making a coasting voyage in the manner of Mediterranean sailors of the same epoch, but an open sea course across the South China Sea. When he went astray and finally found himself off the coast of Shantung, he had unwittingly been blown right through the relatively narrow Taiwan Straight (only eighty miles at one point) and then into the Yellow Sea, as he had to sail twelve days north-west to reach the coast of China. It seems that he was very fortunate not to be cast up on the coasts of either Taiwan, the Ryukyu Islands, or even Japan. There is no evidence for the use of either the maritime compass or the lodestone (its predecessor in China) at this early date, although the magnetic properties of lodestone were already known. The captain navigated by the sun and the stars, and it was when he could see nothing of these heavenly bodies that he lost his reckoning.

The question of whether it was in Sumatra or Java, or even the Malay peninsula, that Fa Hsien passed the five months after sailing from Ceylon is still under dispute. The view that the kingdom of Yeh P'o T'i, which Sanskrit scholars equate with Yavadvipa, was in Java was held by Professor P. Pelliot, an authority not lightly to be challenged. The first two syllables of the Sanskrit name of this kingdom are close enough to modern "Java", and the two great islands, Sumatra and Java, only divided by the narrow Sunda Strait, were often taken to be one island by early navigators. The Chinese records of Han date mention various kingdoms in what is now judged to be north Malaya, along the Gulf of Siam, and also on the coast of Kedah and Perak, countries which were also under Hindu cultural influence. Some years after the date of Fa Hsien's voyage these kingdoms were sending envoys to China.

Funan, the precursor of Cambodia, was visited by the Chinese envoys K'ang T'ai and Chou Ying between the years 245 and 250, that is to say during the Three Kingdoms period in China. Part of their account of the country has been preserved in the dynastic histories. It is clear that the land was already more developed than many of its neighbours. There were walled cities (a point which all early Chinese travellers note as a mark of some degree of civilisation, since it resembled their own). There were also books and archives, written in a script which the Chinese call "Hu"; that is, some derivative of Indian origin. Taxes were paid in gold and silver as well as pearls and perfumes. Silver was used for table-ware. On the other hand the Chinese envoys considered the inhabitants to be black and ugly, and observed that they went barefoot, but they were not given to thieving. In subsequent years in the third century A.D. there were several embassies from Funan to China. The Chinese sources on the early history of Funan, or Cambodia, are the only coherent account which survives, and consequently even the names of the kings are known only in their Chinese form, which can sometimes be equated to a few Sanskrit names found on rare early inscriptions. The books and archives mentioned by Chou Ying were no doubt written on palm leaf as was the case in later centuries, and this is a material which perishes easily. The considerable detail which the Chinese report about early Funan history, and its foundation legends suggest that they were translating, or obtaining a version of a written record. Whether because the Chinese recognised the Khmers as a people of relatively advanced civilisation, and thus more worthy of their notice, or whether they were able to gather more information by means of written records, it is certain that Chinese accounts of Funan are fuller than those of other parts of South-East Asia. A fairly continuous and frequent diplomatic relationship grew up between Funan and the successive Chinese dynasties reigning in the south of China during the third and fourth centuries A.D.

No indication of the political motives for these relations are given; but at the same period the Chinese provinces which are now part of North and Central Vietnam were under constant attack from a newly risen people, based on what is now South Vietnam. These were the Chams, who formed the kingdom of Champa, which the Chinese called Linyi. They began to attack the Chinese territories from the end of the Han dynasty, when the imperial power was dissolving in the mêlée of civil war from which the Three Kingdoms were to emerge. The most southerly Chinese commandery, called Jihnan, the region around modern Hué, became the centre of this kingdom. Hostilities with China continued throughout the third century, China being at the time divided by the Tatar invaders in the north and the Tsin dynasty reigning at Nanking. It would seem possible that the reason why the Chinese maintained such constant relations with Funan may have been to seek a check on the Cham power, since Champa bordered to the south on Funan, and hostilities between the two peoples were frequent. The Chams are believed to have been invaders from the Indonesian islands, whereas the Khmers are the autochthonous inhabitants of southern Indo-China. In the third century the most southerly parts of later Cochin China were Funan territory, later incorporated and colonised by Champa. According to the Chinese sources a certain man named Wen, in origin a Chinese from Yangchou in Kiangsu, became counsellor to the king of Champa in 315 and later usurped the throne at the old king's death. He carried on the northward pressure of the Chams, and extended his kingdom at the expense of the remains of the Chinese commandery of Jihnan. His reign corresponds to the period in China immediately after the expulsion of the Tsin dynasty from north China and its re-establishment at Nanking in the south, an era when Chinese power was weak and preoccupied with the northern nomad invasions.

The system used by the Chinese dynastic historians is to include sections dealing with foreign nations in a part of the work detached from the main line of history. The foreign nations are described, their embassies to China noted, but only rarely are Chinese reciprocal embassies mentioned. It was proper for foreign "barbarians" to send "tribute-bearing missions" to imperial China. It was not seemly to suggest that China, for her part, had some purpose in sending embassies to them. Foreign policy is not therefore expressed; the foreign nation is described, its history briefly noticed, but the reasons for promoting this intercourse are not stated. It can sometimes be adduced from other known facts, and one of the patterns which appears to begin at an early date, after the fall of the Han empire, persists. The kingdom nearest to the Chinese borders, if not submissive, might expect that China would encourage and support, diplomatically, the neighbour, usually hostile to that kingdom, which lay beyond it. Champa could be checked by favours to Funan; at a later time Burma could be held in proper respect by giving encouragement to her hostile neighbour, Thailand (which was not contiguous with the empire). It is a fact which history almost unconsciously reveals, and which merits the attention of statesmen concerned with modern China, as much as that of historians of the past.

The latter half of the sixth century A.D. saw a major change in the relations between China and the South-East Asian kingdoms, and in this area itself. China was reunited in 589 by the Sui dynasty, originating in the north, which conquered south China. Although the Sui themselves collapsed a few years later, they were succeeded by the great T'ang dynasty, which set the pattern of a united empire from that time forward. Periods in which China was divided became short and transitory, and largely the consequence of partial foreign conquest. Consolidation of the united empire resulted in more intensive colonisation of the far southern provinces, which then still included Vietnam, or rather what is now North Vietnam, or Tongking. Henceforward for more than three centuries the kingdoms of the south had to deal with a powerful empire, the most highly organised state then existing anywhere in the world. The T'ang, for their part, were mainly concerned, like all Chinese dynasties reigning from the north, with the frontier along the Great Wall, beyond which were their age-old enemies, the peoples of the steppe. The T'ang empire continued the relations its predecessors had established with the south, and the flow of Buddhist pilgrims also continued actively. On the other hand, without actually undertaking aggressive policies towards the southern neighbours, the power of the now united empire imposed limits upon their freedom of action.

In the sixth century, Champa, under a new dynasty had not only sought investiture from the then reigning southern Chinese Court, an effort to acquire a legitimacy which was in doubt, but a few years later had profited from a revolt in Tongking, which drove out the Chinese authority, to attack that country, only to be defeated. When the southern Ch'en dynasty was overthrown by the Sui, Champa repudiated Chinese suzerainty (595), but when the new Sui emperor, having reconquered Tongking, proceeded to send his armies south and defeat those of Champa, the king of that country promptly acknowledged Sui suzerainty, and with a better realisation of the nature of the Chinese political situation followed this up by equally prompt recognition of T'ang suzerainty (623, 625 and 628) when that dynasty had succeeded the short-lived Sui. Champa, nearest to the Chinese power in Tongking, responded sensitively to the changes occurring in the great empire.

During the same period a great change had also taken place in Funan. That ancient kingdom had collapsed and been replaced by a new régime, equally of Khmer ethnic stock, but originating in outlying territory on the Middle Mekong, the Bassak district, which now lies beyond the frontiers of modern Cambodia. The name of Funan disappears from Chinese records, and the country, which is still modern Cambodia, is henceforth called Chen La, anciently pronounced Ts'ien Lap, a word of unexplained origin, not equivalent to any Khmer or Sanskrit name. The conquest of the old kingdom by the new dynasty (which had some marriage connections with it) took several decades, but by the foundation of the T'ang Chen La was fully established and sent an embassy to the new Chinese Court, which had only been in full control of the empire for one year. The new king of Chen La reigned for many years, dying about 635, and was thus a contemporary of the famous T'ang T'ai Tsung, the real founder of the T'ang dynasty. During the first century of the T'ang dynasty relations with Chen La were close and continuous. The Chinese

B

record no less than fifteen embassies from that kingdom between 686 and 731. No doubt in Chinese eyes these missions amounted to an acceptance of at least nominal Chinese suzerainty, but it is not apparent that this political Chinese influence had any deep effect on the policies of the kings of Chen La in internal matters. The Buddhist pilgrim Yi Tsing in the late seventh century remarks that although Buddhism had formerly prospered in Chen La, an "evil king"—the founder—had persecuted the faith in favour of the Shivaite sect of Hinduism which was then in the ascendancy. In this period the Chinese Court, under the Empress Wu, was itself strongly Buddhist.

Yi Tsing was one of the pilgrims who made the voyage to India by sea, and his records of this experience contain more information about South-East Asia than is to be found in the brief official notices of the dynastic history. It is clear that Chinese envoys now ranged further afield. The kingdoms of the Malay peninsula were visited and described, being at that time under strong Indian influence with numerous Brahmans attending upon the kings. The kingdom of Ho Ling, which is the Sanskrit Kalinga, has been located in central Java, and was also known to the T'ang Court, an envoy being received in 640. At the same period the name Mo Lo Yu, which is the Chinese version of Malayu, appears for the first time as that of a kingdom on the east coast of Sumatra. Yi Tsing visited it and mentions that it had been absorbed by the new rising kingdom of Shrivijaya, which was in the same region, and was to become the dominant sea power in the south-east, replacing the old kingdom of Funan which had held that rôle. Yi Tsing stayed in this kingdom at its capital, probably near modern Palembang, both on his outward voyage to India and on his return. He records that it was a flourishing centre of Buddhist learning and that Chinese pilgrims would do well to stay there for two years or so before proceeding to India, so that they could learn Sanskrit and study the laws and ceremonies of Buddhism as practised in India. Yi Tsing found Buddhist Sanskrit texts available there and spent some years translating them into Chinese. It is clear that eastern Sumatra had become an important centre of Indian, and particularly Buddhist civilisation, at the very time when Buddhism was declining in its native India.

Although the T'ang period saw a considerable increase in contacts with the parts of South-East Asia reached by the sea route, both by pilgrims and by envoys, the Chinese activity seems to have been at least as much receptive as outgoing. The Chinese pilgrims looked upon the island kingdoms as sources of Buddhist knowledge, hardly inferior to India itself. The Chinese Court seems to have been interested in contacts mainly for prestige reasons, and perhaps also from that spirit of enquiry and interest in foreign places, peoples and products, which is the characteristic mark of T'ang society. It was not only the nearer kingdoms of the south which engaged this interest; in these centuries the Chinese had made contacts with western Asia and the Byzantine Empire, with Africa, and with Japan. The influence of China was more directly felt in this period in Yünnan, where close and sometimes hostile relations existed with the kingdom of Nanchao, and in Vietnam, which was in T'ang times a Chinese province. This was the last age of direct Chinese rule in that country, and the longest and most uninterrupted domination. It is in the T'ang period that Vietnam acquired those cultural characteristics which were, whether dependent or free, to mould her civilisation on the Chinese pattern.

Chen La, or Cambodia, had broken into two hostile states at the beginning of the eighth century (706); the Chinese maintained relations with both, but do not seem to have favoured one more than the other. A century later, with the reign of King Jayavarman II, Cambodia was reunited under the first Angkorian dynasty, and a series of cities in the immediate vicinity of the present Angkor Thom became the capitals for the next six hundred years. China was to continue close relations with this country throughout the whole period of Cambodia's golden age, and it is from Chinese accounts that the social life of the country, and much of its history, is best known. Cambodian documents, exclusively inscriptions on stone, record primarily the religious life of the country, the foundation of monasteries, the benefactions of kings, and the restoration of religious monuments. The secular records written on leaf fibre have perished; the story of Cambodia without the Chinese records would be comparable to English history if only monastic charters, ecclesiastical appointments, and religious memorials had survived without any secular literature or history. It is only with the Angkorian period that the Cambodian inscriptions give an adequate record of the names of at least the longer reigning and more effective monarchs; in earlier times these are only known through Chinese transcriptions, and the reconstructions of probable Sanskrit forms made from these renderings.

In the late ninth century the T'ang empire entered into its terminal phase of rebellion and military turmoil; in 907 the last emperor was dethroned and the empire split up into rival warring kingdoms, or empires, as they claimed to be; a period of ephemeral régimes known in Chinese history as the Five Dynasties, from the short-lived power of five successive dynasties ruling only a part of north China. The south was divided among more stable, but weaker and smaller states, seven in number. This confusion was reflected in the southern kingdoms. In 939 Tongking, or North Vietnam, rebelled against the successor state of the fallen T'ang, and became an independent kingdom; it was never to be a Chinese province again, except for very brief periods. Champa, which then occupied what is now South and Central Vietnam was the state most directly concerned with this development, for it portended the opening phase of the long strife between Annam (or North Vietnam) and Champa, which was ultimately to lead to the destruction of the latter kingdom. Already in the years 951 to 958 Champa had sent embassies to the Court of the Later Chou, one of the Five Dynasties ruling north China. There can have been little real hope of aid from so distant a quarter, but the very fact that the king of Champa felt any need to send envoys to north China reflects the growing fear of the new kingdom of Annam.

This diplomatic activity increased with the accession of the Sung dynasty, in 960, which was to end the fifty-year interregnum and soon reunite the empire. The very year which saw the new Chinese dynasty established, the king of Champa, himself just come to the throne, sent an embassy to K'aifeng, the new Chinese capital. It would seem clear that the hope of Champa was that the Sung would restore Chinese authority in Vietnam. Between 972 and 979, years in which the Sung authority was more completely consolidated in south China, thus giving hope of an interest in recovering Annam, Champa sent no less than seven embassies to China. They did not obtain Chinese intervention against Annam. The Sung were essentially a pacific régime; they had come to power not by conquest but by skilful political moves, backed by the general desire to end strife and the fragmentation of the empire. It is evident that they did not wish to extend their authority into regions where the population was clearly hostile to Chinese rule.

It is significant that the great southward expansion of the Vietnamese, their sustained drive against Champa, was not a feature of Chinese rule; during the T'ang and in earlier times the Chinese did not seriously attempt to conquer what is now South and Central Vietnam, they were content if the nearest king, which was that of Champa, paid tribute, and acknowledged Chinese suzerainty. The Vietnamese, after the expulsion of Chinese authority, soon embarked on a prolonged war of conquest accompanied by a massive expulsion of the inhabitants and their replacement with Vietnamese settlers. Perhaps in order to forestall what they feared would happen, in 979 the Chams themselves attacked and invaded Annam, only to meet with heavy defeat. Three years later the Annamites invaded Champa, captured its capital city and slew the king. In 985 the next king of Champa appealed to China for protection, but if any Chinese diplomatic initiative stayed the hand of Annam, it was not for long. In 990 the Annamites reopened the war which was to continue intermittently, almost always with victory on the Annamite side, until in

1068 the Annamites completed the annexation of the three northern provinces of Champa, the modern Central Vietnam, and the kingdom of Champa was reduced to the southern third of Vietnam. Champa had repeatedly invoked Chinese protection, admitting the suzerainty of the Sung emperor in 1042, and continuing to send embassies to K'aifeng. Chinese reaction was slow; it was not until eight years after the loss of Champa's northern provinces that the Sung decided to invade Annam, calling upon both Cambodia and Champa to join the struggle. The war was unsuccessful, and the Chinese and their allies withdrew (1076).

It must be remembered that during this period the Sung dynasty felt itself much more seriously menaced by the power of the Kitan people in what is now Manchuria, and the Hsi Hsia nation, to the north-west. Both these states had retained some areas within the Great Wall, that is to say on the south side of the defensive range along which the Wall is built, and the Sung had never been able to recover this territory. Its possession in hostile hands was a standing menace to the Sung empire, and ultimately a fatal one. It was probably the danger of diverting too great resources to a war in distant Annam when the northern frontier was at risk that deterred the Sung emperors from doing more than encourage Champa with words rather than deeds. In little more than fifty years from the abortive intervention of 1076 the Sung were to lose their capital and all north China to the invading Kin Tatars, who had just destroyed the Liao (Kitan) kingdom in modern Manchuria (1127). Some years passed before the Sung were able to stabilise their authority in south China and set up their capital in Hangchou, where for more than a century they continued to rule half China.

The Southern Sung (1127–1280) was not so powerful an empire as it had been when ruling all China, but it was a very wealthy state. Trade increased enormously in the Southern Sung period, and for the first time in Chinese history the revenues from trade and customs exceeded the land revenue. Much of this contact was with the southern borderlands, and the island countries beyond them. It was not necessary for the Chinese emperors to menace Annam, since this task had been taken up by the rise of Cambodia to the position of dominant power in the south. King Suryavarman II, the builder of Angkor Wat, came to power in 1113, only a few years before the Sung lost north China. In 1123 he attacked both Champa and Annam, and continued these campaigns in 1128 and 1138. In 1145 he turned his armies on Champa, and overran that country, but five years later yet another invasion of Annam failed. These hostilities on the part of their southern neighbour, now grown so strong, were quite enough to keep the Annamites from troubling the Chinese frontier, and an equally powerful reason why the Southern Sung should take no part

in these quarrels. After 1150 the Cambodian kings were more occupied
with wars with Champa, and thus presented no potential threat as future
conquerors of Annam. With the loss of direct rule over Annam the
Chinese emperors of the Sung dynasty seem to have lost any ambition to
push their conquests further south; this would indeed have been impossible on the east coast of southern Asia, unless seaborne invasions were
mounted. The existence of an independent Annam as a buffer between
China and the warlike kingdoms of the south was sufficient.

Beyond the seas, the Sung empire, particularly when at the height of its
power, had been influential in the new kingdom of Shrivijaya, situated
on both sides of the Straits of Malacca, in Sumatra and in Malaya. It was a
commercial country controlling the sea route between India and China,
and constantly frequented by merchants of all nations: Arabs, Chinese,
Indians and the South-East Asians. It had, however, a dangerous and
hostile rival in Java, and early in the Sung dynasty (988), the king of
Shrivijaya sent an embassy to China requesting aid against the Javanese.
It would seem that he must have received diplomatic support, and perhaps
something more, for in 1003 the king took the unusual step of dedicating
a new Buddhist temple to the long life of the Chinese Emperor and
requesting him to bestow a name upon the foundation and send bells for
the monastery. This in Chinese terms amounted to an acknowledgement
of Chinese authority. Three years later Shrivijaya invaded and defeated
Java. It would seem probable that this operation was undertaken with
Chinese encouragement, probably because the Sung thought that Shrivijaya, with whom relations were good, was the more desirable state to
control the narrow seas than Java might turn out to be.

Throughout the Sung period relations both diplomatic and commercial were close and continuous between China and Shrivijaya, which
in effect controlled those parts of the island region with which the
Chinese had useful contact. They were already acquainted with more
remote parts of the region; the first Chinese mention of Borneo occurs in
977 and the presence of Sung porcelain in that island attests the existence,
probably later, of trade. Navigation had become safer and much more
frequent, partly on account of the presence of the Arab traders who had
been frequenting the eastern seas since the T'ang period. Chao Ju-kua, the
Chinese official in charge of foreign trade who in 1225 composed a
celebrated work, *Chu Fan Chih* ("Record of all the Foreign Peoples")
obtained much of his information from Arab sources. His well-known
descriptions of the Mediterranean, the coastal region of Africa and other
distant lands undoubtedly derived from this information. Nearer home
he could no doubt rely on his own countrymen who were now plentiful
in the southern region. In 1154 the Arab historian and traveller Edrisi

reports the existence of many Chinese in Sumatra, significantly relating their presence to the recent troubles in China, which would mean the conquest of the north by the Kin Tatars. They were peaceful, industrious and well-liked. The first two qualities have continued to be characteristic of the overseas Chinese of later centuries; the last is, sadly, not always true.

By the time Chao Ju-kua wrote and other authors mention the presence of Chinese in the south, who would seem to be settled residents and not merely seasonal visitors, China had had more than one thousand years of contact with the peoples of the southern borderlands and the lands beyond the South China Sea. Except in Vietnam, the immediately adjoining territory, and in Champa, just beyond it, the Chinese rulers had never attempted any display of power nor mounted any invasion. They had clearly at varying times exercised a real political influence further south, and in the period when Buddhism was strong in those countries and actively evangelising in China itself, the cultural contact had been at least as much inward to China as outward from her. It is in the Sung period that this situation began to change. Buddhism had virtually collapsed in India; the pilgrims went no more. In Shrivijaya the attractions of wealth and commerce began to gain ascendancy over the mainly religious culture of the earlier kingdoms of the region. In China the development of export industries, particularly porcelain, were soon to give the contact with the south a different character. The evident rise in the wealth of the Southern Sung state due to seaborne commerce, and the perfection, whether by the Chinese themselves or by Arabs using the Chinese invention, of the maritime compass, testify to the increased interest in and importance of non-official contacts.

The wealth and economic advances under the Southern Sung were already, when Chao Ju-kua was writing in 1225, under the shadow of coming catastrophe. Cinggis (Genghiz) had united the tribes of the Mongolian steppe under his own authority and begun the invasion of the Kin empire of northern China in 1210. Although he himself went off after taking Peking, the northern Kin capital, to conquer central Asia, the war against the Kin was continued by his successors (he died in 1227) and in 1233 the Mongols captured the Kin capital at K'aifeng, the old Sung capital of the united empire. Two years later, the invasion of the southern empire of the Sung followed (1235). Thus, after one century of comparative peace and great prosperity the south of China was now subjected to the long devastation of a Mongol invasion, even if this was less ferocious and destructive than it had been in north China. Sung resistance was protracted and stubborn, helped by the terrain of mountains and rice-fields which were unfamiliar and hampering to the Mongol cavalry armies. But although prolonged for forty years the Sung could not in the end resist the power of what was now more nearly a world empire, stretching from the borders of Poland to the Yellow Sea, than any previous state. In 1279 the Sung were finally annihilated in a naval battle fought close to the present city of Hong Kong. The Mongols ruled all China, as well as Asia westward to Russia and beyond.

This conquest of China, the first total conquest by a foreign people, had profound effects upon the southern borderlands. In the late twelfth century and early thirteenth century, when Cinggis (Genghiz) was consolidating his power and beginning the invasion of north China, Jayavarman VII, the last great conquering king of Cambodia, was destroying the power of Champa, and, as it proved, over-straining the resources of his kingdom by his grandiose building projects, which include Angkor Thom in its final form and its great central royal temple, the Bayon. After his death in 1218 even Champa was able to recover some degree of independence, and Cambodia never again embarked on wars of expansion. The Mongols, towards the end of the century, found a power vacuum to their south; Cambodia was still outwardly magnificent and secure; it was in the early years of the next century that the Chinese diplomat Chou Ta-kuan visited the country as a member of an embassy sent by the Mongol emperor Kubilai, and left the best and fullest account of Cambodian life, government and the city of Angkor Thom which we possess. But it was a façade, behind which power was declining. The Mongols inevitably took advantage of this situation to push their power further south than any Chinese régime had even contemplated. The consequences for the southern borderlands were a new relationship with the rulers of China, Mongol for the time being, later the Chinese Ming dynasty.

CHAPTER TWO

CHINESE EXPANSION BY LAND: VIETNAM

Vietnam is the country most open to Chinese expansion and occupation by land. The frontier, although passing along a mountain chain, affords more than one accessible pass, and the sea coast is but an extension of the sea coast of the southern Chinese province of Kuangtung. The Red River delta, the heart of northern Vietnam, is also the best and largest fertile plain south of the Yangtze estuary. Every circumstance seems to dictate that this adjacent country would become, and remain, a part of the Chinese world, and an integral part of the Chinese state. For many centuries this seemed to be its destiny and was the fact. Vietnam was a Chinese province from 111 B.C. until 939, for more than one thousand years. In the next thousand years, from 939 to the present day, the Vietnamese, having won their independence, were able to maintain it with very brief intervals—a Chinese reconquest from 1407 to 1427, and the French rule from the late nineteenth century until 1946. The reasons why the apparent course of history should have been reversed are worth careful examination, as they illuminate the real nature of Chinese contact and expansion in the southern borderlands.

It must first be observed that the part of Vietnam which was formerly subject to Chinese rule is only about one-third of the present country, the delta plain of the Red River and the coastal plain along the shores of the Gulf of Tongking. What is now Central Vietnam, and was before independence known to the French colonial government as the protectorate of Annam, was not for any long period under Chinese rule, and was then the northern part of the kingdom of Champa. South Vietnam was in part Cham territory, and further south, Cambodian. The modern names are largely derived from the terminology used under the French régime and do not correspond either to Vietnamese names or closely to historical regions. "Tongking" is a French coinage, taken from the name of the old capital, the present city of Hanoi, which was colloquially known as *Tong King* (Chinese *Tung Ching*), meaning the Eastern Capital. Annam, from the Chinese *An Nan*, was a name given to the northern area under Chinese rule in the T'ang dynasty, and means "Pacified South". Cochin

China, which used to designate the southerly part of what is today South Vietnam, is a word of foreign coinage, possibly of Portuguese origin. It is not Vietnamese. "Vietnam" itself is the Vietnamese pronunciation of the Chinese words *Yüeh Nan* meaning "Yüeh South", the southern Yüeh, to distinguish it from the other Yüeh kingdoms and regions along the south-east Chinese coast. These had included in antiquity the Yüeh kingdom in what is now Chekiang province, just south of the Yangtze delta; Min Yüeh, which was in modern Fukien province, and Nan Yüeh, or Southern Yüeh, which covered the provinces of Kuangtung and part of Kuangsi with the Red River delta of modern North Vietnam. This last region, as the most southerly part of Nan Yüeh, was called Yüeh Nan, "Yüeh South".

The Yüeh people were thus in early times widely spread along the east coast of Asia, and it is possible that one branch of them was a constituent of the later Japanese people. Chinese conquest, from the third century B.C. onward, gradually absorbed the northern Yüeh, until in 111 B.C. the Han emperor Wu conquered the large southern Yüeh kingdom (Nan Yüeh) and thus came into possession of the Red River delta. Earlier, the conquering Ch'in emperor Shih Huang Ti, the unifier of China, had attacked Nan Yüeh and forced it to acknowledge his supremacy. But at the collapse of the brief Ch'in empire in 205 Nan Yüeh had recovered its independence until finally conquered by the Han emperor Wu a century later. Already in this first age of contact one fact appears; when China was under a strong and unified rule, the independence of any part of the old Yüeh lands was imperilled, or lost. When China was distracted by internal troubles, the Yüeh recovered independence, and kept it until once more conquered by force. Unlike the inner provinces of China the Yüeh regions fought against incorporation in new empires and did not willingly submit to the new central power, as the Chinese provinces usually did.

A seafaring people, the ancient Yüeh always made their settlements on the fertile lands of the river deltas and estuaries which provide the only extensive arable areas in the mountainous south-eastern coastal provinces of China. Thus the first Yüeh kingdom was centred on the estuary of the Ch'ien T'ang River around Hangchou Bay in modern Chekiang province; Min Yüeh, in Fukien, was based on the rich lands at the mouth of the Min River, at Foochow; Nan Yüeh took in the delta of the West River, at Canton, and then spread southwards to incorporate and settle the Red River delta, in modern North Vietnam. These four delta and estuarial regions are the best farming land and the most extensive areas suitable to rice cultivation on the south-east coast. The fifth, the delta of the Mekong, was ultimately to be the last great colony of the Yüeh people, and forms today the heartland of South Vietnam. Fertile lands meant rapid and relatively dense settlement: whereas in their southward movement in the interior of China the northern Chinese immigrants found only a light population along the rather narrow valleys of the Yangtze tributaries, a population more easily absorbed by the immigrants, along the coast they found settlements of Yüeh people who were numerous and occupied compact territories capable of an organised resistance. The ancient state of Yüeh in Chekiang almost destroyed itself, and weakened its people by incessant aggressions upon its neighbours until it was virtually depopulated. The Han emperor Wu resorted to a very large forced transfer of the conquered people when he took over Min Yüeh in Fukien, resettling the population in central China. Nan Yüeh, in Kuangtung, the homeland of the "Cantonese" retains to this day the distinctive character and the restless attitude to northern rule which has always made it a problem region for the central government in China, of whatever character or form.

Cantonese, and also the dialect of Foochow (Hokkiu) as well as other dialects along the south-east coast are the most distinctively different from standard Chinese speech of any of the variations found in the Chinese language. In part this differentiation represents older forms of standard Chinese, imposed upon a non-Chinese speaking population in the past, and as is often the case, retaining in these circumstances an original character which the mainstream of the language has left behind. It can be shown that modern Cantonese is close to the standard spoken Chinese of the T'ang period (seventh–tenth centuries A.D.) which was the period in which the main immigration of northern Chinese to Kuangtung occurred. Foochow dialect is thought to be close to the standard speech of the Han period, when following Emperor Wu's transplantation many northern Chinese were moved into the Min River area. One may compare the eighteenth-century flavour of English as spoken by the Negro population of the West Indies, the differences being the much longer time-span of the south-east Chinese settlements. Underlying this linguistic peculiarity is the ethnic factor; the main constituent of the population in Kuangtung and also in Fukien, is a stock originally non-Chinese, and largely Yüeh. Even within the frontiers of the empire as fixed on lasting lines by the Han emperor Wu in the late second century B.C. Chinese penetration was very largely the imposition of a culture and a more developed civilisation upon non-Chinese peoples.

It is this fact which helps to explain the continuing separate character and identity of the Vietnamese. Vietnam, and the term then meant only the Red River delta, was the extreme limit of the Chinese empire, the "Yüeh South", where Chinese rule meant not immigration of Chinese from the north, but the government of an alien people by northern Chinese officials. There were already many thousands of peasant farmers to till the soil, and provide the revenue for the Chinese government. There was no need to bring in large numbers of Chinese immigrant farmers, and there were plenty of lands nearer to the homes of such people waiting for settlement in the Yangtze valley and its southern tributaries. The Chinese found in the Yüeh people a nation of rice-farming peasants, like their own; it was relatively easy to impose Chinese rule upon them, and thereafter to establish institutions similar in almost all respects to those of China. This is what happened; Vietnamese culture took on a deep Chinese coloration, but the ethnic character of the people continued to be Yüeh, that is "Viet", and they inherited and cherished that consciousness of difference in race and desire for separate nationhood which in a modified form has always characterised their more assimilated cousins, the Cantonese.

Even the Chinese ruling class were few in numbers; it was found more profitable to the imperial power to permit the native chiefs of the Viet (Yüeh) clans and districts to become landlords in the Han manner and establish in the far-off province the new landlord–tenant relationship and land tenure system which had replaced the earlier true feudalism of pre-imperial China. Educated, and encouraged to adopt Chinese customs and ways of thought, this class could be rewarded by employment in the imperial civil service, and in return Chinese rule secured their possession of what had once been tribal common lands. It is characteristic of Vietnamese early history that revolts against Chinese rule were led not by landlord gentry, but by peasants. It is also un-Chinese, but consistent with Vietnamese custom, that some of these leaders should be women. These facts suggest a lasting alienation between the Sinified landlord gentry and the peasantry who, being illiterate, were less susceptible to Chinese cultural influence. If the imposition of Chinese rule and culture on the Cantonese people has, after more than two thousand years, still left this population with many special characteristics and an enduring impatience with northern rule, it is hardly surprising to find that the national identity of the Vietnamese has remained even more strongly marked. "Canton for the Cantonese" was a popular slogan in the early period of the Republic; northerners sometimes wondered whether it did not really mean "China for the Cantonese". In Vietnam a thousand years of Chinese rule was equally unable to efface the sentiment "Vietnam for the Vietnamese"—although the remote situation of the old province, while it made this aspiration more possible, could not inspire any expectation of Vietnam dominating the central government of the empire itself.

The first century of Chinese rule does not record any major revolts by the population of Vietnam; China was under the strong rule of the Early Han dynasty, and it was not until the first years of the first century A.D.

that internal troubles shook that power. Between 9 and 23 the throne was usurped by Wang Mang, and when he fell China was for several years convulsed by the rebellion of the peasant Red Eyebrows and the civil wars between aspirants for the throne. The Later Han dynasty, founded by the collateral prince whose reign title is Emperor Kuang Wu, did not consolidate its power for a decade, and it is at this time that the Vietnamese rose in their first major rebellion. In 39 the two sisters Trung Trac and Trung Nhi, who were members of a family of chiefs, rose in rebellion and maintained their resistance for ten years. The suppression of this rebellion coincides very closely with the consolidation of the power of the newly restored Later Han dynasty and was effected by one of the leading generals of the new Emperor Kuang Wu. The Trung sisters, in spite of their failure, have remained heroines to the Vietnamese people. They had their temple in Hanoi, and are still revered as patriots. Chou En-lai, the Communist Prime Minister of China made the tactful gesture of kneeling before their altar when he made a state visit to North Vietnam. Memories are long in eastern Asia.

The concordance between periods of Chinese weakness and Vietnamese revolts against Chinese rule can be observed in a sequence which continues until the end of Chinese direct rule. In 192 another large-scale revolt shook the Chinese authority, and only three years earlier, in 189, the Han empire, at the death of Emperor Ling, had entered into its final convulsive period of civil war and intense disorder aggravated by another great peasant rebellion, the Yellow Turbans. The rebellion of 192 does not seem to have been primarily Vietnamese, but rather a first upsurge of the Cham people, who established their new kingdom in what had been the most southerly extension of the Chinese province, the commandery of Jihnan (South of the Sun), which corresponded to the coastal plain between modern Da Nang and the "Annam Gate" (Porte d'Annam) near the present demarcation line between North and South Vietnam. This area was lost to the Chinese. After 222, China was divided between the Three Kingdoms, and it was Wu, the south-eastern state, that inherited the Chinese authority in the Red River delta. Although China still claimed Jihnan it is not evident that any real authority was restored so far south. Champa indeed sent embassies to the Court of Wu in 230, but in 248 once more attacked the Chinese province to the north and after winning a considerable victory retained the area of the Song Giang River, south of the Red River delta. Chinese weakness and division were the main causes of these Cham aggressions. In 277 the Three Kingdoms were briefly united by a new dynasty, the Tsin, but this régime lost north China to the Tatar invasions in 316, and henceforward ruled only in the south. For the next two hundred years, under the southern Tsin and their successors in south China, the Vietnamese did not revolt. It seems prob-able that the new threat posed by Cham power was a reason why the Vietnamese preferred Chinese rule to the risks of revolt which would have given Champa an opportunity for further aggression. It was not until 543 that the revolt of the Ly family, whose leader Ly Boh founded the first independent Vietnamese dynasty, the Early Ly, temporarily brought Chinese rule in Vietnam to an end. At that time the Chinese Liang dynasty was approaching its end, and confusion and weakness were soon to overthrow it in favour of the Ch'en dynasty (557–89), a short-lived and feeble dynasty which was not able to control much of southern China, and thus could not re-establish Chinese power in Vietnam. When in 589 the Sui reunified the empire and ended the long division between Tatar dynasties in the north and Chinese dynasties in the south, it was not long before they invaded Vietnam and reimposed Chinese rule. Soon to be succeeded (618) by the great T'ang dynasty, this Sui reconquest was enduring. Revolts, a major one in 722, were suppressed, and the need for the T'ang to keep a large army in the country to guard the frontier with the rising Yünnan kingdom of Nanchao made independence for Viet-nam unattainable. The T'ang, after their conquest, renamed the country An Nan (i.e. Annam), the "Pacified South".

For two hundred and fifty years the T'ang rule in Annam was un-challenged, and this long period during which the country was under Chinese government when that government had never been so highly organised before, and the reigning dynasty fostered what is perhaps the finest age of Chinese culture, made a deep impression on the Vietnamese people. It did not, as events were to prove, induce them to forego their desire to be independent of China in political matters, but it did form the Vietnamese culture in the Chinese mould in which it has since remained. Earlier Chinese authority had begun this work, the T'ang era completed it. When Vietnam became independent she showed no desire to repudiate the cultural heritage which she had acquired from the T'ang.

In 868 the Chinese army in Vietnam, stationed on the frontier with the kingdom of Nanchao (which is now the reverse frontier between China and North Vietnam) mutinied. It had long been unpaid, and the distant court was sinking into incompetence and subservience to military provin-cial commanders. The mutineers went home to China and started that train of civil war and rebellion which was to end the T'ang dynasty in less than forty years. China then broke up into a number of separate and contending states, all claiming the empire, but for the most part only con-trolling one or two provinces or even only one. It was in the midst of this confusion that the Vietnamese, following the general example, rebelled and set up their own separate kingdom, in 934.

The Dinh dynasty, which now took power in Vietnam, was the first of a series which maintained the independence of the country until the French conquest in the nineteenth century, with one brief interval in the early fifteenth century. From the end of Chinese rule in the tenth century Vietnam has in practice governed itself, although a prudent acknowledgement of Chinese suzerainty was made by all the Vietnamese dynasties. In effect this meant very little; precious gifts were tendered as tribute, and the envoys received in return still more magnificent presents to display the power and munificence of the Emperor of China. The kings of Vietnam sought and obtained ratification of their accession from their suzerain. The Vietnamese adopted the calendar of the reigning Chinese dynasty, an act of some religious significance, and in some ways comparable to the flying of the Union Jack on some occasions by the self-governing and effectively independent members of the British Commonwealth. China undertook no obligation to defend Vietnam, neither against external foes, nor to help the reigning dynasty to crush internal rebellion. Vietnam was equally under no obligation to support Chinese wars in arms. It was understood that the tributary state should not further the designs nor give assistance to an enemy of the Emperor, and this also applied to private individuals as well as to foreign states.

This *modus vivendi* was not arrived at immediately: when the chaos which ensued upon the fall of the T'ang dynasty had been ended by the accession of the new Sung dynasty in 960 some years passed before the new empire was fully consolidated by the skilful policy of its founder. The southern states into which the empire had dissolved had one by one to be induced to return to the "true allegiance" or suppressed, usually with very light resistance, if they were recalcitrant. Until this task was accomplished there could be no question of Sung intervention in Vietnam. In 981 the Sung had become fully accepted and established. An expedition was then mounted to reduce the only remaining southern "dissident kingdom", Vietnam. Probably the Sung emperor and his advisers saw no material difference between the former province of Annam and the other kingdoms—or "empires" as they had called themselves—which had arisen in the southern provinces. All had been part of the T'ang empire and thus all should return to allegiance to the Sung. But Vietnam was different; it alone had its real national identity stronger than its bonds to China, especially in the political aspect of that relationship. Vietnam resisted, and with success. The Sung invasion was repelled. It was never attempted again. Vietnam acknowledged Chinese suzerainty, and the Sung emperors accepted this face-saving device. It remained Chinese policy from that time onward, only once reversed. The Sung had indeed other matters to trouble them. Their northern frontier, insecure since the loss of the territories controlling the passes through the Great Wall, which they failed to reconquer, was their constant problem. Vietnam was more a matter of prestige than national security, it could be left alone.

Changes of dynasty in Vietnam, brought about by insurrections or palace plots, did not tempt the Sung to seize any such opportunities. In 1010, only twenty years after the repulse of the Sung invasion, a new dynasty, the Ly, came to power in Vietnam. It promptly renewed the existing tributary–suzerain relationship with the Sung empire, and was accepted. When it in turn was displaced in 1225 the Sung empire had lost north China to the invading Kin Tatars, and was established in the south at Hangchou, controlling the Yangtze valley and all territory to the south of that river. In earlier times the shift of Chinese central power to the south had meant a tendency to expand in the southern borderlands. It is thought that in fact there was a considerable movement of northern population into south China at this time, but it was absorbed within the existing frontiers of the Sung empire. The south of China developed rapidly in this period, but the pressure was not sufficient to push the Sung empire into wars of conquest beyond their dominions. Moreover they had to guard an exposed northern border along the indeterminate margin of the northern rim of the Yangtze basin, a region which has no natural frontier, especially in the eastern section.

The new Vietnamese dynasty, the Tranh, was left in peace by the Southern Sung, but before very many years had passed, had to face the tremendous danger of Mongol invasions. When the Tranh had come to power the Sung were already under attack from the new masters of north China, and of an empire stretching across Asia to the heart of Russia. The conquest of the Southern Sung by the Mongols was a long, slow process, fiercely resisted for forty years. It was not until 1278 that the Sung fleet was finally destroyed off Hong Kong and the dynasty utterly destroyed. Five years later, in 1284, Kubilai Khan, the Mongol Emperor of China whom the Chinese recognise as the first legitimate ruler of the empire (although his forebears back to Genghiz had in fact ruled in north China for seventy years), invaded Vietnam. The Vietnamese, faced with the might of the greatest military power in the world of that age resorted to guerrilla warfare; the cities were abandoned to the invaders, the resistance concentrated in the jungles and mountains. The Mongol armies were mainly cavalry, and the climate as well as the terrain of Vietnam were inimical to their forces. The invasions were repeated for three or four years, but the losses through disease and the inconclusive character of the war finally decided Kubilai that Vietnam was not worth the trouble and loss; he accepted the tribute of the Tranh rulers and withdrew his decimated armies. At this period, it must be emphasised, "Vietnam", or

Annam as it was called by the Chinese, still only comprised the Red River delta and the coastal strip running southward to the region of the 17th parallel of latitude. The great "March to the South" had barely begun. The dynasty of the Tranh ruled only what is now North Vietnam. That dynasty endured beyond the Mongol Yüan dynasty of China itself. In 1400, when it fell, the Ming, representing the Chinese counter-thrust, had driven the Mongols from China and under the vigorous Emperor Yung Lo was pushing its claims to allegiance into the world of the southern kingdoms, both by sea and by land. A few years after the fall of the Tranh, in 1407, Emperor Yung Lo, presumably deciding that he need not recognise its successors, invaded Vietnam and achieved the conquest of the country. As will be seen the kingdom already extended as far south as Da Nang, but it would seem that Chinese rule was never very firmly established in these new southern lands. In any case it did not last long. Yung Lo himself died in 1425, and there was a rapid succession of short-lived emperors in China, which weakened the government. In 1427, a revolt which had already broken out nine years earlier in 1418 under Le Loi, who defeated the Chinese near the border city of Lang Son, achieved decisive victory and recaptured the capital, Hanoi. The Ming emperors, like their Sung predecessors, then accepted the tribute offered by Le Loi, who founded the new Vietnamese dynasty. The invasion of Emperor Yung Lo was the last attempt by the rulers of China to incorporate Vietnam into the Chinese empire as a province. When the Manchus succeeded to the throne in the seventeenth century they made some military demonstrations against Vietnam, but quickly accepted the existing political relationship first established in Sung times. Thus for over a thousand years, since the achievement of independence in 939 to the French conquest in the later part of the nineteenth century, Vietnam was effectively an independent state, even if it remained one under strong and continuing Chinese cultural influence.

Chinese rule had been exercised over what was a much smaller area than the kingdom which arose after independence was achieved. That is perhaps, one reason why the T'ang and earlier, weaker empires such as those of south China between the Han and the T'ang were able to maintain their authority in the distant province. The Vietnamese for their part were in those centuries barred from southward expansion by the presence of the warlike Cham kingdom which engaged in frequent piratical sea-borne attacks upon the coast. The protection of the Chinese empire was needed and had to be paid for with the price of direct Chinese rule. Almost immediately after independence was achieved in the early tenth century A.D. this situation changed. One cause was the increase in population of the fertile Red River delta under the long and peaceful T'ang rule.

Pressure demanded fresh lands for settlement, and being essentially a rice-cultivating people, the Vietnamese sought these new lands along the fertile coastal strip, not in the western mountain region which borders upon Yünnan. The mountains were then, as now, largely inhabited by tribes of non-Vietnamese stock, usually hostile to the men of the plains; it was more worthwhile to seize good land along the coast than engage in difficult conquests for poorer land in the mountains.

In 982 the new Dinh dynasty, which had come to power only some forty years earlier, was strong enough to invade the kingdom of Champa and sack its capital, then in the northern part of the country. Vietnam retained some of the conquered territory, but the southward march was resumed by the next Vietnamese dynasty, the Ly (1010–1225), which by 1069 had annexed all Cham lands down to the region of the 17th parallel, that is to say, what is now North Vietnam. It is clear that the Cham inhabitants were not merely conquered—or slain—the survivors were driven out, to take refuge in the southern parts of their homeland. Vietnamese conquest was not mere aggression to impose rule and collect revenue, it was consciously designed to win new territory for Vietnamese settlement. This objective proved to be the unifying force and inspiration of the new independent régime. The peasants, crowded upon the inadequate lands of the Red River delta, wanted new lands to escape the increasing poverty of over-populated villages. The landlord class—whom the Communists today call "feudalists", but who were in fact a landed gentry largely employed by the government as officials in the Chinese manner—wanted new estates; both classes therefore supported the wars of conquest and settlement. The characteristic of Vietnamese southward migration is thus very similar to that of Chinese southern expansion within what are now the southern provinces of China. But in Vietnam there was neither room nor desire for Chinese settlers: Vietnamese were themselves all too numerous. They carried Chinese culture and custom with them to the south, but the great expansion was neither Chinese in manpower nor in direction. Chinese rule in Vietnam had ended before it began.

When the Ly dynasty fell, the new Tranh, 1225–1400, took up the task and followed the same policy. By 1306 they had reached Da Nang, now in South Vietnam. The relative delay in achieving this objective may be a consequence of the great Mongol invasions of 1284 and the devastation that they caused. Vietnam could afford no southern adventures while this danger lasted. By 1306 Kubilai Khan was dead, and his successors, ephemeral and short-reigning monarchs, had abandoned their dream of world-wide conquest. In the later Yüan (Mongol) dynasty China was quiescent in respect of southern policy. The Tranh kings of Vietnam were therefore able to resume the "March to the South", as far as Da Nang, but it is probable that this long step was more than a dynasty already past its prime could safely afford. In 1371 the Chams, in a last effective resurgence, swept north and actually took and sacked Hanoi itself. This disaster plunged the Tranh dynasty into a confusion from which it never recovered. Thirty years later it was displaced in 1400 and in the confusion that followed the Chinese emperor Yung Lo achieved his brief reconquest of Vietnam (1407–27). This in turn ended with the successful resistance of the new Le dynasty, but it was fifty years before the March to the South could be resumed on a large scale. The Cham counter-attack in 1371, aided by these circumstances which were coincidental to it, had won Champa a reprieve of one hundred years.

In 1471 the Vietnamese monarch invaded Champa in strength and was wholly victorious. The capital was taken, a large-scale massacre of the inhabitants carried out, and the kingdom of Champa virtually destroyed. Cham remnants in the far south, the region of the Mekong delta, were divided among several small principalities all under Vietnamese suzerainty. The Vietnamese had largely achieved their objective, the conquest of the south, but this fact proved to be a new problem in itself. The expansion into new lands, where population was less, meant that the immigrants tended to acquire those characteristics which have always distinguished a migrant population. They became less amenable to the distant central government, more independent in their thinking and way of life. They had discovered that by moving south one could largely leave an oppressive government behind; if it followed up, one had only to move on to newer, still more fertile lands. Before long the government in Hanoi found the distant south hard to control. The Le dynasty had passed its zenith by the middle of the sixteenth century. Two great official families dominated the Court, and their intrigues and mutual hostility threatened the régime. Of the two the Trinh had the greater power in Hanoi, and in 1558 they contrived to rid themselves of their rivals, the Nguyen, by getting the head of that family appointed as viceroy of the south, with headquarters at Hué. This both left the Trinh in unmolested authority over the weak Le kings, and left the problems of the south for their rivals to solve as best they could.

The Nguyen proved very capable of dealing with them. There was now what amounted to, and steadily developed as, a new central government located in the south itself, at Hué. It was in the interest of the Nguyen to expand once more, so as to increase their domain and strengthen themselves against the Trinh in the north. Expansion would bring new settlers from the north, and the south was still much less populous. Within just over a century, by 1692, the Nguyen rulers at Hué had totally suppressed the remaining Cham principalities and virtually annihilated that nation. Some communities of Chams still exist along the far south coast of Vietnam, and in the neighbouring districts of Cambodia, but as a nation the Chams disappear from history. The Nguyen had taken Saigon in 1691. This event was only a very few years after the new Manchu dynasty of China, under the vigorous young ruler Emperor K'ang Hsi, had finally suppressed all his Chinese opponents in south China and conquered the whole empire (1688). The fact that the Nguyen found it possible to undertake the last great conquest of the south, that of the Mekong delta, at a time when their northern rivals at Hanoi, the Trinh, had to reckon with the possible ambition and hostility of a new warlike and victorious Emperor of China is certainly significant. Trinh embarrassment was Nguyen opportunity.

The Nguyen were not very much afraid of K'ang Hsi; they admitted to their newly-conquered lands not only Vietnamese settlers but also Chinese refugees from the Manchu conquest of south China; some of these founded Cholon, the still Chinese-inhabited sister town of Saigon. Others settled in the Mekong delta. In earlier times no Vietnamese régime dared to harbour the enemies of the Emperor of China. The Trinh in Hanoi were still in this exposed position, but the Nguyen in the south could afford to flout the old prohibition and ignore China; they had the Trinh in between. This fact illuminates the great change which the March to the South had brought about in the relations between the Chinese Empire and its "tributary", Annam. The tributary was now a large kingdom, and the southern half of it was almost inaccessible to direct Chinese power. The Manchus, a land people, never took to the sea, nor maintained large efficient naval forces. The Manchu empire was at this very time ready to engage in far-ranging campaigns to conquer Mongolia, central Asia and Tibet. A century later it was to carry out the remarkable feat of crossing the Himalayas and conquering Nepal, but it did not attempt to reconquer Vietnam, north or south, Trinh or Nguyen. The system, now tried for centuries, by which Vietnam was ready to acknowledge the suzerainty of the Emperor and participate fully in the Chinese civilisation was sufficient for the pride and less expensive to the purse of Chinese rulers.

The elimination of Champa, and its survival for so long, were intimately related to the fortunes of a country with which the Vietnamese had previously less direct contact, Cambodia. The long pause in the March to the South which followed the advance to the 17th parallel region in 1069, before the great step forward to Da Nang in 1306, is in part the same period in which the great Cambodian king Jayavarman VII was pursuing his conquests in southern Champa. He held that country till his death, in 1218, although it regained independence after that.

Even before his reign Vietnam had had to reckon with Cambodian power as a competitor for the Cham inheritance. Throughout the twelfth century from 1123 onward when King Suryavarman II attacked Annam itself (as was done again in 1150), Cambodian power was active in the southern part of what is now Vietnam, both against the Chams and sometimes in alliance with them. The relative passivity of the Sung in China, which should have encouraged the Vietnamese to push forward the March to the South, had been matched by the activity of Cambodia in the region to which such a March was directed. King Jayavarman VII was the last great Cambodian conqueror; his campaigns, and his buildings, over-strained the resources of the kingdom, and in the thirteenth century Cambodia enters first a period of tranquillity which passed in the next century into decline. This easing of Cambodian pressure permitted the Chams to mount their last great counter-attack on Vietnam in 1371 and equally, after the Ming conquest of Vietnam by Emperor Yung Lo had been terminated in 1427, gave Vietnam the freedom of action required to conquer Champa in 1471.

By the time the Vietnamese were moving into the Mekong delta, Cambodia, under constant pressure from the Thais, former tributaries now become powerful enemies, had been forced to abandon Angkor; and her kings were rather precariously established on the Mekong lower course, including much of what is now the upper delta. Thus the Vietnamese after destroying the Cham principalities found a common frontier with a weak and harassed Cambodia. The pressure formerly put upon the Chams was transferred to the Khmers, who were gradually forced out of the delta region. This confrontation between a weakened Cambodia and an expanding Vietnam under the Nguyen viceroys gave rise to the long-standing hostility between the two nations. The Khmers fear the fate of the Chams, and see their own fertile Mekong basin country as the next field for Vietnamese expansion; the Vietnamese have not ceased the March to the South, and under French rule did in fact continue to infiltrate settlers into Cambodia.

The March to the South, especially its later phases when some proportion of the conquered population was assimilated into the victorious Vietnamese people, had the effect of diluting and subtly altering the character of that Chinese culture which the northern Vietnamese had so long adopted. The population of the southern provinces was less heavily infiltrated and controlled by the educated—Confucian Chinese educated—class than it had been in the north. Estates were larger, the proportion of peasants higher to that of landlords. Consequently northern Confucian culture was challenged by southern partly pre-Vietnamese, partly spontaneous new sects and trends. Buddhism flourished, and took on the character of a popular as opposed to an official cult. It no doubt drew strength from the Buddhist character of the Cham and Cambodian elements in the population. Later indigenous sects arose, some of which still continue. After the introduction of Christianity Catholicism made rapid progress. These movements can be seen as in part due to the weakening of the impact of purely Chinese civilisation at a greater distance from the source, and in part due to social causes, the independent character of a pioneer peasant population in opposition to the pretensions of a landlord class.

The fact that it was to the south that the first European voyagers and traders came, bringing with them new ideas and a new religion, added to this developing regional distinction. It was some twenty years before the southern viceroyalty was set up under the Nguyen leader (1558), that the first Portuguese ship touched upon the coast of Vietnam (1535). Missionaries soon followed the early navigators and found in the far southern region, the Mekong delta, a relatively fertile field for their endeavours. The factors outlined above weakened the popular opposition to a new religion, and the ease and progress of Catholic conversions in the south certainly illustrates a side to the South Vietnamese character, indeed to that of all Vietnamese, which marks a clear difference between them and the people of China itself. It may be that a people is always uneasily conscious of the fact that its culture is alien and was originally imposed by conquest. Similar traditions of opposition, covert and popular rather than overt and aristocratic, to foreign imposed cultures appear in many parts of the world (Ireland is a good example). A manifestation of this attitude, of great importance to the future culture of Vietnam and its relationship with China, was an indirect consequence of missionary endeavour.

Faced with the double difficulty of the complexity and range of the Chinese ideographic script and the fact that most of the population was illiterate, the missionaries decided to create an alphabetic rendering of Vietnamese (a language which permits of this treatment) and invented *Quoc Ngu*, the romanised rendering of the spoken Vietnamese language. They then translated religious works into Vietnamese using this system of writing. Such a development would never have been possible in China: firstly the nature of a language largely homophonic does not lend itself to alphabetic transcription; secondly the Chinese reverence for and pride in their own ideographic system would at once have stigmatised any new transcription as barbarous. The early Catholic missionaries in China, pursuing the exact opposite course to their colleagues in Vietnam, learned Chinese and became proficient scholars in the literature and classical language. *Quoc Ngu* spread quickly, and far beyond Christian convert circles. It naturally aroused the alarm of the Confucian-educated official and landowning class, since it cut at the foundations of their authority and prestige. Also, it was not a system adapted to transcribing the classical Chinese language, and thus offered no help to traditional educators. Just as in China the ultimate major influence of Christian teaching, present from the very first Jesuits used by the Court as astronomers and mathematicians, was to sow the seeds of interest in the natural sciences, so in Vietnam the ultimate major influence was the creation (also from the first) of an instrument fitted to spread and strengthen the national culture in opposition to the alien civilisation of Chinese origin.

Christian influence was before long introduced into the northern part of Vietnam also, but it does not seem to have been quite so powerful as it was in the south. It was also associated with the growth in trade and the appearance of a merchant class in the ports and cities, who were equally uneasy subjects for the Confucian official ruling class. The division between the Nguyen viceroys in the south and the Trinh regents dominating the northern Court was tiresome and hampering to traders, and offended the sense of unity of the whole people. It continued to trouble the country with civil wars and strife throughout the seventeenth century and the first part of the eighteenth century also. Confucian tradition despised commerce and the government did little to foster it and much to harass and fleece the merchant class. Foreign visitors remarked on the poverty of the peasantry and observed that the merchants, although often wealthy, did their best to conceal their condition from a hostile government. Here again the over-emphasis on a trait of imported culture is observable in Vietnam. In China the official class intellectually despised merchants, but in practice frequently co-operated with them in lucrative ventures and winked at their evasions of the law against purchase of land and of official rank.

The tensions of Vietnamese society, occasioned in part by the virtual cessation of the March to the South after the incorporation of the Mekong delta at the end of the seventeenth century (1622) exploded some eighty years later in the great Tay Son rebellion (1772–1802), led by three brothers Nguyen, who seem to have had a merchant background. Their rebellion arose in the south and was in part based on the mountainous and jungle-covered region north-west of the Mekong delta, from which it took its name Tay Son, meaning Western Mountains. It was extremely successful for many years. Saigon was taken in 1776, and ten years later the rebels, having virtually overthrown the Nguyen viceroyalty of the south, attacked the northern region and took the royal capital of Hanoi in 1786. The distracted Trinh regents and their supporters then appealed to China to help them. Emperor Ch'ien Lung of the Manchu dynasty, the third of the great trio of Manchu rulers, was then on the throne, which he had already occupied for forty years. He decided that the Tay Son revolt and the collapse of all recognised Vietnamese authorities opened another opportunity for Chinese intervention. His armies had during his reign completed the conquest of Mongolia, Chinese central Asia and Tibet. In 1789 he dispatched a large army to northern Vietnam, but it was met and defeated by the Tay Son forces near the frontier. Ch'ien Lung abandoned any further intervention.

Only a year or two later the forces which were to defeat the Tay Son movement had come into action. The French adventurer and *émigré* from the French Revolution, Pigneau de Behaine, gathered in the eastern possessions of France in India, which had not yet accepted the Revolution, a mixed force of European adventurers nominally in the service of Nguyen Anh, last claimant for the fallen Nguyen viceroys of the south, who had fled abroad. Naval raids and small-scale invasions were organised by Pigneau de Behaine and his Vietnamese ally upon the south coast. They met with some support largely from the Christian converts. In 1791 they recaptured Saigon, and from this essential base steadily pursued their purpose, raiding and invading up the coast with every south-east monsoon (summer). Hué was taken in 1801; and Hanoi itself the next year, 1802, an event which marks the end of the Tay Son revolt. That rebellion had been characterised by a markedly national and anti-Confucian aspect. *Quoc Ngu* became its official language in place of traditional Chinese; one of the original brothers who started the revolt was a Buddhist monk, and the support of the Catholic converts for the counter-revolution forecast an alignment which has persisted to the present time.

The other striking facts about the Tay Son movement are firstly, that it was consciously and successfully "pan-Vietnamese". It reunified the country, refused to perpetuate the separation of the southern viceroyalty, and set up its capital in Hanoi, the old centre of government. In this way it certainly represented a very deep feeling of unity in the Vietnamese people which subsequent imposed divisions have failed to eradicate. Secondly the movement was defeated by foreign intervention, and not by Chinese intervention, which was repelled. The activities of the seaborne forces of Pigneau de Behaine thus foreshadowed the coming French conquest, and the apparent triumph of Nguyen Anh was the prelude to the domination of his allies. The fact that the defeated Trinh had preferred to risk the consequences of Chinese invasion rather than accept the national character of the Tay Son movement also illustrates a new trend in the development of Vietnamese history. National movements become more and more hostile to the rule of Sinified officials and a Chinese-orientated culture; when in the nineteenth century Chinese power ceased to be the urgent question, and French penetration took its place, the national movements of revolt and protest turned against the new foreign danger.

There are similarities between the Tay Son revolt in Vietnam and the Tai Ping rebellion in China some fifty years later. Both were popular movements based on the peasantry and hostile to the ruling Confucian ideology, both came within an ace of total victory and the consequent profound re-orientation of the culture of their country. Both were largely defeated by foreign intervention based on sea power. Saigon in the hands of Pigneau de Behaine foreshadowed the rôle of Shanghai as the military base for General Gordon's "Ever Victorious Army" and the financial base for Li Hung-chang's rather more powerful and ultimately effective Anhui imperialist army. Both movements also point to a new attitude, as yet couched in antique forms, from which later national and popular movements drew inspiration. Tay Son embodies the ideal of a united Vietnam, national in culture and popular in support. The Tai Pings are recognised by the Chinese Communists today as the forerunners, even if often on the wrong track, of their own triumphant revolution.

Nguyen Anh, who took the throne of an united Vietnam, which was in fact the work of his enemies, reigned as the Emperor Gia Long of the new dynasty of the Nguyen. His forebears had been the viceroys of the south, he himself made Hué his capital, and forsook Hanoi. Gia Long made it his policy to reinforce the Chinese character of his rule in every possible way. His new title of Emperor, which might have been somewhat presumptuous in Chinese eyes, did not incur the active wrath of Ch'ien Lung's harassed successors, nor prevent a formal acknowledgement of Chinese suzerainty. The government was rigidly centralised; Nguyen Anh, descendant of the southern viceroys, did not intend that others should emulate the history of his own family. The Chinese examination system for the Civil Service was reinforced and remodelled on lines close to Chinese practice. Confucian learning was stressed, Buddhism was restricted and often persecuted, the régime, in spite of its debt to French mercenaries, became markedly anti-Catholic. In the south the colonisation of the delta region was intensified by planting military farmer-soldier colonies along the borders with Cambodia and in the sparsely inhabited new lands along the lower Mekong. The active resistance to French conquest which these colonies later demonstrated shows that Emperor Gia Long was probably already aware that his southern provinces were the most exposed to foreign dangers, not the northern frontier with Manchu China.

Four successive emperors of Vietnam reigned and ruled from 1802 to 1883, the year in which French conquest or imposed protectorate, ended real Vietnamese independence. Gia Long (1802–20) was not directly involved in conflict with the French, and followed his own strictly traditional and authoritarian policy, including anti-Catholic measures, undisturbed. His two immediate successors, Minh Mang, died 1841, and Thieu Tri, died 1847, were still able to hold off the increasing pressures which in part generated by the missionaries and their converts, in part deriving from the growing mood of European nineteenth century imperialism, were mounting around them. Until the end of Gia Long's reign the Napoleonic Wars and the exhaustion of France by this long struggle made foreign invasion from that quarter impossible. Until the English had revealed the inherent weakness of the Manchu dynasty in China by their easy victories in the Opium War (1840-2) the European nations still had a respect for the strength of the eastern empires which might have been justified in the eighteenth century, but was now out of date. It is significant that the first French military initiative, an attack upon the port city of Da Nang, occurred in 1847, only five years after China's defeat in the Opium War. It was an isolated instance, without lasting consequences, but it happened in the year that Emperor Thieu Tri died; his successor, Tu Duc, last independent monarch of Vietnam, was to struggle all his life against increasing encroachment.

In 1858 Admiral Rigault de Genouilly attacked Da Nang again, and in the next year captured Saigon. From that event there began a series of encroachments and annexations which have some similarity to the career of Pigneau de Behaine and Gia Long himself in their war against the Tay Son only sixty years earlier. Saigon became the base; the conquered area was enlarged around it, and interior regions thus cut off from the rule of the government in Hué. In 1862 the eastern part of what was to be called Cochin China, Saigon, Mytho and Bien Hoa, was ceded to the French by the Emperor Tu Duc, who feared further aggressions if he resisted, and their consequences upon the internal stability of his régime. In 1864 the French envoy on the spot was induced to agree to a retrocession of these areas, and signed such an instrument. His action was repudiated in Paris, where a powerful colonialist political lobby was now forming. Three years later in 1867 the French governor in Saigon on his own initiative invaded and occupied, then annexed, the remains of the delta region of South Vietnam up to the Cambodian border. At the same time a protectorate was imposed upon the weak kingdom of Cambodia, which indeed almost welcomed this protection from Vietnamese and Thai aggressions.

It may be observed that these important French advances were concurrent with the decline of Chinese political power due first to the Tai Ping rebellion in the fifties and early sixties of the century and then to the Anglo-French War against China from 1858 to 1860, which imposed new and far-reaching restrictions on the declining empire. Tu Duc could not hope for help from China in this troubled epoch. On the other hand France's own disaster in 1870 only called a very temporary halt to the progress of conquest and domination in Vietnam. By 1873 the government in Saigon was strong enough to eliminate all remnant of Vietnamese administration and bring in direct French colonial rule. The officials ("mandarins") of Tu Duc had refused to co-operate, and in many cases had withdrawn from the area; the French therefore claimed that this created an administrative vacuum which they must fill themselves. They did; taxation increased ten times in the next twenty years. The age of colonial exploitation had begun.

In the same year, 1873, the French first moved against the northern part of Vietnam, where an officer acting almost independently of the home government, but not without political backing in France, seized Hanoi. He was killed there the next year, and the French evacuated the city in return for a new treaty signed by Tu Duc granting open trade in Tongking and the free navigation of the Red River. Meanwhile in China there had been what Chinese historians call the T'ung Chih Restoration (Revival would be a better term) which followed the suppression of the Tai Ping rebellion in 1862 and the subsequent suppression of the lesser rebellions of the Nien Fei in central China and of the Moslems in the western provinces and in Yünnan. The dynasty was once more in control, and the great Chinese viceroys who had re-established it were making cautious attempts to modernise the armies and create a minimum of modern industry, mainly for armaments. Tu Duc was induced to believe that China could, after all, once more offer a counterpoise to the aggressions of France. In 1880 he sent a tribute mission, not merely to the frontier, as had long been customary, but to Peking itself. This was clearly a political demonstration of faith in China and an indirect appeal for Chinese protection. It infuriated the French colonialist party.

Within two years the French, accusing the Vietnamese government of infractions of the Treaty (the standard excuse for forceful action throughout the Far East at this period) seized Hanoi (1882), this time intending to stay; and although the commander of the expedition, Rivière, was killed the next year, the French did not withdraw. War in the Red River delta continued for nearly twenty years, the French meeting guerrilla resistance which is described by contemporaries in words which might be used by the Americans today. The invisible enemy, who melts in the presence of powerful forces, but reappears when they leave, who cannot be distinguished from the peasantry in the fields, because he is often one of them himself. Tu Duc died in 1883 and dynastic troubles at his succession opened the way for the French to occupy Hué and set up a puppet emperor. Another claimant withdrew to lead the guerrilla resistance until his death. Meanwhile China had intervened, both with the action of guerrilla irregulars called the Black Flags (themselves successors to Tai Ping refugees who had fled into the frontier mountains) and with regular forces. These won a victory over the French at Lang Son, but the French command of the sea, which made it possible for them to bombard the Chinese port of Foochow and attack other coastal areas, coupled with China's preoccupations in Korea with Japan, made the Chinese Court willing to make peace, abandoning its claim, millennial in duration, of suzerainty over Vietnam. This event formally terminated Chinese authority of any kind in the country; French imposition of direct colonial rule in Tongking in 1887 and the increasing power of the protectorate over the shrunken empire of Annam at Hué ended for more than fifty years the independence of Vietnam itself.

CHAPTER THREE

CHINESE EXPANSION BY LAND: YÜNNAN

Yünnan, the most south-westerly of the provinces of China, has been an integral part of the Empire and later Republic since the middle of the thirteenth century, when it was conquered by the Mongols, then ruling in a great part of China. The thirteenth century is in Chinese history almost the modern epoch, certainly not a period of high antiquity. For fifteen centuries preceding the Mongol conquest China had known Yünnan not as a province, but as the seat of an alien and often hostile kingdom. It was first given the name Yünnan in the third century A.D. when the western dynasty of Shu Han, one of the Three Kingdoms, briefly imposed suzerainty on some part of the country. Yünnan means "South of the Clouds" and this seemingly poetic name actually describes the principal climatic feature of the country. The high plateau of Yünnan, in the west at around 7,000 feet, sloping in the south-east to about 4,000 feet, is literally south of the clouds, the moist cloudy provinces of Ssuchuan and Kueichou. Of the first the proverb unkindly says "Dogs of Ssuchuan bark when the sun shines", implying the rarity of this event. Of the second, Kueichou, it is said "Kueichou has never three fine days (together)"— adding that it has never three flat "li" (miles) nor three pieces of silver, a jingle which rhymes in Chinese. ("Kueichou mei yu san t'ien ch'ing, san li p'ing, san k'uai yin.") But in Yünnan the climate is dry and warm, its tropical latitude moderated by high altitude, the long dry winter compensated by abundant permanent streams and rivers flowing down from its high ranges.

Great ranges rib this plateau, from north to south, dividing the country in the west into deep narrow valleys, in the eastern part into wider, more open valleys many of which contain large lakes, or are formed from the beds of lakes which have drained away. To the north-west the mountains attain 20,000 feet, declining as they run south to less than half that altitude. But the mountains are rarely less than four or five thousand feet higher than the plateau in any district. The mountains are steep and still in many parts heavily forested, unsuitable for agriculture; the plateaux and the valleys are rich lands well watered at all seasons, never in danger of

39

drought, and usually free from flood risk also. It is a country designed by nature to favour local heavy settlement by agricultural peoples separated by high uninhabited ranges from their nearest neighbours. This indeed has been the ethnic history of Yünnan, one of fragmentation, not only into differing racial groups in different valleys, but also between one people on the good lands and less advanced peoples in the ranges above them. Thus there has always been, and still persists, vertical as well as horizontal divisions among the inhabitants of Yünnan. The stronger peoples took the rice-growing valleys, the weaker were pushed up into the mountains, very often driving still more primitive peoples into the highest levels. Peoples who lived by hunting and food collecting could there survive, for game is plentiful. Lower down the "slash and burn" type of cultivation, destructive to forests, was widely practised. The evidence of the surviving layers of varying peoples, very distinct in culture, language and way of life, suggests that the Chinese were by no means the first invaders to displace the cultivators of the rich valleys and lake shores.

Yünnan has been many times invaded, and settled, in part or on a wide scale by newcomers. The origin of these prehistoric movements and the peoples who made them cannot be discovered, and archaeology has as yet thrown little light on the prehistory of Yünnan. It can at least be said that the routes by which they must have come can be conjectured, if only because there are so few available. Some peoples descended from the Tibetan plateau, still higher than that of Yünnan, by the high valley of the Yangtze and the upper Mekong, routes which are still in use as highways from Yünnan to Tibet. The passes are high, the valleys often very narrow, and the rivers too swift and rocky for navigation. Such routes can only be used with the consent of the valley dwellers, for they are easily blocked. It is more likely that infiltration rather than invasion was the pattern of northern movement into Yünnan. To the north-east a somewhat easier route leads to Yünnan from western Ssuchuan, the city of Suifu on the upper Yangtze being the starting-point. This route, although, as is inevitable on any journey in Yünnan, crossing several high ranges, is mainly across the plateau. It was still used on a large scale by mule and pony caravans carrying Ssuchuanese silk to Burma and thence, by river steamer and sea passage to Calcutta, up to the Second World War. The caravan road from Suifu to Bhamo on the Irrawaddy was over six hundred miles in length. This route was one which many armies were to follow, especially in the earlier centuries when Kueichou was not pacified.

The most obvious route, from the limit of navigation on the rivers of western Hunan province, rivers which are tributaries of the Yangtze, was across Kueichou province. The ranges are here lower, though rugged; the border range with Yünnan itself being the highest. This was in late imperial times (the Manchu dynasty) the trunk road from Peking to Yünnan. It was also by this route that the Ming emperor Yung Lo had the great marble slabs, which still decorate the stairways of the Forbidden City, hauled for hundreds of miles over mountains and valleys till they could be rafted in western Hunan and reach Peking via the Yangtze and the Grand Canal, a distance of somewhat more than 3,000 miles. In earlier times the Kueichou route was less used, because the province was not pacified and remained divided among hostile tribal groups until the Manchu emperors conquered it in the early eighteenth century. Less direct, although important for some trade, was the route from the limit of navigation on the West River (which flows to the sea below Canton) across north-west Kuangsi province and then across the Yünnan plateau to K'unming, the provincial capital. This was a road which connected Yünnan with south China, not with the northern provinces from whence authority, armies and power usually emanated.

Very few, if any, of the rivers of Yünnan are avenues of travel or trade, and none are navigable within the borders of the province. In the west, the three great rivers, Salween, Mekong and Yangtze, run in tremendous deep parallel valleys for several hundreds of miles, only separated by high rugged ranges. Then they diverge, the Yangtze turning north and then east, the Mekong continuing south to Cambodia and Laos, the Salween passing into Burma. Three rivers whose courses are respectively barely thirty miles apart in western Yünnan reach the sea at points so far apart as the vicinity of Shanghai, Saigon and Rangoon. Their high valleys are several thousand feet higher in the east than in the west: the Salween runs at about 2,000 feet in Yünnan, the Mekong at about 4,000, and the high Yangtze is 6,000 feet above sea level when it bends abruptly to the north and east, cutting in half a range of mountains 20,000 feet in height. Between these deep valleys are ranges which often exceed 12,000 feet and grow higher to the east. The valleys are narrow, affording very little cultivable soil, and the rise and fall of the river between summer and winter (summer being the season of high water) can be scores of feet. These valleys, especially those of the Mekong and Salween, are infested with a peculiarly virulent type of malaria, and Chinese will not settle in them; even travellers hurry through them and never spend the night in the valley. The West River, which forms the artery of the south China provinces of Kuangsi and Kuangtung, rises on the Yünnan plateau, but is not navigable until after it has reached Kuangsi.

The barriers to intercourse with outside peoples seem, and are, more formidable on the western borders of Yünnan than in the east or south;

yet they have been crossed for many centuries by traders and travellers, if much less frequently by armies. Once the traveller has passed the Salween and its divide the descent to Burma and the Irrawaddy valley is relatively easy, if at times unhealthy. The great river gives easy access to the sea, and coasting voyages could link Burma and India. There is little doubt that some sort of contact existed along this indirect route from very early times, even if it was at first confined to intertribal trade. The direct route to India, across the jungles of northern Burma to Manipur and the valleys of Assam was more difficult and much less safe. Even in modern times these jungles have been the stronghold of head-hunting tribes who offered only a grim welcome to travellers. The connection between Yünnan was with South-East Asia, Burma and Vietnam, not directly with India. The route to Vietnam, today the line of the railway built in the early years of the twentieth century by the French, was not easy nor much travelled in antiquity. The descent from the Yünnan plateau is very steep, and the gorges of many rivers lie across the way. The valley of the Red River, which forms the rich delta of Tongking, is malarial and narrow, although this river, rising on the Yünnan plateau, might seem to afford the obvious and natural link between Yünnan and Vietnam. As is so often the case in Yünnan the river is virtually useless for this purpose, and travellers must find a seemingly more arduous road across the mountains. When the French obtained their concession for the railway the Chinese imperial government refused to consent to the Red River valley route, which would have been relatively easy to construct, on the grounds that the area was too unhealthy and that a railway would serve no economic purpose there. The real reason was that they believed the mountain route to be so difficult and steep that no railway could in fact be built on that alignment. The French built it none the less, one of the most spectacular lines in the world, spanning profound gorges and tunnelling through range after range. Strategically, as was proved in the Second World War, it was useless; it was only necessary to blow a few bridges and block a few tunnels to make it impassable. The Japanese never penetrated into Yünnan by this route. Economically it was barely worthwhile, but as feat of engineering, it was superb.

The first recorded contacts between China and Yünnan date from the late fourth century B.C., and were not made by the Chinese kingdoms of that date in north China, but by Ch'u, the southern kingdom which was centred on the middle Yangtze, but also comprised the modern province of Hunan. Ch'u was not strictly a Chinese kingdom; it had never been freely accepted as one of the members of the ancient concept, the Middle Kingdom, over which the Chou kings reigned rather than ruled. Ch'u was possibly basically of T'ai or Miao ethnic stock, or as some writers consider, of mixed stock, incorporating a wide variety of the ancient peoples of south and central China. That it was in culture under strong Chinese influence is certain from the numerous archaeological finds which have been made in areas which were part of Ch'u and also from much Chinese literary evidence. At the end of the fourth century B.C. the contest between the kingdoms of China for supreme mastery of the Chinese world was growing intense. The chief rivals were already the north-western kingdom of Ch'in, which is believed to have been only partly Chinese (Han) in ethnic character, and the southern kingdom of Ch'u, which was, as has been seen, certainly of largely southern non-Han stock. Ch'in was steadily annexing large parts of the old northern kingdoms, and thus growing stronger. Ch'u, which had rivals lower down the Yangtze river, had been prevented from effective competition for the northern heritage by these distractions, and in the late fourth century sought some compensation in expanding southward, into the regions beyond Hunan, then occupied by a number of less advanced peoples.

King Wei of Ch'u (339-329 B.C.) sent a general, member of the royal family, named Chuang Ch'iao to extend his power in this direction. Chuang Ch'iao seems to have taken the route across Kueichou for at least part of his forces, although other contingents may have taken the route from the high Yangtze at Suifu through Chaot'ung to K'unming. This route would then have passed through the south Ssuchuan kingdom of Pa, which was at war with its northern neighbour, Shu, and probably therefore unable to bar the passage of the Ch'u army. Chuang Ch'iao was able to force his way through to the K'unming plain, on the shores of the great Tien Lake. This is the largest and one of the most fertile areas of rice cultivation in Yünnan, and the present city of K'unming, capital of the province, is situated there. Chuang Ch'iao annexed the region to Ch'u, and called it Tien. This word has no other meaning in Chinese other than as a place-name for the lake and region, except a probably derivative adjective meaning "boundless, vast". It is likely that it is a name derived from the previous masters of the district.

Very little is known of who these people may have been. A recent archaeological discovery not far from K'unming, at a hill-site called Shih Chia Chai, has brought to light bronze objects decorated with figures in relief which are of a markedly non-Chinese character, and seem to depict a people of pastoral pursuits, for domestic animals are plentifully shown. The date of these objects has been conjectured on stylistic grounds to be near or contemporary with the Ch'u conquest, but if the objects prove the introduction of Chinese bronze technique, they also exhibit the strength of a non-Chinese art tradition. The Ch'u army was certainly not strong enough to oust the natives of the soil, and was probably not accompanied

c

by many of its womenfolk. Before long developments in western China were to make the distant colony still more isolated.

In 316 B.C. the aggressive kingdom of Ch'in, profiting by the inter-necine war between the two Ssuchuanese kingdoms of Shu and Pa (respectively centred on modern Ch'engtu and Chungking) invaded and conquered both kingdoms, incorporating the whole of the great province of Ssuchuan into Ch'in. This event which enormously increased the power and resources of Ch'in was perhaps a decisive factor in her ultimate victory in the incessant conflicts of the Warring States. Its immediate consequence was to cut off the colony at Tien from direct contact with Ch'u. Chuang Ch'iao seems to have tried to re-establish communications across Kueichou, but found the resistance of the local tribes too powerful. Ch'u itself was now in greater danger from Ch'in aggression which continued to menace it until some ninety years later, in 223 B.C. it was conquered by Ch'in in the general collapse of the old kingdoms. Ch'in, having unified China for the first time was not interested in following up this conquest with a campaign into the remote south-west, and Tien was left in peace. Chuang Ch'iao ruled it as a viceroy of Ch'u, but his successors became kings of Tien.

It is probable (there are some literary indications of the fact) that many refugees from the former kingdom of Pa in Ssuchuan fled south to Tien. It became an isolated focus of Chinese culture in an area still mainly untouched by such influences, and K'unming, its modern successor has remained the chief centre of Chinese power and civilisation in Yünnan up to modern times. During the following two centuries of the great Han empire in China Tien was able to retain independence until the reign of Emperor Wu (140–86 B.C.). That monarch undertook many expeditions and wars to expand his dominions, and the king of Tien, no doubt impressed by the Han conquest of Nan Yüeh (Canton) and the concurrent diplomatic penetration of the Kueichou principality of Yeh Lang (around modern Ts'unyi) sought of his own accord recognition by acknowledging the suzerainty of the Emperor of Han. This was granted, and his kingdom was nominally renamed the Yi Chou Commandery. As the King was confirmed as ruler, this made little difference, but permitted him to feel safe and secure. It also opened a new channel for contact with China, and so strengthened Chinese influence in the region. It does not appear that either the Emperor Wu or his successors made any attempt to impose more direct Chinese rule or extend their domains in Yünnan.

They retained an interest in the remote province for another reason. In 138 B.C. the Emperor Wu had dispatched an envoy, Chang Ch'ien, to the central Asian kingdoms which had been formed from the débris of Alexander's empire in what is now Russian central Asia. The envoy saw there cloth and large bamboos, traded from India, which he recognised as products of Ssuchuan, the great western province of the Han empire. On his return he reported this fact, among much other information, and the Chinese Court for the first time discovered that a trade route to India existed from Ssuchuan across Yünnan. Many envoys were then sent to explore it, but it is recorded that none ever completed the journey, and that most never returned. It has been doubted whether Chang Ch'ien might not have mistaken some Indian product for those of Ssuchuan, but the mention of "big bamboo" seems to suggest that he was correct. The very large bamboos of which one joint can make a useful small bucket, are only known in China. If the "cloth" of Shu were some form of raw silk material, which could only have come from China at that time, the identification would be certain.

The route existed in later times, as has been mentioned, crossing Yünnan to Burma. Possibly even at that time the trade then went down the Irrawaddy and by sea to India. Indian navigation, as the Hindu influence throughout South-East Asia attests, was already well developed. The Han envoys may have hesitated to go so far across unknown seas (as the envoy sent by China to Rome was later discouraged from crossing either the Persian Gulf or the Black Sea) or possibly they sought to reach India by the direct route through northern Burma. If so, their fate would have been settled by the head-hunting tribes of the region. This proclivity would not necessarily mean that no trade route could exist through their country, for in very recent times Chinese merchants did carry on such a trade, on special and exclusive terms.

The jungles of northern Burma are one of the last resorts of the Asiatic rhinoceros and also produce many rare herbs, which like the horn of the rhinoceros, are very valuable commodities in the Chinese medicine trade. Up to the Second World War buyers from all over China, and from South-East Asia also, used to gather at Tali in western Yünnan at an annual fair held in April where these products could be bought at prices profitable to those who had collected them, and still very profitable to those who would sell them in the great cities of China and the south. The collectors were local Chinese merchants belonging to families who had established intimate relations with the head-hunting tribes and who alone were able to enter their country in safety. Only members of these families could enter tribal territory. They brought goods such as tools and weapons which the tribes valued, in return they collected their herbs and, if lucky, a rhinoceros horn, either by barter or by their own efforts. If they wished to increase their numbers, even by a single man, they had first to negotiate with the tribal leaders, who would usually only accept one new member, who must be a close relation of those who were already admitted. Anyone else would lose his head, even if he accompanied a recognised trader. Numbers were kept low, and competition was minimal. But trade profitable to both parties was systematically carried on year after year. In the further districts the Chinese came only in the dry winter season and were not allowed, on pain of death, to remain throughout the year. No women were permitted. On the fringes of the region it was sometimes possible to pass the summer, if the trading family were well known and the reason for a longer delay, such as illness, was apparent.

This system has continued for many generations, and is perhaps much older than any surviving record or remembrance. It seems at least possible that this type of trade, known from other parts of the world, already existed in Han times and that some Chinese products passed from tribe to tribe across northern Burma to India. But if the conditions of trade were then as they have been in modern times, it is very unlikely that any Chinese envoy from a distant region could have been accepted, or survived an attempt to penetrate the tribal lands.

Possibly as a consequence of these attempts to find a route to India across Burma the Han authorities established a claim to administer the region west of the Mekong River. There they established, or named, a Commandery called Yungch'ang on the site of the city which bore the same name till the end of the Manchu dynasty, but has been renamed Paoshan under the Republic. The Han also bestowed the name Lan Ts'ang Chiang on the Mekong, a name which the river still bears in Yünnan and is generally known to the Chinese by this name throughout its course. The boundaries of the Commandery of Yungch'ang were claimed to extend beyond the Salween as far as the present city of Tengyüeh, which is the last administrative centre of modern western Yünnan. This westward penetration was not accompanied by any comparable expansion into the south of Yünnan, where although the ranges are lower, malaria is more prevalent. The Chinese were probably aware that this southern area of Yünnan bordered on Vietnam, which they already ruled, and to which access by the border with modern Kuangsi province was much more direct and easy. There was no particular incentive to establish authority in southern Yünnan. On the other hand Yungch'ang (or Paoshan) is still the centre for communications with northern Burma. It occupies a fertile plain on the plateau between the Mekong and Salween and is the natural centre for administration of the western region of Yünnan. As at Tien (K'unming), it is probable that Chinese rule was indirect, a local chieftain being recognised as the governor, but required to give protection and support to official envoys and travellers from China.

Han policy was thus indirect rule, but it had established footholds across the whole breadth of Yünnan nearly as far as the present frontier with Burma. The actual border claimed was the western edge of the Yünnan plateau, before the "great descent" into the valley of the Irrawaddy, which Marco Polo was to describe in these words many centuries later. Even in modern times this country is wild and only lightly inhabited: the great valleys of the Mekong and Salween, highly malarial, were major barriers, and the heavily forested ranges between them are also formidable obstacles rising steeply from the deep gorges of the rivers. Twelve centuries later, in Ming times, the Chinese bridged both rivers with suspension bridges swung on great iron chains, but this aid to travel was lacking in Han times. The rise of the rivers in summer is often over seventy feet, so that ferrying is difficult and indeed almost impossible when the river is in spate. The Commandery of Yungch'ang must have been isolated from all communication with K'unming and China for many months at a time. It needed a strong motive to establish any claim to this country, and it is difficult to see what other motive than the quest for a trade route to India, which would be shorter than the immense journey across central Asia and over the Hindu Kush, could have inspired the distant Court.

The Chinese seem to have made no further expansion, either in exploration or in the extension of their administration during the two centuries of the Later Han dynasty (25–221). The claims to suzerainty were maintained, but no closer political control established. At the fall of the Han dynasty the empire was contested by three major claimants who set up the Three Kingdoms, of which the weakest was Shu Han (or the Han dynasty of Ssuchuan) which ruled little more than that province. Perhaps because its hopes of expansion were denied by the more powerful Wei in the north and Wu in the east, Shu Han tried to expand southwestwards into Yünnan. This was the policy of the famous minister Chu-ko Liang, who dominated the Court of the second (and last) ruler of Shu Han. Chu-ko is famous in Chinese history as both a loyal minister who refrained from usurping the throne of a weak monarch, and also as a wily and skilful general, master of ruse and surprise, who extended Chinese authority far to the south-west. These exploits have become the subject of romance and drama which somewhat obscure the real character of the enterprise. Chu-ko reduced the former vassal state of Tien to the status of a directly ruled Chinese Commandery, and then extended his authority westward about one hundred miles to Ch'uhsiung.

These areas are easily accessible from Ssuchuan by the northern road from Suifu, and could be held by any Chinese power established in the province of Ssuchuan, the base land of Shu Han. Further west, where Chu-ko Liang campaigned beyond the Mekong down to the present Burma border, he refrained from establishing direct Chinese rule and even refused to station permanent garrisons. He based his policy on three arguments. First, permanent garrisons in such distant inaccessible regions could easily run out of food supplies. No doubt this reflected the great difficulty in crossing the deep river gorges in the high water season. Secondly weak garrisons would be subject to attack by tribesmen still hostile after defeat. Thirdly he contended that a permanent occupation would breed distrust of Chinese policy, leading the tribes to believe that full conquest was intended. He also rejected the policy of raising tribal levies or requisitioning grain. Knowing the country from his own campaigns he realised its poverty and saw that harsh direct administration would only lead to turbulence and revolt.

It was therefore from this early date that Chinese colonial policy, if one may use a term so often deemed derogatory, assumed a character which it was to retain for centuries. The direct control of the Chinese government was to be the last stage of penetration. First came the adventurous trader, or envoy; next the chiefs of important tribes were persuaded and flattered with titles to acknowledge Chinese suzerainty and give protection to travellers. When Chinese power had become firmly established in the adjoining region, the nearest tribal territories at a suitable opportunity could be brought under Chinese authority. More distant tribes, after punitive campaigns, were once more left to rule themselves under Chinese suzerainty. In Yünnan the distinction between fully incorporated territories and their inhabitants and those still left outside the direct authority of the provincial officials was termed that between "*shu*" and "*sheng*", literally "cooked" (or "ripe") and "raw". The tribal population which had accepted Chinese customs and fully submitted, even if it still used a non-Chinese language for colloquial speech, was accepted as "cooked". Those tribes which still lived beyond direct rule and had accepted very little or no Chinese culture, were "raw". It was clearly understood that that which is raw today can be cooked tomorrow.

Chu-ko Liang has remained a local hero in Yünnan, typifying, in Chinese eyes, the ideal administrator of newly-conquered lands, firm, cautious, humane and far-sighted. Yet his work proved, in one sense, transitory. The Shu Han conquest of Yünnan endured very little longer than the Shu Han dynasty itself, which succumbed to conquest by the new Tsin dynasty, based on north China, in 264. Tsin's reign was brief over all China, for in 316 the north was lost to the great invasion of Tatar peoples which was to keep China divided between two empires, north and south, for nearly three hundred years. The successive southern empires, and briefly one established mainly in north-west China (the Northern Chou 558–81) claimed to rule over the former territories of the Shu Han in Yünnan. In practice this claim was either nominal suzerainty, or lacked any foundation. Yünnan, in the period of the division between north and south, regained tribal independence, and relapsed into tribal turbulence.

It would also seem that in this period the early influence of China upon its culture was challenged, and in part replaced by a new foreign influence coming from the south-west. Buddhism, which had spread in China itself since the late Han period, and become very strong in both the northern and southern empires, had reached China by the central Asian trade route from India. Later the sea route from Ceylon and south India to south China became important. But in Yünnan Buddhism seeped in from Burma, a country more directly in touch with India. Consequently there is in the earliest monuments of Buddhism in Yünnan a strong and obvious South-East Asian influence derived from India, and not from China. The surviving monuments and works of art are few and often fragmentary, but their stylistic character is clear. In the far west of the province, between the Salween and the borders of Burma, the local tribes adopted the Theravada (or Hinayana) form of Buddhism, prevalent in Burma, Cambodia and Thailand, and deriving from Ceylon. They still retain this cult today.

Yünnan was thus to become in the next age a point of contact and of conflict between Chinese and Indian civilisation. The political control of China had lapsed, and its reimposition was to be strongly resisted by a new and powerful kingdom, covering all Yünnan. This kingdom of Nanchao was under considerable Indian cultural influence expressed in its Buddhist art as its surviving monuments testify. It was also centred on a city which is not mentioned as one of the old Han Commanderies or tributary chieftaincies, Tali. Yünnan was therefore not to have the same history as the old kingdom of Nan Yüeh, the modern Canton region. After a preliminary Chinese conquest and partial occupation, Yünnan regained independence, formed a powerful kingdom, long resisted a most powerful Chinese dynasty, the T'ang, and did not succumb until subjected to the overwhelming power of the Mongol invasion. In some ways its history seemed to parallel that of Vietnam, but the ultimate result was the opposite.

In 589 the Sui dynasty, founded by a north Chinese family intermarried with the Tatar ruling families of the former northern empire, reunited China by a swift and easy conquest of the weak southern Ch'en dynasty. But in taking over their domains and their tenuous claim to suzerainty in the south-west the Sui were to find that the situation in that region had greatly changed. Much of Kueichou and most of Yünnan were now organised into a number of kingdoms which could muster considerable armies. They were no longer barbarous tribes split up into small territorial

units of a single valley or plain. The Sui dynasty itself was soon en-
gulfed in the troubles which followed upon its unsuccessful wars with
Korea (North Korea, the kingdom of Koryugo) and China fell once more
into confusion. This interlude was brief: in 618 the T'ang dynasty, victor
in the complex civil war, emerged to reunify China on a lasting basis. It
was not long before it made its power felt in the far south. The T'ang
adopted the old and tried policy which the Han empire had followed.
Chiefs or kings were invited to admit the suzerainty of China, receiving
in return confirmation of their authority and titles of honour. This system
seemed to work well enough for several years, and there can be no doubt
that the spread of Chinese culture and custom was stimulated. The T'ang
authorities, however, were not satisfied with the division of the region
into so many relatively small kingdoms, finding this situation complicated
and hard to manage. They conceived the idea that by uniting many of the
smaller kingdoms under one ruler the whole political management of the
fringe of the empire would be facilitated. This was, from their point of
view, a major error. It made possible the rise of the kingdom of Nanchao
which was to become formidable and completely independent from as
well as hostile to the T'ang empire.

Nanchao had been one of six kingdoms, the Six Chaos (the word is
T'ai for king) which divided up west and central Yünnan. The Nanchao
were so named because the original headquarters of the chief had been at
Menghua, south of Tali, which later became their capital, and also because
the other five Chao were either west or north of Menghua. Nanchao was
thus originally the Southern (Nan) Chao. The choice of Tali as capital was
wise, for it is one of the most perfectly protected sites imaginable. Why it
had never, it would seem, been conspicuous in Han times is obscure, for
its situation calls for the establishment of at least a local power. The plain
on which the city stands is about thirty miles in length, bordered to the
east by the large Erh Hai lake, which is up to five miles wide at points,
and on the west by the towering Ts'ang Shan range, a precipitous barrier
rising to 14,000 feet, or 7,000 feet higher than the plain of Tali. That plain
is at both ends confined by narrow passes between the lake, its feeding and
discharging rivers, and the Ts'ang Shan range. The northern pass is
known as Lung T'ou Kuan, the Dragon's Head Pass, or colloquially as
Shangkuan, the Upper Pass; the lower, guarded by the fortress of Hsiakuan, the Lower Pass, is Lung Wei Kuan, the Dragon's Tail Pass. The
Dragon is the Erh Hai lake ("Ear Lake", from its shape). The two passes,
even if they had not been fortified, would be ideal positions to defend the
plain and bar out a much superior force. They were fortified by the strongly
walled city of Hsia Kuan on the southern entrance which bars the route to
K'unming to the east, and the narrow pass by which the road passes west-

ward to Yungch'ang and the Mekong crossing. It is thus the strategic crossroads of western Yünnan, and although it is possible to detour round the Tali plain and travel to the north, this road is much harder. (It was, none the less, the one taken by the Communists on the Long March in 1935, since they could not break through into the Tali plain.) The northern entrance to the Tali plain is commanded by the fort at Shangkuan, where a deep gorge runs down from the Ts'ang Shan range to the lake at the mouth of the Erh Hai River, which feeds the lake. The fortress is built across the only passage between the gorge and the lake.

The Tali plain is fertile rice land, never endangered by flood, and never at risk from drought, for the perpetual streams which flow down from the great Ts'ang Shan (snow-capped for about five months) make constant irrigation possible. It is able to produce large quantities of cereal and the summer crop of rice is alternated with beans and legumes in winter. High, at 7,000 feet, but within the tropic line, Tali has an almost ideal climate with a long dry autumn and winter, and a wet but relatively cool short summer season, when the south-west monsoon brings heavy rain to the mountain barrier. It is not clear what tribe or group were displaced or conquered by the rulers of Nanchao when they moved north to seize Tali. The inhabitants today, and certainly for many centuries past, are not a pure T'ai people, but are known as Pai (which in its Chinese rendering simply means "White"). The Pai words are *Ber Wa Tze*, which mean "people (or posterity) of the White King". Who this legendary monarch may have been is unrecorded, but an ancient and large tomb, long since violated, on the slope of Ts'ang Shan near to Tali city is locally venerated as the tomb of the White King. It seems more probably to have been a tomb of one of the Nanchao kings, and the legendary White King may be a folk memory of one of the warrior kings of Nanchao. It seems clear enough that the rulers of Nanchao themselves, and probably their followers, were T'ai, but it is doubtful whether the Pai people by their surviving customs and language can be classed as T'ai.

Yünnan today, as in the past, is an intricate patchwork of what are now called "national minority peoples"—or formerly tribes—of very varying cultural levels. The Pai are essentially a rice-farming people; they inhabit not only the Tali plain but the valleys to the north almost as far as the high Yangtze, but Tali is their real centre. To the south, only a few miles beyond Hsiakuan, other peoples occupy the land. Therefore the kingdom of Nanchao which before long was to incorporate all Yünnan and far beyond the borders of the present province cannot be described as a T'ai kingdom, in the sense that the later kingdom in Thailand itself, and in Laos were T'ai in ethnic composition of their population. Nanchao was a kingdom ruled by a family of T'ai origin, supported, probably, by a ruling class of the same stock, but governing a wide variety of differing peoples including, as they grew stronger, many districts in which Chinese settlement had taken root. This character differentiates Nanchao very sharply from Vietnam to the south. In Vietnam the Chinese ruled a single people, fringed, it is true, by mountain tribes, but these were peripheral and hardly brought under direct administration. When Vietnam threw off Chinese rule the Vietnamese became the dominant race and ruled the tribes as feudatories.

However, in Nanchao there was no large widespread, or compact, dominant people. The Pai of Tali may have even then been numerous, but their area is confined and makes up only a small part of Yünnan. The Miao are scattered along many mountain ranges; the Na Khi are found around Lichiang in the north, but not elsewhere, and so the list could be continued; many smaller or greater peoples occupying detached fertile valleys and lake plains, widely separated by wild mountain ranges which are inhabited, if at all, by less advanced tribes such as the Lisu. This fragmentation was an aid to the establishment of a strongly based monarchy at a strategic point, but it was a fatal handicap to the evolution of a nation. It was the national identity of the old Yüeh stock of Vietnam which even a thousand years of direct Chinese rule was unable to break down; it was the lack of any such national identity in Yünnan which made the ultimate survival of a strong and militant kingdom such as Nanchao, which subsisted for six hundred years, impossible in the face of the cohesion and power of China. The Vietnamese, even when independent, continued under strong Chinese cultural influence, but refused to accept political control. The peoples of Yünnan were not so deeply influenced by Chinese civilisation, and still are in part untouched by it, but they were not able to maintain their independence and ended wholly incorporated in the Chinese empire.

It is an irony of history that Nanchao, which was to be for a long period the principal obstacle to the extension of Chinese authority and influence in the south, was fostered by the Chinese empire itself. The kingdom which was encouraged in the early years of the T'ang dynasty to consolidate the former Six Chaos and set up its capital at Tali (629) was still seen as a successor to the petty states which had received Han patronage four hundred years earlier. Nanchao seemed at first to accept this rôle. In 647 it acknowledged the suzerainty of China, and the kingdom was officially described as the "Department of Ming" within the new enormous southern province of Chien Nan. The T'ang had abandoned the old Han Commandery system for a new one, which in its major forms has survived till today, of *Tao* (later *sheng*), provinces of great area. Chien Nan was the western and south-western province, comprising all of western

Ssuchuan south of the modern border with Kansu province, and such parts of Yünnan and Kueichou as the T'ang claimed or administered. Relations between the king of Nanchao and the early emperors of the T'ang were good. Envoys came and went, and the sons of the king went to Ch'angan on visits or for education. It must be recalled that at this time the T'ang empire was at the very acme of its power. The great T'ai Tsung, the real founder, did not die until 649 and the long reign of his real successor the Empress Wu, or her domination of the government, which lasted for half a century until 705, ensured continuing order and power. That of her grandson Hsüan Tsung (or Ming Huang, "the Brilliant Emperor") is best known from its tragic conclusion, in the turmoil of the rebellion of An Lu-shan (755) but it was for nearly half a century a glorious age in which the Chinese civilisation shone with a brilliance which has never been equalled.

These were not the circumstances under which a relatively small southern state would wisely challenge Chinese suzerainty. King P'i-lo-ko of Nanchao was an able ruler. He used the T'ang alliance and suzerainty to consolidate his power in western Yünnan, and this was acceptable to the T'ang governors of Chien Nan who wanted no frontier troubles. In 731 King P'i-lo-ko rid himself of all competitors in western Yünnan by a ruthless act of treachery. He invited his five chief rivals, the princes of Menghua, Paoshan, Chiench'uan, Mitu and Tengch'uan, all of which are cities of western Yünnan, to a banquet at his new capital, Tali. This was held in a pagoda, or two-storeyed building, and when the party had dined well and was partly intoxicated, the King withdrew, leaving his guests. The lower storey of the building had been filled with hay and straw, which was then set on fire, all the princes perishing in the conflagration. It is related in Tali legend that the Prince of Tengch'uan had been suspicious of this invitation, but finally went to the meeting, wearing an iron bracelet given him by his wife, perhaps as a charm. After the tragedy the wives of the dead princes came to reclaim the bodies for burial. Only the Princess of Tengch'uan was able to recognise her husband's charred corpse by the iron bracelet which he still wore. The Tali people have made a festival of this tragic event. A small temple marks the site of the fatal pagoda, and on the 24th of the 6th month (approximately 30 July) the women of Tali dye their finger-tips red to recall the fact that the Princess of Tengch'uan burned her fingers recovering the iron bracelet. There are other ceremonies including the burning of a large haystack, to symbolise the pagoda, and a play is staged which seems to be of purely local origin based on the story of the massacre. Curiously this ceremony and its associated superstitions is one of the very few by which the present people of Tali recall their history in Nanchao days, although it might well be thought that King P'i-lo-ko was hardly well pleased to have this particular exploit perpetuated in popular memory.

In 738 he enlarged his kingdom by reducing the tribes to his north, the Tibetans (T'ufan) and Lolo (or Nosu) who dwelt in the high Yangtze valley and neighbouring districts. These tribes had been a nuisance to the T'ang Court, raiding the border; P'i-lo-ko's action was welcome, and he was rewarded with fresh titles, including that of "king of Yünnan"—one of the earliest uses of the modern name for a wide region of the province. In Han times it had applied only to the K'unming district. In 742 the king of Nanchao's grandson went to the Chinese capital, Ch'angan, was received in audience and married to an imperial princess. The visit of the Prince Feng-chia-yi represents the high point of the friendly relations between the T'ang and Nanchao; soon a fatal change was to transform the previous amity to long-lasting hostility. The Emperor Hsüan Tsung was growing old; the history of his reign confirms his loss of judgement and grip in these years—usually and popularly attributed to the influence of his favourite the concubine Yang Kuei Fei, one of the most celebrated beauties in Chinese history. More significant probably, was the great power and influence of her brother Yang Kuo-cheng, the chief minister, and the Court eunuchs. King P'i-lo-ko was succeeded by his son Ko-lo-feng. These names are as the Chinese record them, and are not Chinese in formation, but clearly represent three syllable words in the T'ai language. Their apparent Chinese form does not mean that the process of sinification had yet reached the stage when Chinese names displaced the native words. Chinese can (or at that period could) only be written in Chinese ideographs, and it was necessary to choose words which were approximate in sound to those of the foreign words transcribed. Chinese pronunciation in the T'ang period was more like modern Cantonese than modern Standard Speech (Mandarin) and the sound of these Nanchao names would have been largely unlike their modern equivalents.

In 750 King Ko-lo-feng travelled across Yünnan to pay respects to the Chinese viceroy of Chien Nan, no doubt to obtain confirmation of his accession to the throne. On his return journey he was pestered by the extortionate demands of a local Chinese official, and when he complained to Ch'angan, his representations were ignored. He repeated his complaints, sending a more important mission to bear them. Once more they were ignored, as it is said because they were never brought to the notice of the ageing Emperor by eunuchs too concerned themselves in the extortions to risk detection. King Ko-lo-feng then raised an army and attacked the neighbouring T'ang-ruled districts of eastern Yünnan and western Kueichou (where T'ang rule was rather nominal) and speedily overran many of them. The T'ang provincial officials then raised an army

of 80,000 men to subdue the "rebel". Ko-lo-feng, alarmed at these consequences, again sent missions to Ch'angan, but their purpose, which was
apology and explanation, was never allowed to reach the Emperor's
knowledge. The Chinese army reached the neighbourhood of Hsiakuan,
at the southern entrance to the Tali plain. There it was met and totally
defeated by the forces of Nanchao (751). It was reported that 60,000 of
the T'ang troops were slain, surrounded and fighting to the death. A great
mound is still shown to travellers as marking their mass grave. The battle
is still remembered by the people of Tali and the district. A small temple
stands on the mountain slope above the grave mound of the T'ang
soldiers, and is dedicated to Li Ming, the T'ang general who lost his life
in the great disaster. His statue stands on the altar, and when, in 1938, news
finally reached Tali that Nanking had fallen to the Japanese invaders, it
was declared that General Li Ming's right arm began to bleed. Pilgrims
were attracted from far and wide to see the miracle, which was generally
interpreted as a very bad omen.

The Chinese did not accept the battle of Hsiakuan as final: in 754 another
huge army was raised, which this time attempted to invade the Tali
region from the north-east, but it too was met and routed in the
Tengch'uan valley, one of the rivers flowing southward to the Tali lake.
The defeat was concealed from the emperor, who indeed was misled into
believing that it had been a victory. In any case the Emperor Hsüan
Tsung had soon more pressing worries than the lack of success on a distant
frontier. The great rebellion of An Lu-shan broke out in 755 and for ten
years, after taking the capital itself and driving the aged Emperor into
flight to Ssuchuan, raged across north China. When it was finally suppressed Hsüan Tsung had abdicated, and his successor, painfully recovering
authority in the north, and that but imperfectly, had no resources to spare
for wars in the far south-west. Nanchao had profited by the rebellion to
consolidate its victory. Allied with the Tibetans it carried on raids and
incursions into T'ang territory which greatly enlarged the realm of
Nanchao. In the west Ko-lo-feng, now realising that his quarrel with the
T'ang was not likely to be ended soon, turned his attention to opening
another route of contact with the world beyond his kingdom. In the
years from 757 to 763 he invaded Burma and conquered the fertile
lands of the upper Irrawaddy valley. This conquest had the effect of dis-
integrating the early kingdom of Pyu, in lower Burma, and ultimately
made the incursions of the Burmese people possible, and, it would seem,
the more or less complete elimination of the original inhabitants of Mon
race.

Nanchao was now a power to be reckoned with, and as the T'ang
dynasty never fully recovered from the effects of the rebellion of An

Lu-shan, it was never able to contemplate the reconquest of Yünnan. On the contrary, the Nanchao kingdom continued its aggressions upon the weakened empire for a full century, with only brief intervals of peace. In the years that followed the end of the An Lu-shan rebellion (763), the armies of Nanchao repeatedly invaded Ssuchuan in alliance with the Tibetans who were then an active and aggressive people constantly raiding the Chinese frontiers and even penetrating far into the provinces. Much of southern Ssuchuan was brought into the Nanchao kingdom in these years. Peace was established for a while in 793, when Nanchao acknowledged Chinese suzerainty, sent nominal tribute, but retained its effective independence. Recent failures in campaigns in Ssuchuan may have induced the king of Nanchao to make this gesture, but it was also due to the fact that the Chinese practice of that age (and of many later periods) did not admit of any relationship between China and a neighbouring kingdom other than that of the suzerain-tributary status. Tribute could be small, or much less than the gifts which the Chinese emperor bestowed in return, but the acknowledgement of suzerainty was essential.

After a generation of comparative peace, Nanchao resumed her warlike policy in 829 with an invasion of Ssuchuan which actually took the capital, Ch'engtu, and reached the northern parts of the province. Ssuchuan was, of course, by far the most desirable conquest within the range of the Nanchao power. It is a province of very great fertility, an immense rice plain, and very closely settled. The permanent conquest of Ssuchuan would have created a new great power in the south-west which might have never again submitted to the dynasties ruling in north China. More or less continuous fighting prevailed to decide the fate of this province until 873 when a great Nanchao invasion was defeated and driven out of the province after laying siege to Ch'engtu and other important cities. Concurrently, and in order to outflank the defences of Ssuchuan, Nanchao had repeatedly attacked the Chinese-held parts of eastern Kueichou and western Hunan, occupying and incorporating several districts within the kingdom. The Chinese then ruled in what is now North Vietnam, the Red River delta, and this province too was invaded by Nanchao three times between 861 and 866, only the last invasion being decisively defeated. While these southern invasions were in progress the Nanchao armies had penetrated into western Kuangsi, to cut off the Chinese in Annam (North Vietnam) from direct communication with their home country.

The defeat of the last great invasion of Ssuchuan in 879 and that of Annam a few years earlier marked the decline of Nanchao's aggressive militarism. It came just too soon to achieve a lasting success. From 868 when the great rebellion of Huang Tsao shook the declining T'ang dynasty and inaugurated a period of thirty years of deepening confusion and civil war ending in the collapse of the centralised empire and of the T'ang dynasty itself, an opportunity was offered which would, a century or less earlier, have resulted in a Nanchao conquest of most of south China. The rebellion and its aftermath of civil wars between satraps nominally loyal, or rebellious, to an impotent Court, was an opening which could have been exploited with minimal opposition. On the fall of the T'ang south China was to be divided up for fifty years into a number of states, all claiming to be the "empire", but in effect ruling only one or at most two provinces. Yet in this era of division and weakness China was more immune from Nanchao attacks than before. It has been seen that during this period Vietnam threw off the Chinese yoke, which was already gravely weakened by the mutiny of the Chinese army on the Nanchao–Annam frontier, a mutiny which inaugurated the great rebellion of Huang Tsao. But Nanchao took no advantage to push her claims in now independent Vietnam, nor to harry the local monarchs who arose in south China after the fall of the T'ang.

In the last disastrous years of the T'ang there was peace between the kingdom and the failing empire. A Chinese princess was sought and married to the King as late as 881 and in 924 Nanchao sought alliance and friendship with the successor kingdom of southern Han, established at Canton. It would seem that having in the late ninth century decided that China was too strong to make the permanent conquest of Ssuchuan a feasible project, in the tenth century Nanchao was content to watch the break-up of the T'ang empire in the assurance that no further menace to her independence could come from China while this condition lasted. Internal troubles were also disturbing Nanchao itself, and these seem to have taken their origin in the discords between large conquered Chinese populations, or populations more wholly assimilated into Chinese culture, and the more national non-Chinese elements of the old western parts of the kingdom. The further seizure of Chinese regions or districts at such a time could only have added to these problems, and this consideration may have played an important part in the more peaceful demeanour which Nanchao now assumed.

It was not yet clear, nor was it to be so for very many years, that the limitation set upon the expansion of Nanchao would ultimately lead to contraction and finally to extinction of independence. Unlike Vietnam, which could and did expand into the almost empty southern part of the modern country, after overcoming the relatively weak Champa, Nanchao could only expand at China's expense. The conquest of upper Burma was difficult to hold; the climate is against a Yünnanese army, and the communications between the plateau and the Irrawaddy valley some of the worst in the world. To gain real strength beyond the narrow rice plains and valleys of Yünnan, separated as they are by great tracts of empty mountain country, Nanchao must occupy permanently and then fully colonise and assimilate a truly rich region of heavy population. Such were Ssuchuan and Hunan; but the former is close to the main strength of any power ruling north China, and the latter is separated from Yünnan by the poor and mountainous Kueichou province. In view of the difficulties which had to be overcome in the campaigns conducted by Nanchao against the T'ang their success is surprising, and the ultimate failure to consolidate is to be expected. Nanchao, in that age, faced with a disintegrated Chinese empire, whose disunion might last for many years, or even prove final—no one could tell—could believe that she was immune and could become firmly established in the region which she had fully incorporated.

The area of the kingdom was indeed large at the conclusion of the wars with T'ang. It comprised all of Yünnan, part of upper Burma, that part of Ssuchuan which lies south of the Yangtze, the western half of Kueichou, a small part of western Hunan, and some border districts of what is now Kuangsi province. A large kingdom, but still only the size of one of the ten great Chinese provinces into which the T'ang had organised their empire. Moreover much of this territory was either uninhabited or the home of tribes less advanced than the Nanchao ruling groups or the Chinese settlers they had conquered. Fifty years later, by the date of the foundation of the Sung dynasty in China, Nanchao had lost effective control over the Kueichou tribes, and thus lost the Hunan districts; and had moreover abandoned south Yünnan to its tribal inhabitants and left the Irrawaddy valley. These territories had not then reverted to China; they had simply relapsed into the multi-tribal divisions which King Ko-lo-feng and his successors had forcibly suppressed.

The history of Vietnam and of Nanchao thus runs in some ways parallel, then diverges. Both owed their first culture to Chinese conquest; both successfully expelled the Chinese authority, while retaining the culture; Nanchao achieving this independence two centuries before Vietnam did so. But once free from Chinese rule, the Vietnamese began that "March to the South" which was to expand their country on the lasting basis of settlement and colonisation, even when political unity was weak. They sought no territory from China; at no time in history did a Vietnamese ruler try to profit from Chinese passing weakness to invade the empire. Nanchao did just the opposite. There was no March to the South, because there was no great alluring but almost vacant territory to occupy. Expansion must be into China, which meant confronting a power which even when in decline was still very formidable, and once reunited would be irresistible. Nanchao established the fatal reputation of being a potential threat to the unity of the Chinese empire; Vietnam established the harmless reputation of being interested in expansion to the south, away from China, but carrying Chinese culture—and nominal suzerainty—with it. Nanchao might, and did, adopt Chinese culture almost as fully as contemporary Vietnam had done, but it did not have the same consequences. In Vietnam it acted as a valid reason for the later Chinese policy of non-intervention in that country, for Vietnam could not be seen as an enemy to the empire. In Nanchao, which was an active enemy, Chinese culture provided a reason and a way to overcome the enemy and ultimately incorporate the kingdom.

CHAPTER FOUR

THE CHINESE CONQUEST OF YÜNNAN

The power of Nanchao began to decline after 877 at the very time that her great antagonist, the T'ang dynasty, was entering upon its final age of turbulence and confusion. This paradox may be in part explained by the consequences of the early victories of the Nanchao kings. Great areas of Chinese settled country had been seized, and thousands of captives from these regions and those raided and temporarily occupied had been transported to the interior of Yünnan. Nanchao thus unwittingly built up within its own frontiers a kind of cultural "Fifth Column", a growing population of Chinese culture and speech, literate in large measure, and thus equipped to play an increasingly important part in the government of the country which had involuntarily become theirs. The incentive to revolt and rejoin the T'ang empire, or to hope for its intervention, was virtually eliminated by the contemporary decline and confusion of the T'ang empire itself. In an atmosphere where Chinese learning was admired and sought, where a Chinese education was a valuable social asset, the captive or fugitive Chinese could aspire to rise in power and influence so long as they proved loyal to the king of Nanchao. Once the T'ang empire was in the throes of contests between rival dynasts, whose chances of ultimate victory seemed slight, there was little reason to prefer any one of them to the ruler of Nanchao.

In spite of the long hostility towards the Chinese empire the Yünnan kingdom had continued to admire, accept, adopt and imitate the civilisation of the T'ang. Ko-lo-feng's victory inscription near Tali, which still survives in a partially legible condition, is written in classical Chinese and was composed by a Chinese scholar. The few remaining examples of Nanchao architecture at Tali and elsewhere, pagodas of a distinctive style, and dating from the early eighth century, are none the less variations of the style of the Chinese architecture of that period, not Indian nor Burmese. Nanchao had an art which had characteristics differing from that of China, and in which Indian influence played some part, but it was not a dominant rôle. Buddhism was Mahayana Buddhism, not the Hinayana of Burma, although, perhaps at a later time the people of the border districts, T'ai and others, were converted to the Hinayana faith.

The government was formed on the basis of Chinese administrative practice, although there appears no positive evidence for the introduction of the public civil service examination. Probably tribal feudalism was still too strong for this step; Chinese of distinction seem, on the contrary, to have established themselves on grants of land in positions not very dissimilar to those held by native lords. The evidence of successive generations of Chinese holding high positions in the government points to something more than hereditary ability; it suggests continuing political power and influence based in part at least on descent. In this way it would appear that Nanchao society had more affinity with pre-T'ang China; the age of the division between north and south when a military aristocracy monopolised political power, although using the forms of civil service appointments to cover what was in fact hereditary authority. Something not too dissimilar was happening in Japan at this same period, where the imperial Court borrowed Chinese (T'ang) forms and titles, but had to recognise the continuing power of the native clan aristocracy. In China itself the transformation of an aristocratic society into a bureaucratic gentry-ruled empire was not sudden nor swift; it took place during the T'ang period, but was not fully achieved until the Sung dynasty.

The kings of Nanchao continued to welcome T'ang princesses as brides, and some nominal dependence on the empire was still admitted. In 924, some sixteen years after the total elimination of the T'ang dynasty, the Nanchao king obtained as a bride the daughter of the Chinese claimant "emperor" who controlled the most southerly provinces of the T'ang, Kuangtung and Kuangsi, under the name of Nan Han (southern Han). This ruler was neither powerful nor warlike; his chance of becoming emperor of all China was very slight; but he was the Chinese prince nearest to Nanchao, and as such seems to have been considered the nearest to a legitimate successor to the fallen empire of T'ang. On the other hand the Nanchao dynasty itself was losing authority and probably failing to produce competent kings. Late in the tenth century the native dynasty was dethroned by a sanguinary revolution (in which it seems the royal family were virtually extirpated) and power was taken by Tseng Mai-ssu, a grandee of Chinese descent, whose ancestor in the seventh generation had been Tseng Hui, a Chinese official from Ssuchuan who took service with King Ko-lo-feng. The new king abandoned the distinctively T'ai name of the kingdom (Nanchao, i.e. southern kingdom) and called his new dynasty Ta Li (Great Order), a name which later attached itself to the capital city. Early in the Sung period a further revolution in Tali brought to power the Tuan family, also of Chinese ancestry, and this dynasty was to endure until the final age of the Yünnan kingdom. The political dominance of families of Chinese origin had furthered the process of sinification; it is evident that in the later period, the Tuan dynasty, the former Nanchao kingdom was becoming a sinicised state and also that it no longer presented any real threat to the authority of the Chinese empire in south-west China.

The new central power in China, the Sung dynasty, whose reunion of the fragmented empire of the T'ang took nearly thirty years, more of diplomacy than war, was still unwilling to attempt the conquest and incorporation of Yünnan. When, after the conquest of the local pretender in Ssuchuan in 967 the conquering general told the new Sung emperor that it would be easy to invade and seize the Tali kingdom also, the Emperor, after studying the map, rejected any such plan, declaring that all country south of the Tatu River, which is a tributary of the Yangtze, was not his, and he had no ambitions upon it. The Sung thus acknowledged the right of the old Nanchao, now Tali, kingdom to total independence. They do not seem to have even exacted the formal acknowledgement of Chinese suzerainty. The Tuan kings for their part were also willing to live in peace with China, and undertook no raids or invasions. When a rebel in 1053 took refuge in Tali after defeat in China, the King delivered him to the Chinese emperor.

The Sung had good reason to renounce any ambition to conquer Tali. They did not fully control all north China, for the region of north-east Hopei, including Peking, and the north-west including most of Kansu province, remained beyond their authority, under the Liao Tatar dynasty in the north-east and the Hsia kingdom, of Tibetan–Tangut dominance, in the north-west. These two states were usually hostile, and controlled the passes which lead from the Mongolian steppe into China. Border warfare was frequent and the potential threat to the Sung was real and, ultimately, very dangerous. T'ang experience seemed to prove that Yünnan could be the graveyard of Chinese armies from the north. Thus for a long period, more than three hundred years, there was no Chinese pressure upon Yünnan in the sense of political expansion. There was certainly a continuing cultural influence, which did not grow weaker, but it must have seemed to men of that age that China had renounced her ambition to incorporate Yünnan, just as surely as she had renounced a similar ambition in Vietnam. The final independence of the latter country from China was ratified by the unwarlike policy of the Sung, and it would appear that they had made the same decision in respect of Yünnan.

Three centuries and more is a long time; a situation consolidated by this duration could be expected to be a permanent one. The Sung never changed their policy, and neither did Tali. There were no more invasions of Chinese provinces, no border raids, and no aggression against the frontiers. Tali, or Nanchao, did not in fact retain its former power over the outlying districts. Those which had not reverted to Chinese rule, as did all the Ssuchuan region, drifted into virtual tribal independence, as in Kueichou, western Yünnan and northern Burma. The kingdom was smaller, but secure. Perhaps too secure; there is little in the sparse record of this period that reveals any very active cultural life, or any development of a national identity. Unlike Vietnam, independence and security seem to have had a more emollient effect on the people of Tali. Chinese culture was dominant, but seems to have been provincial in its expression. The warlike character of the Nanchao period was replaced by military weakness. The Sung general who tried to persuade his emperor to conquer Tali in 967 may have been too optimistic in thinking that the operation would be easy. Three centuries later the Mongol invaders found it to be almost unopposed.

With inadequate records it is hard to discover what social factors had brought about this transformation. The Sung, as they did not claim suzerainty, and did not suffer from Tali hostility, are generally silent in their historical records of the Tali kingdom. The affairs of Tali did not matter to the Emperor so they were not recorded. If Tali kept records on the model of the Chinese histories, these have not survived. It would seem that one probable reason for the failure to build a cohesive nation in Yünnan, as was done in Vietnam, was due in part to the rule of Chinese families whose cultural allegiance was always to China, and who ignored or failed to patronise native trends and aspirations. The other essential difference between the two countries was the inherent divisive nature of the topography of Yünnan. Each valley lived (and largely still lives) to itself. Trade was slight, and only affected light articles, such as medicinal plants of high value. It is impossible to move a significant quantity of rice from one valley to the next, across fifty or more miles of wild mountains, by means of porters or mules, and sell it at an economic price in a valley which has probably had an equally abundant harvest of its own.

The western districts of Yünnan are still less easily accessible and produce less surplus. The people of that region were either still primitive hunters, slash and burn mountain cultivators, or formed a thin settlement in deep valleys which are very malarial. Beyond these valleys and the high ranges which divide them lay Burma and the fertile upper Irrawaddy valley. This could have been the region which would have played for Yünnan the rôle which South Vietnam played in the history of Vietnam: the southern eldorado to which the poor could move, and where the nation found a common objective; but it was in these obscure centuries of the later Nanchao or Tali kingdom that the present ruling race of Burma, the Burmese themselves, descended from the Tibetan borderlands and occupied the Irrawaddy valley. It is probable that their entry had been made possible by Nanchao's early victories over the kingdom of Pyu, which it had conquered and destroyed, but whose territory it had failed to hold and settle. There is very little record of the stages of Burmese occupation and conquest, but it is certain that it was accomplished on a large scale during the three centuries of the Tali kingdom's existence. Thus the Irrawaddy valley was lost to any prospect of incorporation in a greater Nanchao. Ultimately this development made a Chinese incorporation of Yünnan inevitable, for the growth of Nanchao within Yünnan itself could never in time match the expansion in numbers of population and power of the united Chinese empire, nor afford a sufficient base for permanent independence.

That independence was safeguarded for so long more by the weakness of the later Sung than by the strength or determination of the Tali kingdom. After the loss of north China in 1126 the Sung empire had a dangerous neighbour, at first the Kin Tatar empire, later the new Mongol empire, upon its northern frontier. When the Kin, who could be held at bay, succumbed to the Mongols in 1234 the fate of the Sung was almost inevitable. By the middle of the thirteenth century the Mongols ruled the whole Asian world, from Korea to the western borders of Russia. No kingdom had withstood them, most had fallen at the first campaign. Since their conquest of the Kin dynasty the Mongol Great Khans had made no secret of their ambition and intention to conquer the Sung also, and they had already begun to encroach upon the frontiers as soon as the occupation of the north was consolidated.

The Sung offered a tenacious resistance, which has been rather underestimated by historians. They had no allies, and could hardly hope to find any of power in the world of their age. They never drove the Mongols out of a conquered district but they did successfully defend strong places for many years, and frustrated the invasions directed against the Yangtze provinces. The Mongols, recognising the difficulties of a frontal assault, decided to outflank the Sung empire by seizing its western province, Ssuchuan, and moving into the south-western region, thus by-passing the line of the Yangtze River and cutting into Sung territory from the southwest. Under Mangu Khan this policy was entrusted to one of his sons, Kubilai (Kublai), later to reign as first Mongol emperor of all China, and to become, thanks to Marco Polo, the Venetian in his service, the best known of all rulers of China to the Western world.

In 1252 Kubilai mustered his forces in southern Kansu, and undertook a surprise march through the western borders of Ssuchuan (the province not yet being fully under Mongol occupation) along an "unknown route, among mountains and precipices" which must have closely paralleled the famous way across the grass lands of eastern Tibet taken, in the reverse direction, by the Communist armies on their Long March in 1935. The Mongols passed the Tatu River, then the frontier between Ssuchuan and the Tali kingdom, and swept down into Yünnan. Their coming was wholly unexpected, for they had made a march of more than six hundred miles through wild country almost unknown to travellers. Tali made virtually no resistance, the king submitted, and the kingdom was reduced to a Mongol province. Before long the Mongols were to penetrate to the western borders and invade Burma, where, however, they found the climate unfavourable to their permanent occupation. Outflanked, the Sung empire's ability to resist was greatly reduced; in little more than twenty years after the conquest of Yünnan the Sung had been wholly destroyed and Kubilai reigned as Emperor of all China over a realm larger than any which had preceded it. He was also the acknowledged lord of the Mongol Khans, his relatives who ruled in central Asia, eastern Russia, Persia and much of the Middle East.

The conquest of Yünnan was thus not an enterprise of the Chinese empire under Chinese rulers, but a by-product of the Mongol conquest of China itself. It may be that it would never have occurred without the Mongol invasions, or it might have been delayed until a stronger Chinese dynasty had succeeded to the Sung, but having been accomplished in this way, it was never to be reversed. The people of Yünnan did not have the sense of national identity which could inspire them to revolt, when the Mongol power declined, or to keep out the authority of the Chinese dynasty which drove the Mongols out of China. The Mongols first gave to the whole region which incorporated the fallen kingdom of Tali, as well as other districts which it had not ruled for many years, the name of Yünnan province, reviving the ancient Han name which had been applied only to the eastern part of the Yünnan plateau. They handed over the government of the new province to a Muslim from central Asia in the service of the Great Khan, and this man, and his successors of the same race and faith, introduced large numbers of their compatriots as garrison troops settled in the major centres of agriculture and government. This was the origin of the Yünnan Muslim community, which was at one time much larger than it has been since their great rebellion in the nineteenth century, but still remains an important element in the population.

Although the resistance of Tali itself had been insignificant, it is evident that tribal opposition to the Mongol conquest must have been more formidable, for Marco Polo, who travelled through Yünnan to Burma some years after the conquest, describes the country as still suffering from extensive devastation, cities almost uninhabited, villages abandoned, and rice lands gone back to grass and weeds. It is a picture which could have been drawn of many of the countries which experienced the Mongol onslaught. Now a remote border province, Yünnan does not seem to have enjoyed much prosperity from its first union with China. Almost the only monument of Mongol rule is an inscription set up outside Tali city on a large marble slab which contains, in a barbarous mixture of Mongolised and colloquial Chinese, an injunction to the soldiers of the Mongol ruler not to molest the Buddhist monks of the great Three Pagoda monastery, whose ruins still attest the glories of Nanchao architecture of the eighth century.

Yünnan was the first of the southern Chinese provinces to come under Mongol rule, and it was also the last province in China which the Mongols held, even when they had lost Peking and been driven from the northern provinces. In all they held Yünnan for one hundred and thirty years. It was not until the founder of the Ming dynasty had been acknowledged ruler of all the Chinese empire for fifteen years that he sent his armies to oust the Mongols from their last foothold, which was Yünnan. It is thus possible that the Ming Emperor did not at first see the conquest of Yünnan, which had not been a Chinese possession in any real sense under earlier dynasties, as a logical outcome of his conquest of the Mongol dynasty. Had the Mongols themselves not been the actual rulers in Yünnan it is conceivable that the Ming would have left a native dynasty in peace, as the Sung had done four hundred years earlier. But in Yünnan the Mongols still poised a threat, even if only a slight one, to the victorious Ming; they could form an outpost which a reviving Mongol power could use for another invasion. So Yünnan was invaded in 1382 by the armies of Emperor Hung Wu of the Ming, conquered again, and thus finally incorporated into a Chinese empire under a Chinese sovereign. The last humble representatives of the Tuan dynasty, who had enjoyed some minimal authority under the Mongols, were eliminated, and Yünnan became a province of the new empire on the same footing as any other.

Another massive influx of settlers came with the Ming armies. They were Chinese, mainly from the Yangtze provinces, which were then the main centre of Ming power. They became established as landowners and local gentry in all the chief urban centres and major agricultural plains. The oldest and proudest families of Tali today are (or rather, before the Peoples' Republic, were) the descendants not of Nanchao chiefs or even of Tali kingdom sinicised Yünnanese, but of the officers of the armies of Ming Hung Wu. The Ming stamp upon Yünnan has been enduring and remains conspicuous. Temples and monuments of Ming date are numerous; the remarkable iron chain suspension bridges which span the Mekong and Salween, as well as many lesser rivers in western Yünnan attest the vigour of the new régime and its concern with improving communications. Many of the cities of Yünnan owe their modern form to Ming builders, and many reflect in their rectilinear walls and cross streets the common city plan of north China, miniature copies of Peking. The old caravan road system, now far gone in decay, was originally a network of paved pathways crossing ranges and rivers and connecting up every city in the province with the rest of China, and ultimately with Peking. This, too, was Ming work. Along these roads the Ming emperor Yung Lo, when building the present imperial palace at Peking in 1405, had the great slabs of marble, quarried at Tali high on the mountain slope, pulled and rolled for hundreds of miles until they could be shipped on rafts on the upper reaches of the Hunan rivers. They are 18 feet in length, nearly 5 feet wide, and presumably of a thickness commensurate with these measurements.

There was considerable and continuous immigration of Chinese into Yünnan during the Ming period. Many families claim descent from Ming soldiers or administrators, and say that they originated in "Nanking", by which they mean the province of Kiangsu and the lower Yangtze region. The practice of sending exiles to various places in Yünnan seems to have also begun in Ming times. These people were always sent to the same Yünnan district to which preceding exiles from the same district in interior China had come. Thus dialects tended to become stabilised and various. The inhabitants of Paoshan (the ancient Yungch'ang) between the Mekong and Salween, are largely descended from exiles from the lower Yangtze region, and do in fact speak the dialect of Nanking with very little difference from the native speakers in the southern capital, with whom they have never had the slightest contact. Similar differences appear elsewhere; the people of Tali have a very strong local Pai accent, even those families which claim paternal Chinese ancestry. The inhabitants of K'unming, the provincial capital, speak a tongue with recognisable close affinities to that of Peking colloquial speech. There is a special reason for this, which derives from one of the episodes of late Ming history, very significant in the history of Yünnan and its assimilation into the Chinese civilisation.

After the Ming conquest there does not appear to have been any important movement for liberation from Chinese rule. Whether the forces of the new imperial power were too strong, or whether, in view of the undoubted benefits Ming rule conferred, the people of Yünnan had no inclination to struggle for independence, it seems that the Ming reigned unchallenged in Yünnan until the end of the dynasty. However in the years following the Manchu entry into China in 1644, a series of events brought about a situation which seemed likely to revive the independent state of Yünnan, albeit under a Chinese, not a native dynast. General

Wu San-kuei is not today a hero to the Chinese people; he it was who allowed the Manchus to enter China and then helped them to stamp out the resistance offered by Ming claimants. In late life he in turn revolted against the Manchu Emperor and died fighting him. But it was Wu San-kuei who made the Manchu conquest possible. A distinguished general, he was in command of the frontier army stationed at Shan-haikuan, where the Great Wall reaches the sea, the strategic gate between Manchuria and China proper. The Manchu kingdom already ruled in the former Chinese province of Liaotung (Wu San-kuei's native land) beyond the Wall. In 1644 the rebel Li Tzu-ch'eng captured Peking and the Ming Emperor took his own life. The rebel Li proclaimed himself emperor and sent word to Wu San-kuei, two hundred miles to the east, to submit to the new dynasty, promising great rewards. If Wu had accepted these offers the Manchus would never have entered China. Li and Wu between them would have made a strong defence of the frontier, and the new Shun dynasty of Li would have replaced the Ming. But a personal quarrel divided Wu San-keui from his prospective new sovereign. He hesitated, then decided instead to invite the Manchus in to help him to destroy the rebel Li Tzu-ch'eng. This was the first cause of the Manchu conquest.

Once the Manchus were installed in Peking they gave Wu high honours, and before long sent him and his troops off to pursue the beaten rebels, and then to crush movements of resistance in favour of Ming pretenders. For thirty years Wu San-kuei served them well in these duties, and in 1657 he invaded Yünnan which was the last province under Ming rule, and having conquered it, drove the last Ming claimant into flight to Burma. In 1661 he invaded Burma, defeated a joint Sino-Burmese army, and advanced to within sixty miles of Mandalay, the capital. At that point the king of Burma found treachery to be the better part of valour; he surrendered the Ming Prince to Wu San-kuei on condition that the Chinese army should leave the country. Wu took his captive back to K'unming and put him to death, thus extinguishing the Ming dynasty. The Manchus rewarded him by making him both civil and military governor of Yünnan and Kueichou with princely rank. His influence was very powerful in the neighbouring recently pacified provinces of Hunan and Ssuchuan, and even as far north west as Shensi and Kansu. In all these areas Wu San-kuei appointed the officials, or had to be consulted before any were appointed. He was very nearly a sovereign prince.

After ten years of this uneasy relationship, which was paralleled by two other so-called "feudatory" Chinese princes, former Ming generals like Wu himself, in other parts of south China, the Manchu Court felt strong enough to challenge their power and crush it if it proved recalcitrant.

High honours were conferred on the Chinese princes, but their independent position was abolished. The others accepted, Wu San-kuei repudiated his allegiance, declared independence and in 1673 proclaimed himself Great Commander-in-Chief of a new Chou dynasty. He did not at once take the title of emperor, in conformity with an old Chinese custom which required, or expected, a new claimant emperor to prove himself victorious—thus having the Mandate of Heaven—before assuming the title of supreme monarch, Heaven's viceroy on earth. In point of fact when Wu San-kuei did take the imperial title, in 1678, his movement was not making rapid progress. He had had five years of stiff struggle with the Manchus in Hunan and Ssuchuan, and had recently met with reverses in Kiangsi also. Five and a half months after proclaiming himself Emperor Chao Wu of the Chou dynasty, Wu San-kuei died. It would seem probable that he decided to take the final step knowing he had not long to live and in order to facilitate the succession of his grandson, Wu Shih-fan, who took the throne at K'unming, which was the capital of this Chou empire.

It is far from certain that if Wu San-kuei had been a younger man when he threw off allegiance to the distant and alien Manchu Court he would not have succeeded in refounding a new kingdom of Nanchao, or whatever he might have called it, in Yünnan. He was sixty-six when he died; had he lived he could not, perhaps, have dislodged the Manchus from north China, where they met little opposition, but he might have shaken their new power in the south and consolidated his own in the south-west. His son had not his ability; by 1681 the Manchus were besieging him in K'unming itself, and when he had no hope of deliverance he took his own life. The city fell, the Manchus massacred the followers of the Wu family, but left the mass of their soldiers, men of northern origin, as quasi-exiles in K'unming, which ever since has retained something of the air of a northern city and miniature Peking which Wu San-kuei bestowed upon it in his twenty years' sojourn. Thus a possible revival of the independent kingdom in Yünnan collapsed. Further exiles and Manchu rule enhanced the sinification of the country, which Wu San-kuei, himself a northerner, had indeed promoted.

For two hundred years, until the Manchu power itself was well into decline, no movement of any significance for the independence of Yünnan arose. When such a revolt did occur in the middle of the nineteenth century it was not led by Yünnan-settled Chinese, nor by the native inhabitants, but by the Muslim settlers. This community had, as has been mentioned, originated under the Mongol rule as mercenary soldiers brought in from central Asia. By the late nineteenth century it was large, rich and also felt itself oppressed. Monopolising the caravan trade, which was the only means of transport in the mountainous province, the Yünnan Muslims were settled in all the major cities along the main roads. They were thus well placed to revolt, but also well placed to be fleeced by corrupt officials, who by the middle of the nineteenth century were numerous. It would seem probable that after the Ming conquest, the Muslim settlers, servants of the defeated Mongols, were not trusted or accepted as loyal subjects. They had lost status, and although inheriting warlike traditions from their military forebears, were not enlisted as soldiers. They turned to transport and related industries, some relatively small number of them taking up agriculture.

In 1855 the Manchu empire was in a sorry state; it had recently been defeated in the Opium War by Britain; in 1851 the Tai Ping rebellion had broken out in the southern provinces, and in 1853, after sweeping across south China and down the Yangtze, the rebels had taken Nanking, the southern capital, and proclaimed there the Great Kingdom of Heavenly Peace (T'ai P'ing T'ien Kuo). Since the rebels were in control of most of the Yangtze valley, and threatening to move north on Peking, communications between north China and the south-western provinces were precarious or very roundabout. To the Yünnan Muslims these events seemed to offer an unsurpassed opportunity to revolt and drive the Manchu power out of Yünnan. Unlike the revolt of Wu San-kuei, which although Yünnan-based, aimed at the expulsion of the Manchus from all China, the Yünnan Muslims sought only to gain power in Yünnan itself and there set up a Muslim kingdom. They had no links with the heretical Christian Tai Ping rebels, except that Tai Ping victories facilitated their own rebellion in Yünnan.

The spiritual leader of the movement was a Tali-born Muslim named Ma Te-hsin, who lived at K'unming, and was a Mullah or Muslim priest. In spite of his connection with the revolt the Manchu government did not for many years apprehend him, though he seems to have lived in the area they dominated for most of that time. The military leader was a certain Tu Wen-hsiu, also from Tali, who definitely proclaimed his intention to set up a Muslim kingdom. This he called P'ing Nan Kuo (Peaceful Southern Kingdom), and he himself took the Muslim title of Sultan under the Arabic name of Suleiman. This in itself proves the local and national (Muslim) character of his movement. No "Sultan" could aspire to rule China, no man with a foreign name would be acceptable as a Chinese emperor. Tu was not only aware of the international connections of men of Muslim faith, but appreciated the situation of Yünnan in this respect. He rapidly conquered all western Yünnan, until his kingdom marched with the kingdom of Burma, which before long was to succumb to British conquest. Tu knew of Burma's weakness; he sought no alliance with these Buddhist rulers, but did approach the British, already in southern Burma, with a letter to Queen Victoria asking for recognition as king of P'ing Nan. It was not acceptable to the Queen nor her advisers; they were not at that time ready to promote the dissolution of the Manchu empire. Had they done otherwise, it is at least quite probable that an independent Muslim-ruled Yünnan could have emerged and survived.

The weakness of Tu Wen-hsiu and his supporters was that they represented only a sectional interest in Yünnan, a land ever divided by geography and also by race and local feeling. There seems to have been no rally of the native peoples to the Sultan's cause; equally there was no overt opposition to it from these elements. The Chinese population, if not actively opposed, remained passive also. The real opposition came from the armies of the Manchu dynasty, although these were in fact Chinese forces under a Chinese commander. Ts'en Yu-ying was an unusual man. Coming from a family of Chinese origin long settled in the tribal areas of Kuangsi province, his family had been the recognised local feudal lords of one such tribe for several centuries, yet they had retained Chinese culture, speech and won official positions. Ts'en himself was thus a man of the south-west, no northern intruder like Wu San-kuei, and perhaps could have more easily made himself the sovereign of a detached southwest than the Muslim Tu Wen-hsiu. But Ts'en was loyal to the Court at Peking, and that Court, no longer in a position to exert much influence for its own part in the far-off south-western provinces, entrusted him with full powers.

It was a long and devastating war, waged mostly on the Yünnan plateau between Tali and K'unming. As early as 1857 Ts'en Yu-ying advanced to Tali, but was driven off. In the same year the Muslims besieged K'unming, repeating the attempt in 1861, and finally, under Tu Wen-hsiu, briefly taking the city in 1863. But Muslim dissensions and jealousies, the submission of some of their leaders, and the quarrels which broke out between others, ruined their chances of consolidating their victories. Gradually Ts'en Yu-ying recovered and stabilised the eastern part of the province. As late as 1868 Tu Wen-hsiu was able to besiege K'unming for a year, but when the siege had to be abandoned in 1869 it was a turning-point in the long war. These repeated and long sieges of a walled city in the middle of the nineteenth century must be among the last examples of this ancient form of warfare in history.* Ts'en was now appointed viceroy of Yünnan and left his subordinate, Yang Yu-k'o, to

---

* Perhaps the very last example was the siege of Peking for six weeks in December 1948 and January 1949 by the Communist Peoples' Liberation Army. At that time the city of Peking was wholly contained within its ancient walls.

deal the final blow. Yang advanced on Tali in 1872 and forced the passage of the Hsiakuan at the southern end of the lake. He then laid siege to the city itself and took it after a prolonged and fierce resistance. Even after the death of Tu Wen-hsiu (who tried to take his own life but was surrendered by his guards before he could do so), the Muslims resisted in and out of the city for nearly a year. They were massacred in thousands, but fought on. When pacification was complete it was estimated that the population of the province had fallen from eight million to about three million, although it is thought that many of the missing had in fact fled to more peaceful regions.

Thus ended the last attempt to separate Yünnan from China, for it was a conscious attempt to do that, to set up an independent Muslim kingdom. It has never been repeated. The Muslim community although it survived and has recovered some of its numbers, never won back the strong position it had held before 1873. The city of Tali which had been the traditional capital for an independent kingdom, as opposed to K'unming, the stronghold of Chinese administration, was almost destroyed at the imperialist capture. Today more than half the enclosure within the walls is still open fields and the grass-grown ruins of houses; much damage was done by the great earthquake of 1925, and this used to be the official explanation of the desolate areas, but the older inhabitants knew well that it was false: the open lanes which were once residential streets were then inhabited by the Muslim population, which, after the fall of the city, was forbidden to dwell within it.

The Muslims were themselves responsible for severe damage to cultural monuments of the further past. The great Buddhist monastery called San T'a Ssu, Monastery of the Three Pagodas, is today a heap of ruins. This was not the consequence of the earthquake, for the three ancient pagodas which give the monastery its name survived the earthquake, as they had survived Muslim, Ming and Mongol. In the one small hall of the ancient monastery which has been later restored there is a mutilated fragment of a life-size bronze Buddha, long famous as a work of the Nanchao period. Only part of the torso escaped Muslim abhorrence of sculpture, but this fragment shows a style very strongly Indian in character, with relatively little sign of direct Chinese artistic inspiration. This is, or rather was, the most important evidence for the Indian strain in the civilisation of Nanchao which had come down to modern times. There are other indications of this underlying influence in the culture of contemporary Yünnan, particularly in the Tali region. Until comparatively recent times tombstones carried the inscription and identification of the deceased in Chinese on the front of the stone, in Sanskrit on the reverse: a custom unique to Yünnan, and in particular characteristic of

Tali. Many scores of such tombs are still standing on the slopes of the mountain above the city.

The people of Tali decorate their houses and also temples—even mosques—with a design sometimes in low relief, sometimes painted, of a snake-like monster, which is believed to be the god of earthquakes, locally called Ao Yu; there can be little doubt that it is a somewhat modified representation of the Naga, the serpent deity of Hinduism. The Naga motif is very common in all decoration in the Tali district; in the legs of tables and chairs, and conspicuously in the form of the headdress worn by Pai girls of the Tali plain before marriage. This is not a Chinese art motif, and is almost certainly a relic of the pre-Chinese culture of early Nanchao.

Such survivals are few; the casual traveller would find little in western Yünnan which did not appear to be of Chinese origin, until he draws close to the Burmese border where the inhabitants are of T'ai race (Shans) or Kachin tribespeople. But very often the Chinese form of a building, a work of art, or an artifact conceals an element derived from the older culture of this region. Curiously, in spite of their long residence and brief domination, the Muslim component of the population has produced few clear evidences of any cultural influences brought with them from central Asia. The style of black and white arabesque decoration used in Tali under the eaves of houses is perhaps almost the only detectable artistic influence. This, too, is confined to the Tali district.

It is therefore clear enough that the Chinese assimilation of the older culture in Yünnan is very nearly absolute. Memories of a former independence are vague and shadowy among the common people; known as historical facts, but seen through Chinese education, by the literate. National feeling does not exist among the peoples now called National Minorities. They are aware of their difference from Chinese, but feel no particular pride, nor inferiority. Educated men of these peoples are literate in Chinese, but have never (until perhaps under the Peoples' Republic) attempted to devise a system of writing of their own. This seems to have always been true with very few exceptions. The literature, in so far as any has survived, of Nanchao was in Chinese, or perhaps also in Sanskrit. Educated Pai at Tali, although speaking their own language colloquially at home, are quite unaware of its special grammatical characteristics and quite without interest in the language as such. It is just common speech for the home and the farm, never used in polite circles. The factor which determined social status in pre-Communist times was education; a man who read and spoke Chinese was an equal of any pure-blood Chinese (if in fact there were any such people in Yünnan) and one who could not read was an inferior, even if his native language was Chinese.

If he could only speak some non-Chinese language he was in practice classed as a "*man tzu*", i.e. a barbarian, or perhaps more accurately as a "native" in the pejorative sense of that word. A Pai who could only speak Chinese very badly was heard to abuse a Nosu herdsman who obstructed the road as "*hu tu man tzu*"—a "stupid native". Colonial attitudes were not confined to European colonialists.

Yet Chinese colonial policy, for such it must be called in Yünnan, was in some ways enlightened. The population was seen as divided between "shu" and "sheng"—ripe and raw. Ripe for Chinese civilisation, full acceptance and official employment if they had acquired a Chinese education and conformed, more or less, to Chinese social customs. This last requisite was not too rigidly applied. The Pai of Tali have a family system which is non-Chinese, and based more on local origin in a village than on patrilineal descent. Exogamy was no part of it, and is still often ignored by men of education. Chinese from other parts of the country who see tombs recording the marriage of families of the same surname are surprised, if no longer shocked; but the educated Tali Pai find this quite normal. In some parts of Yünnan assimilation is not so far advanced. The Na Khi people who live around Lichiang, one hundred miles north of Tali, in an area once under strong Tibetan influence, had developed a simple system of ideograph script, or picture writing, which may have been an imitation of Chinese, but was different. It was still in use on tomb monuments in the late thirties, but fast dying out. A certain number of longer manuscripts have been preserved. This people suffered from the stress of having changed their social customs, to conform with Chinese morality, at a very recent period. Formerly pre-marital intercourse was recognised and normal; under Chinese influence it became disgraceful and condemned. In consequence the suicide rate among girls in Lichiang was very high, and was associated with romantic attitudes of protest.

The "raw", or "uncivilised" in Chinese terms, were largely left to themselves. Very little conscious and planned effort was made to bring them under Chinese influence, so long as they kept the peace. For the most part dwellers in the high ranges and forests which did not attract Chinese settlement, their main contact with the agricultural population was at markets to which they came to buy cloth or trinkets and to sell the forest products, particularly medicinal herbs, which are valued by Chinese. It is very probable that in spite of this easy tolerance, the "raw" tribes felt neglected and deprived of influence. The remarkable success which, in the early twentieth century, Protestant missionaries scored in converting large numbers of Li Su, a mountain tribe, was perhaps as much due to the feelings that these people derived from conversion; security, influence and assistance from powerful friends—the foreigners—than from religious convictions. Chinese policy, on the other hand, lethargic although it seemed to be, was based on the conviction that time would bring all the peoples of Yünnan within the full pale of Chinese civilisation; a century this way or that did not matter. History had shown that opposition melted away, that nothing better could be offered than Chinese culture, and that those who adopted it were proud of their achievement and unwilling to abandon their new status.

The Muslims, in recent centuries, alone offered an apparent alternative, and for this reason were much more harshly suppressed than dissident "raw" tribes who could be expected to be refractory from time to time, but were never a real threat. There seems to be very little evidence that this basic Chinese approach has changed under the present régime. It is now more theoretical; the Minority Peoples have a right to their own culture, and the right to be educated in it, if that is what they want. But they also learn Chinese; they are brought up, whether within a non-Chinese community or in a mixed one, as followers of the Communist ethic and under the teaching of Mao Tse-tung. More is done for the people, not only the Chinese settlers, than the imperial or early republican government ever contemplated, but this, too, is an assimilative force, bringing a backward province into the full stream of contemporary Chinese culture. The rude or contemptuous terms used for non-Chinese in former times are abandoned and condemned, even when they were long sanctioned by use and no longer meant very much to either Chinese or non-Chinese. The Min Chia (literally "common people") of Tali are now to be called *Pai*; but this word is the Chinese form of the native *Ber*, which is a contraction of *Ber Wa Dser*, "People of the White Prince". It does not seem that they may be called, in Chinese, *Pai Wang Tzu*; perhaps this is too feudal and reactionary a term.

Yünnanese, of all races, used to have a distinctly provincial attitude to the rest of China: while this could hardly be called "Yünnanese nationalism" since it had no political motives nor undertones, it was markedly self-centred. Although Yünnan is a border province, and very far from the centre of the country, the Yünnanese always spoke of other parts of China as "*wai sheng*", "outer provinces"—an expression which greatly surprised, shocked or amused visitors from such "outer provinces" as Peking, Shanghai or Canton. If some different, and perhaps more desirable custom existed elsewhere, and was mentioned, the normal reaction was "we do not do this in Yünnan", and the implication was that Yünnan was therefore superior. Much of this sort of provincialism can be found in other parts of China (notably Ssuchuan) but there did seem, in Yünnan, to be a stronger sense of particularity than is found elsewhere. This could

D

be explained, at least in Tali, by the continuing use of customs and manners which are not of Chinese origin, and were known to be native to the region.

As a corollary to the attitude to "outside provinces" there was a very distinct recognition of non-Yünnanese as in some way unlike, even almost alien. Where settlers from Ssuchuan were numerous, even the place-names recorded their alien origin, as at Pinch'uan, "Guests (from Ssu) Ch'uan". Muslims were never allowed to forget that they were an alien people (Hui Tzu) even though they all spoke the local dialect and dressed in the Chinese manner—only being distinctive in their religion. Since the fall of the empire the old imperial practice of never employing natives of a province on service in their own province had fallen into complete dis-use. Officials were Yünnanese, the governor of the province was Yün-nanese, and if he attempted, not always successfully, to distribute the holders of office to districts other than their own native places, he often found it convenient to ignore this rule in practice. In this sense Yünnan had recovered more practical independence from the central government than it had enjoyed since the Mongol conquest. During the "Warlord Era", 1916–34, the Yünnanese never saw an army from outside the pro-vince, nor submitted to a governor who was not a native of it. When the armies of the Nanking government, following at a discreet distance the Long March of the Communist forces in 1934–5, penetrated Yünnan, they were not very welcome. The communists did not take cities, nor occupy the land for long; the Nationalists would have done both if they could have spared the troops. The attitude to the Communists was thus ambivalent; true, they were "*wai sheng jen*"—outsiders—but so were the Nationalists. True, too, that the Communists were the enemies of land-lords and the official class, but these people took refuge in the cities which were not taken by the Communists. The common people liked what they had seen of the Communist Long Marchers; they paid for goods, they gave fair wages for porter hire, and the only trouble with them was that they marched so far and so fast that even the seasoned Yünnanese porter found it a gruelling experience. When the Japanese invasion began the Yünnan forces made a contribution to the national defence. The divisions which were bound for the front were given a fine send-off with banquets and compliments; everyone was really rather glad to see them go, soldiers away in the "wai sheng" were well employed, and better than they might be at home. No one seriously expected that many, if any, would ever return.

Yünnan is now integrated as a province of the Peoples' Republic, but there have been not a few indications in the course of the Cultural Revolu-tion that the old particularism is not dead. It will probably last for very many years, for even the present improved communications leave the country still remote, relatively inaccessible, and far from the centre of power. Yet it is equally certain that the process of incorporation in the Chinese state and nation is now complete in the political sense and very nearly as thorough in the cultural aspect. Yünnan thus presents a history of Chinese expansion from its early beginnings with relations between a distant Court and local barbarian rulers, through a period of cultural infusion contemporary with political rejection, and then through the successive stages of conquest, occupation and assimilation. The same process, or similar events certainly marked the Chinese incorporation of Kuangtung and the south-east coastal province of Fukien: at an earlier period still one may dimly perceive very similar events and a like sequence in the incorporation of the Yangtze valley. Yünnan was the last in a long series.

The question must then arise: is it in fact the last, or only the latest? A history of Chinese southward movement both politically and culturally which has already continued for more than two thousand years, perhaps for nearly three thousand, cannot be assumed to have come to an end for all time just because present political configurations do not seem to favour its continuance. There was the long period of Nanchao power which must have seemed to have brought Chinese progress to an end, followed as it was by the Sung rejection of a policy of expansion. Nevertheless the process resumed and was brought to a culmination within five centuries of the fall of Nanchao. Today the prospects seem no less unfavourable than those which confronted the first Sung emperor in the late tenth century. Burma is a vigorously national state, and reasonably well populated. This is no empty land waiting for settlers. Vietnam has for centuries shown its willingness to receive Chinese culture and its equally firm rejection of Chinese rule. Nothing today shows that this pattern of response has changed. Even if some of the other countries of South-East Asia are accessible to China by land, if only after considerable effort has been expended on improved communications, they are in fact already more closely in touch by sea. Thailand, Cambodia and even Laos have not taken their Chinese immigrants from the land route, but by sea. The Chinese influx into these countries is therefore not a part of Chinese expansion by land.

It may be, therefore, that the expansion by land has reached its natural limit, where other peoples of advanced civilisation have already installed themselves, and cannot be either assimilated or ejected. In modern times expansion by sea may be both easier in the transport of settlers and travellers, and more efficient at the stage of political control which could follow. But these conditions would only be fulfilled if the Chinese in future turned their minds and energies to ruling the seas, something which they have very rarely tried to do in the past. However, the power they developed during the brief effort in this direction which they made in the early fifteenth century stands as a signal to what could be accomplished if this ambition became established state policy.

CHAPTER FIVE

MONGOL AND MING IN SOUTH-EAST ASIA

From the early years of the thirteenth century the Mongol conquerors of China were already in possession of Peking and north China;
Genghiz Khan having been proclaimed emperor of the Yüan dynasty in
1206: but it was not until 1234 that he and his successor finished the conquest of the Kin dynasty, which had ruled the northern half of China for
over a century. Only when the Kin were overthrown did the Mongols
begin their invasions of the southern half of China, governed by the Sung
dynasty. Fully forty years passed before in 1280 Kubilai Khan, grandson
of Genghiz, completed the conquest of Sung China. Yünnan had been
seized several years earlier, in 1253, but this operation had been undertaken to outflank the Sung empire from the west and facilitate the conquest of the southern and south-eastern provinces. The Mongols had not
immediately followed it up with any fresh invasion of the other southern
neighbours of China. Had their ambitions really been confined to conquering the Sung, who had claims upon the whole Chinese empire which
must have appeared unacceptable, the Mongols had no need to go further.
Vietnam had not been under direct Sung rule at any time, nor had any
other South-East Asian kingdom. But the Great Khan, who was also to
attempt to extend his rule to Japan, was not content to accept any
frontier which might be shown to be weak or ill-defended; he set no
limits to the Mongol empire, which already reached far into eastern
Europe.

It might have been thought that the simultaneous invasions of Japan,
Burma, Vietnam and plans for reducing Java also to subservience were
rather too much even for the irresistible Mongols to contemplate,
especially as the final phase of the war against the Sung still continued; yet
Kubilai ordered his first invasion of Japan in 1274, an earlier ultimatum in
1268 requiring the "king of Japan" to come to Peking and pay homage
having been rejected after time-spinning negotiations. This first invasion
being too weak and encountering bad weather, the next attempt was put
off until after the Sung war was over, in 1281, when the much larger
second expedition set forth. In the same year active preparations were also

afoot to invade Annam, Champa, Cambodia and Burma. These various campaigns as they developed did not in the end prove very successful to the Mongols and were ultimately to add nothing of any importance to their empire, but it would seem that they did mark the high-tide mark of Mongol power, reaching out to regions which were either too remote or too difficult to conquer and to hold. The Japanese invasions were a catastrophic failure, and were never renewed after 1281. The invasion of Java was undertaken some years later, but led to inconclusive results. Burma resisted for fifteen years, and was devastated, but left to local princes to govern. The Mongols failed to conquer either Champa or Annam, and were content with a demonstration against Cambodia which secured an offer of tribute.

The pattern of Mongol aggression was in all cases similar. First an envoy was sent who demanded that the King of the selected kingdom proceed to Peking to pay personal homage to the Great Khan; this was rather more than Chinese diplomacy had ever exacted even when the power of China was very strong. Tribute missions, and acknowledgement of suzerainty had been the age-old requirement, not personal homage. If, as was usually the case, the South-East Asian kings, like the Shogun of Japan, refused to go to Peking, preparations for an invasion and conquest were put on foot. There was no suggestion of any lesser demand. In South-East Asia at least the Mongols seemed to have little to fear from such resistance, for important changes in strength had arisen among these kingdoms during the period when Sung China was slowly succumbing to Mongol attack. Since the early years of the thirteenth century the Tai peoples, known to their neighbours as "Syam" (from which the earlier European name for Thailand, Siam, comes) had been moving down from Yünnan and its western borders into the lower valley of the Mekong, in what is now Laos, and also into the Menam valley in Thailand itself. They were warriors, sometimes in the service of the kings of Cambodia, more often, and later essentially, enemies to that empire. By 1220 they had solid establishments and principalities in the Menam valley and along the middle Mekong.

At about the same time—the exact date is not known—as the Mongol conquest of the Sung, between 1283 and 1292, King Rama Khamheng founded a strong Tai kingdom by amalgamating several of these principalities and conquering much territory in modern Thailand and Laos from Cambodia. He was also able to profit from the dissolution of the Burmese kingdom under Mongol attack to dominate lower Burma. This new kingdom of Sukotai was the origin of modern Thailand. King Rama modelled his institutions closely on Mongol examples; his great inscription, which records most of what is known of his life and work, seems to have echoed the language of Genghiz Khan, and the King may have been an actual ally of the Great Khan. It is clear that the Mongols favoured him; he was not subjected to any invasion, he visited Peking in 1294, paid tribute, and brought back with him Chinese experts in the making of porcelain who started that industry in Thailand. Thus the rise of Sukotai was a significant factor in the affairs of the south-east, weakening the other kingdoms who were exposed to direct Mongol pressure.

As early as 1271 Kubilai had demanded tribute and homage from the king of Burma; refused, he renewed the demand in 1273, and on this occasion the Burmese king emphasised his rejection of the demands by putting the Mongol ambassadors to death. It was not an action which the Great Khan was likely to overlook, but the final stages of the war against the Sung, and the invasion of Japan postponed the day of reckoning. The Burmese had followed up their provocation by attacking a tribe on the Yünnan border who had submitted to the Mongols; in 1277 an expedition was sent from Yünnan to invade Burma, and after winning a victory in the Nam Ti valley east of Bhamo, the Mongols apparently expected more compliance from the Burmese king, distant though his capital at Pagan was. The results of this Burmese expedition were judged to be inadequate and a new one was set in motion in 1278; but although the Mongols took a strong place on the Irrawaddy not far from Bhamo, they still had not seriously penetrated the heart of the kingdom. The climate, the heat and the tropical maladies of the country took a heavy toll of their northern or Yünnan-based troops. Nevertheless Kubilai persisted; in 1283 a new army commanded by a Mongol chief, Singtur, instead of by the Muslim officers used hitherto, invaded the Irrawaddy valley and pressed on towards the capital, from which the king of Burma withdrew into the delta and its swamps. Peace negotiations led to no result, and in 1287 the Mongols finally took Pagan and dissolved the kingdom.

They clearly found it a profitless conquest; Mongol troops could not stand the climate, and as an army of occupation risked being reduced to weakness by disease, they decided to evacuate Burma, leaving Tai princes, mercenary soldiers in origin, in power in a large number of small principalities. Burma under the Mongol suzerainty was reduced to a warring chaos of petty princes of Tai descent, all of whom were nominal feudatories of the Mongol emperor. The confusion was so great that in 1300 the Mongols returned once more, to restore order, but very soon withdrew, leaving things much as they had been before. Mongol action in this part of South-East Asia was more disruptive than effective; it destroyed the Burmese kingdom, but left nothing in its place. Perhaps the only clear and lasting result was the establishment of a claim to suzerainty over Burma by the emperors of China, for the Mongol Great Khan was in the eyes of South-East Asians primarily the emperor of China. This claim, fortified by the Mongol conquest of Yünnan, was to be inherited, and pressed, by their Chinese successors.

Several years before the final conquest of the Sung, the Mongols in possession of Yünnan since 1253, had in 1257 invaded Annam and captured and sacked Hanoi, the capital. Vietnamese resistance had then forced them to withdraw from this ephemeral conquest, and for the next thirty years, at recurrent intervals the Mongol attempt to conquer Vietnam—both Annam in the north and Champa in the south—was continued, offering a strangely disturbing parallel to the efforts of successive Western powers to do the same thing in the same country since 1945. The Mongols did not learn any lessons from Sung forbearance. Well before the Sung were eliminated, Kubilai sent his general Sogatu to invade Champa by sea, intending to force Annam to surrender by a concurrent invasion of that country by land, from the north. Both efforts failed. The Chams aided by their swampy jungle country, successfully and strongly resisted much superior forces, and finally Sogatu had to go north to help his compatriots who had invaded Annam under Prince Togan, a son of Kubilai. Togan again took Hanoi, in 1285, but this conquest of the Annamite capital failed as before to bring the country to submission. Resistance gathered in the mountains and jungles; Togan was defeated by the Annamite Prince Tran Nhon Ton, and his expected aid by Sogatu from the south was intercepted and defeated, Sogatu losing his life in the battle. The Mongols had once more to withdraw from Hanoi and the whole country. Two years later Kubilai ordered a third invasion; once more Hanoi was taken, and as in the previous instances, the guerrilla resistance in the countryside, the climate, the heat and the unsuitability of the terrain for Mongol cavalry tactics, forced the Mongol army to withdraw. This evacuation proved final. Both Annam and Champa, enemies although they usually were, had been forced into alliance by the common danger. Both having repulsed the armed invasion, were swift to placate the Mongol Khan by offering tribute and acknowledgement of suzerainty on the old Chinese pattern. The attempt to substitute direct Mongol domination for that well-tested diplomatic device had signally failed.

In 1283, before the final defeat in Annam and Champa, Sogatu had raided northern Cambodia, and promptly received and accepted an offer of tribute and admission of Mongol suzerainty from the failing power of the Khmer empire. Why Cambodia was treated with such restraint, while an insensate attempt to conquer Champa and Annam was still continued, remains obscure. Cambodia is further from the Chinese homelands, but this factor certainly did not deter Kubilai in his war against Japan, Burma or Java. It might be significant that in the same year, 1283 (if not in fact a little earlier) the new king of Sukotai (Thailand), Rama Khamheng, who was so openly pro-Mongol, had come to power and was known as the powerful enemy of Cambodia, which he had already stripped of its Menam valley provinces. Mongol policy, in this respect following traditional Chinese policy, tended to discourage the strong and support the weaker party in the quarrels of South-East Asia. King Rama might be something of a pupil and friend, but that was no reason to allow him a better chance of conquering Cambodia.

Within a very few years, in 1296—only four years after King Rama had composed his famous inscription which manifestly admires Mongol customs and manners—the Mongol Court was on good terms with the king of Cambodia. In that year a Mongol embassy reached Angkor Thom, where it remained for a year, and one member of it, Chou Ta-kuan, occupied his time by recording and noting facts and impressions about Cambodia which he later embodied in a famous book. This work remains the only complete, eye-witness account of Angkor Thom and its associated monuments as they were in their glory; and moreover the only extant account of the manners and social life of the country, the ceremonies of the Court, the royal palace as it then appeared, and the uses to which many of the existing monuments were put in their prime. Chou mentions that there had recently been a disastrous war with Sukotai; that the purpose of the long embassy to which he was attached may have been to keep the peace in that part of the world and prevent further Tai attacks on Cambodia, is not stated, but may well explain the unusual fact of an embassy *from* China, rather than *to* the imperial Court being so much as recorded, let alone described in detail. Chou also refers to resident Chinese, and descendants of Chinese immigrants; "men from the sea", he says, rather contemptuously, inferring that many of them may well have started life as pirates. His testimony is the first evidence of a truly historical nature for a resident Chinese community in South-East Asia. Chou Ta-kuan also comments on the monuments and religion of the Khmer, noting the frequent *linga* symbolic stones, and observing that they had much the same appearance as the stone at the Altar of the God of the Soil in the imperial palace at Peking. The *linga* is a phallic symbol: that the stone at the Altar of the God of the Soil in China, one of the most ancient of the imperial cults, has the same origin has long been conjectured by Western students, but never confirmed in Chinese literature. Chou Ta-kuan discreetly avoids such confirmation, but shows that he saw the resemblance, for the nature of the *linga* could not be misunderstood.

As in the cases of Burma, Annam and Champa, Kubilai did not wait until the war against the Sung was finally over before extending his demands to more distant Java. Already in 1279 he had sent envoys to the king of Singosari, in Java, then the predominant power in the island, requiring the usual homage personally paid in Peking. King Kertanagara was a man of great ambition and far-reaching designs. He not only had no intention of submitting to the Mongol power, but he aimed to form a confederation of the Indonesian kingdoms to oppose Mongol intrusion. He rejected the demand, and set about expanding his authority with a view to meeting a Mongol invasion if it came. There is some conflict among the authorities whether the King carried out these designs by actual force, in Madura and in Bali, or by winning the rulers of these smaller kingdoms to his side by religious activities designed to display him as the chosen of the gods, the destined victor. Java, as yet, was still Hindu in culture and Buddhist in religion. Whether founder of a "Holy Alliance" or scheming conqueror, King Kertanagara was probably encouraged by the Mongol failure in Champa and in Annam. The former country had ancient links with Java, and the religion and culture of both was Hindu–Buddhist. In 1289, when the Mongols had clearly been driven out of both Annam and Champa, a new embassy was received in Java renewing the old demands. King Kertanagara not only rejected them but it is said "disfigured the faces" of the envoys before sending them back to Peking. Authorities differ as to whether this means that he cut off their noses, or merely inflicted humiliations upon them, causing them in the Chinese phrase to "lose face".

Mongol sea expeditions needed some time to prepare, but the Great Khan was not willing to allow Java to escape unpunished. By 1292 the armada of the Mongols, manned by Chinese sailors and commanded both by Mongol and Chinese admirals, had sailed down the coast of Champa and crossed towards Borneo and so on to Java; but when it arrived off the coast of the great island, it found the situation entirely transformed. It is believed that King Kertanagara, who had sent an expedition to reduce the Sumatran state of Malayu, had hoped to intercept the Mongol armada at sea. He did not succeed, and late in 1292 a sudden revolt in the home country overtook him while his forces were mainly out of the country; his palace was surprised and stormed, the King being slain. Prince Vijaya, the ousted heir to the kingdom, then invited the Mongols to land and co-operate with him in defeating the usurper and slayer of his father. The Mongol commanders deemed this an easy way to accomplish their mission. They landed, and with the aid of Prince Vijaya and his followers defeated the usurper and retook the capital, where Vijaya was enthroned as King, offering the usual tribute and accepting Mongol suzerainty. Whether he was also expected in due course to go to Peking to pay personal homage is not clear; it would probably have been an unreasonable demand at a time when the kingdom was still unsettled. The Mongols relaxed their guard; they dispersed their troops in small garrisons, whether with the intention of remaining permanently, or only for a certain period; but they had not reckoned with the distrust which their presence inspired, and the secret determination of the new King to carry on the policy of his father. When he judged them sufficiently off-guard and broken up into small groups, he attacked these garrisons individually, prevented the regrouping of the army, and finally drove them to re-embark. Once more South-East Asian delaying tactics, guerrilla-style war, the jungle and the climate had been too much for Mongol power. The fleet returned to China; Vijaya sent tribute, and Kubilai gave up his plans on Java, or perhaps, more probably, they were abandoned by his successor, when he died the next year in 1294.

The Mongol empire was never the same again after the Great Khan had passed away. Succession troubles disturbed the peace, the rulers were short-lived and mostly ineffective, and from the middle of the next century after 1350, they were faced with a complex and continuous revolt of their Chinese subjects. Control over south China was lost, and although the Mongols retained Yünnan until the very end, they lost all power at sea with the southern provinces. As on previous occasions the decline of Chinese power meant that the kingdoms of the south were left to their own quarrels without any fear of Chinese intervention. But there were consequences of the Mongol incursion which were of lasting importance. In the first place, as in Yünnan, which the Mongols brought finally within the Chinese empire, the claims of China whenever she was strong enough to exert them were enhanced. All the South-East Asian kingdoms including those of Malaya (the peninsula) from 1293 onward had acknowledged the suzerainty of Peking. Nominal allegiance of this sort had extended to Burma, Thailand (Sukotai), the Khmer empire, or what was left of it, Champa, Annam and Java. These claims were not forgotten by the successors of the Mongols, the Chinese Ming dynasty, which was the ultimate victor in the chaotic civil wars, only partly directed against the failing Mongol power, which racked China until Chu Yüan-chang, founder of the Ming dynasty, destroyed all Chinese rivals and drove the Mongols out of the country in 1368.

Among the rivals he overcame was one who had ruled the southern coastal provinces for nineteen years. Fang Kuo-chen was originally a salt merchant, a lucrative profession, since salt merchants operated under licence from the imperial monopoly of that commodity. He was suspected of connivance with the pirates of the south coast, and rather than face this accusation used his wealth and connections to start a rebellion, one of the first against the Mongols, as early as 1348. Fang made his campaigns by sea, gaining complete mastery of the southern waters, and thus intercepting the tribute and rice trade with the north of China. This was in any case a severe blow to the Mongol régime and put an end to their sea power. Their attempts to suppress Fang were uniformly unsuccessful, and he held power until finally conquered not by the Mongols, but by the rival rebel, Chu Yüan-chang, founder of the Ming dynasty. The importance of this incident is that it illuminates some of the reasons for the decline of Mongol influence in South-East Asia, their relatively early loss of control of the sea and trade routes, and foreshadows the rôle which the early Ming dynasty was to play by means of sea power. The rise of Chinese navigation had begun in the Southern Sung period when there is positive evidence of the use of the maritime compass (originally an instrument for determining the most benign aspect for graves) as an aid to navigation.

It was precisely in Fukien, the maritime southern province, that Taoist alchemy flourished, and that the early invention of the compass was developed in the preceding centuries. It was also Fukien which became the main centre of Chinese maritime enterprises, both civil and naval, from the Southern Sung onward. There can be little doubt that these two facts are related; the mariners came to know of and use for practical navigation the instrument which the Taoist priests had perfected for quite different purposes. The voyages of the Mongol fleets, and the heavy reliance on naval power as its last defence by the Southern Sung dynasty, were made possible by better navigation. It is still uncertain whether the Arabs made the first use of the Chinese invention of the compass for navigation, or borrowed it from Chinese sailors. Thus well before the great Ming maritime expeditions of the early fifteenth century there had been a steady and important development of sea travel and naval power. It is against this background, often overlooked, that the Ming expeditions must be considered. The Chinese movement to the south was turning to the sea, away from the old land routes of expansion, which with the independence of Annam and the conquest of Yünnan had reached a natural limit. In both cases Mongol power had acted as a catalyst, realising in practice the tendencies which were at work before they appeared, and which would have developed under a Chinese dynasty had their conquest not precipitated the change.

By the last decades of the fourteenth century the Ming dynasty was firmly established by the first emperor, Hung Wu (Chu Yüan-chang). He had conquered all China in sixteen years, beginning as a man of the poorest class, a destitute beggar turned bandit and then rebel. But his empire had been racked by civil war and uprisings against the Mongols for more than twenty years. A period of consolidation was essential. It was not until his son, who is known by his reign title of Yung Lo, had mounted the throne, that serious attention was turned to the southern countries. From 1405 to 1433 the Ming Court mounted seven major seaborne expeditions which extended the bounds of Chinese knowledge and contact with the southern world and the oceans beyond it to a point never before attained, and in naval terms, never matched since. There are many strange aspects to the Ming maritime expeditions which preceded by just under a century the great voyages of the Portuguese. Unlike the European ventures they were very large operations carrying strong forces, and using many ships. They were not openly commercial, nor privately sponsored, but supported by the personal authority of the emperor himself, and, strangest of all, commanded and organised by the Court eunuchs. The regular civil service of the Empire had only a smaller part in them—and disliked them for that reason. Further, they had no direct military purpose in mind; they did not conquer, nor establish colonies, nor even bases under Chinese authority, although they ranged the whole of the southern seas, across the Indian Ocean to the coasts of the Red Sea, Persian Gulf and east African coast. From these far-off places they brought back as "tribute" curiosities and valuables, and gave rich presents in return to distant kings whom the Chinese could hardly have hoped to bring into lasting submission.

They displayed the power of China in lands where she had hitherto been little more than a legend, but they did all this for the apparently empty satisfaction of winning professions of purely nominal allegiance or admission of a remote suzerainty which could not be effective. It has been suggested that the original motives were to search out and destroy possible refugee enemies of the Ming—southern Chinese more than Mongols—and also to assert the power of the Ming in lands where the Mongols had rather conspicuously failed to profit from their own expeditions. If this was so, it would seem that before long the motives changed. No refugee Chinese were likely to be found in Arabia, Persia or the African coastal countries; very few would have gone to India, and if they had, they could well have been left in obscurity. Very early in the programme the motive changed to one of exploration, of discovery, imperial regulated trade, and what might be called scientific curiosity. The Mongols had never been known in Arabia, nor southern India, still less in eastern Africa. These countries did not need a Ming fleet to convince them that the Mongol power was fallen. China equally could not at that period expect, or indeed wish to settle migrants in those lands, nor establish colonies or bases.

On any understanding the Ming maritime expeditions must remain unusual, indeed unique in Chinese history, and the motives for such lavishly equipped and very costly adventures have seemed inadequate. It is possible to assess some of the factors; the Mongols had devastated north China, and after depopulating huge areas, had forbidden the resettlement of a very extensive tract of country in northern Anhui and western Shantung provinces, with neighbouring parts of Honan. This was reserved for an imperial hunting park, and no agriculture was allowed. The huge territory became a wilderness, and so remained for more than a century. No doubt it was a great help to the rebels against the Mongol dynasty to have this refuge, where no emperor dared any longer to hunt, and where no organised civil administration existed. When the Ming acquired the empire the dynasty took over, as its own property, the former possessions of the fallen Mongols. They did not need vast desolate hunting parks, but a source of revenue outside the regular taxation, which was handled by the imperial civil service, was a valuable asset. The Emperor Yung Lo sold off the desolate region to immigrant farmers and landlords; with the large sums so gained he financed the maritime expeditions, as a Court activity, beyond civil service control, and therefore directed by the servants of the Court itself, the eunuchs.

It may still seem curious that eunuchs could be found fitted to command great fleets—an activity hardly consistent with their normal duties—but it was an old tradition in China that the emperors should rely on these men to perform many tasks which would normally be entrusted to civil servants or to military officers. Eunuchs by definition could have no family ambitions; they could be trusted with power because they could not transmit it to descendants. This was more than could be said of any minister or general, and this factor was perhaps particularly significant at a time when a new dynasty was lately come to power, risen from a completely obscure background, and with only the prestige of its own achievements, all recent, to sustain it. Yung Lo was himself a very able soldier, who had campaigned against the Mongols and his father's rivals for years; he had no need to fear too great eunuch influence, such as had undermined the last Han emperors, men who were bred in the palace and knew nothing of the outside world.

Yung Lo could also reflect that the rival who had held the field longest against his father was that Fang Kuo-chen, the sea king of the south. It was desirable that naval power be re-created, and that that power should not be commanded by any man capable of setting himself up as a rival. A hard-bitten soldier like the Emperor would not have too much respect for civil advisers and ministers, men of education superior to his own, but also men of much slighter achievement. Faithful, competent, unambitious and wholly dependent servants such as the eunuchs were the men to command his fleet. It is unfortunately not known how, or even if, they were trained to undertake these responsibilities. They certainly had the assistance of competent and experienced seamen of whom there must have been no lack in that age. Cheng Ho, the commander-in-chief and some of his staff also, were Muslims, still rather an unusual religion for pure Chinese to follow, but probably more common after the Mongol period which had seen such numbers of central and west Asian Muslims employed in China. There was also the advantage that a Muslim would have an understanding of the customs and prejudices of many of the rulers of the southern kingdoms where in the past two centuries Islam had made large-scale conversions. The rulers of Malay states, and of other Indonesian kingdoms were converting to Islam. Even more important was the fact that western Asia, beyond the Indian Ocean, was a region of exclusive Islamic culture where an infidel, even if representing the Emperor of China, might not be a very welcome envoy. The choice of eunuchs and the religion of the commander-in-chief were therefore not such inexplicable aberrations as they may have appeared to be. It was certain that the diplomatic skill of the leader of the expeditions must be as necessary as naval or military prowess; the countries to be visited were very distant, no Chinese base was to be found, the fleet would need the goodwill and friendship of the rulers of remote ports, which if denied, could imperil the whole enterprise.

The first expedition carried 27,000 men, some of the later voyages as many as 37,000, and there were sixty-two ships of special construction and very large dimensions. They are given in the accounts of the voyages preserved in the writings of those who took part in them as being, in our measurements, 517 feet long, 212 feet wide, with four decks, and the hull divided by watertight compartments—a detail which may be the first example of this type of construction. They could make six knots with favourable winds. These ships were specially designed for long-range voyages and were fitted with the type of sail which permitted them to "bore the wind" as the Chinese phrase put it, that is, to sail against the wind, as later European vessels did. It would seem that this very important invention was probably not Chinese, but borrowed from the Oceanic peoples of the Pacific. It had been adopted in China from the eighth century, the T'ang period onward. It is also now known that the Chinese were using the maritime compass by the tenth century A.D. and very possibly earlier.

The further modern scholarship has advanced in the study of the Chinese maritime activity of the twelfth, thirteenth, fourteenth and fifteenth centuries, the more it has become clear that the aspects of the great Ming expeditions which had attracted attention as strange and unexpected, are in fact closely related to a longer development and a continuing tradition of shipbuilding and naval power. The Ming were the last of a series of governments which had increasingly expanded the naval forces and encouraged, in their own rather peculiar way, commerce with distant countries. By the end of the T'ang dynasty the factors which were to turn China's southward expansion from the land frontiers to the sea routes were increasingly operative. The capital was moved from Ch'angan in the western province of Shensi, to K'aifeng, which is very much nearer to the eastern coast. After the fall of K'aifeng and the loss of north China to the Kin invaders in the early twelfth century, the capital of the Southern Sung was at Hangchou, actually on the coast, and then a considerable port. It has been suggested that from this same period the north-western provinces, and beyond them the land route to western Asia which had carried the great silk traffic of earlier times, began to suffer from increasing dessication, one cause for the new emphasis on sea communication and the rising prosperity of the south-east coastal provinces. The question cannot be regarded as settled; there were other factors making for the shift in trade routes and political focus quite distinct from any climatic change.

The T'ang dynasty had settled and colonised the southern provinces, and the consequences of this development of their rich resources was a steady growth in their population and economic importance. This began to be clear in the Sung period, and to become of major importance in the Southern Sung dynasty (1127–1280). The north-west suffered heavily in the wars that marked the close of the T'ang dynasty, the south largely escaped any similar devastation. Once again the Kin invasion, and the later Mongol invasion fell most heavily on the north and north-west, the south was either spared or escaped more lightly. The great clan names of high antiquity which were still borne by well-known statesmen in the Northern Sung period (tenth and eleventh centuries) and still originated in the north-west, their ancient home, are in later times, down to the present, only found in Kuangtung; the ancestors of these southern branches having migrated there mostly during the Southern Sung period. Many other evidences of a great shift of wealth and power from the north-west to the east and south-east coast could be cited, but the consequences for the growth of Chinese sea power were for long ignored, partly due to the faithful reliance on the dynastic histories, which with their traditional approach and formulae tend to obscure such facts. It is now seen that the long resistance of the Southern Sung to Mongol conquest, so contrary to the rapid collapse of the northern Kin empire, is connected with this development.

The Kin, a Tatar people, were warlike, but land bound; the still more powerful Mongols were also a land people from the northern steppes. Like overcame like. The southern Chinese, now become a numerous and prosperous people, were not the best of soldiers, but they were good seamen. Moreover the concentration of wealth in the coastal areas of the south was now such as to make the Southern Sung dynasty the first Chinese government to which the land revenue was less profitable than taxes on seaborne commerce. The commerce, constantly expanding and enriching the government, had to be protected, and naval forces were created to perform this task. It was the control of the sea along its coasts which for long defended the Southern Sung from land attacks by Mongol armies. To overcome the Southern Sung the Mongols had to create their own fleet, manned from the natives of eastern coast provinces already conquered, and it was a sea battle off the south coast of Kuangtung, near Hong Kong, which finally set the seal on Kubilai's conquest of south China. Unlike the later Manchus who neglected the sea and its defences, the Mongols set about recruiting the former seamen of the Sung, and rebuilding the fleet with the knowledge and expertise of those whom they had recently conquered. This was the foundation of Mongol sea power, which although not always used with much skill, and undoubtedly handicapped by the lack of cordial co-operation from the Chinese who manned the fleets, was nevertheless a very formidable power. In 1279, the last year of the war against the Sung, the Mongol Court ordered the building of 1,500 ships, which figure was increased to 3,000 in 1281 and 4,000 in 1293. The invasions of Japan, in which the Korean fleet also participated, are said to have been effected with more than 4,000 ships, and those of Champa and Java, in which only Chinese ships took part, with over one thousand on each occasion.

Many of these vessels were not large enough nor sufficiently seaworthy for the stormy seas on which they were employed; the Mongols seem to have believed that mere numbers would suffice, and off Japan they suffered heavily for this mistake. The Ming, when they came to power corrected this error; their fleet, built under the first two Ming emperors, Hung Wu and Yung Lo, did not exceed 3,500 ships, half of which were reconnaissance light vessels, and the rest men-of-war. The main naval base was near Nanking, charged with the defence of the coasts and the approaches to the capital, which was located at that city in the reign of Hung Wu. Four hundred men-of-war were assigned to this task. A similar number were given the duty of convoying the grain fleets which sailed north along the coast carrying the tribute rice to the northern garrisons and cities, including the later capital, Peking. The great Ming innovation was the building of real "capital ships", huge for their period, and known as "Precious Vessels". They could each carry five hundred men, and their average tonnage was about 500 tons. Sixty-two of these great ships formed the core of Cheng Ho's fleets of exploration and oceanic travel. They were the product of a long tradition of developing naval construction, and it may be assumed that the sea king Fang Kuo-chen, the determined rival of Chu Yüan-chang, had taken over from the dissolving Mongol navy both ships and men, as well as the skill and knowledge of the shipbuilders of the southern ports. These were all inherited by the early Ming emperors.

A study of the actual records of Cheng Ho's expeditions, and the nature of the products of far-off countries which they brought back to China also goes some way towards correcting the impression, derived from later hostile accounts, that these expeditions were concerned only with the collection of valuable or prestige articles, for presentation to the Emperor. Valuable timbers from tropical lands, drugs, hides and other articles which were not produced in China, or in insufficient quantities, figure in the lists of "tribute" sent to China in the great fleets. In return the Ming Court sent "presents", but these were often, if not always, of a less commercial character: State umbrellas, embroideries, porcelain, books. Even the "golden seals", granted as emblems of local sovereignty were made of silver plated with gold. The Ming Court, under the cover of the conventional exchanges of "tribute" and "presents" was in fact conducting a profitable foreign trade in certain specialised lines of imports. The strikingly different aspect of this trade, compared with the later European seaborne trade with the same parts of the world, was that the Chinese trade was exclusively official; no private trader was permitted to take part in it. It was carried on by the Emperor's own private servants, the eunuchs in command of the fleets, and the Court was the sole importer of "tribute" and the sole dispenser of export "presents". The Mongols had actually forbidden private overseas trade with severe penalties attached to transgressors, although it would seem that some merchants were licensed to act for the state in this capacity, and no doubt made a good profit out of this grace. It was characteristic of China from very ancient times to treat trade as a state monopoly whenever its nature made this system easy to enforce. In Han times iron-working was a state monopoly; salt remained so throughout history down to the present day, and such huge enterprises as the imperial potteries at Ching Te Chen in Kiangsi, the home of porcelain, were essentially similar in character. Private capitalism in China was always under pressure, always insecure; only the state could finance great enterprises and it was also determined to keep their profits. This factor in the development of the Chinese economy, very significant for past history as for present practice, was also a major determinant of the form which early Chinese expansion overseas was to take. When the state favoured such activity, it flourished; if the state withdrew its patronage and its funds, it forthwith withered away.

The question of the motives which impelled Yung Lo to mount six great Ming expeditions (the last of the seven was promoted under his successor) is now interpreted rather differently from the views which the first European scholars to give attention to these phenomena adopted. The Chinese Ming history itself, compiled from official records centuries later, lays great stress on the alleged search for the missing grandson of the first Ming emperor, whose throne Yung Lo had usurped, and who, at the age of sixteen, disappeared when the palace at Nanking was set on fire during Yung Lo's capture of the city. The Emperor Yung Lo is alleged to have been unconvinced that the youth perished in the fire. Such a motive, discreet enquiries in near-by foreign lands, might have their part, but it is hardly possible that Yung Lo can have been looking for his lost nephew in Arabia or Africa. The view that the expeditions were something wholly novel, and owed their existence to an imperial whim, or the desire to display power and acquire prestige cannot now be sustained without considerable modification. The building of a great fleet was not new, even if the Ming Navy was better equipped and used larger vessels than the Sung or the Mongols. Yung Lo was a very able ruler; there is no similar evidence for other vain and extravagant caprices. Power and prestige certainly played their part, but they were not used to conquer distant lands nor even to establish Chinese colonies at strategic points, as the Portuguese were before long to do. The Chinese purpose was to carry on a special type of imperial-directed and imperial profit-making trade; the exchange of "tribute" for "presents"; the "tribute" having great commercial value in China, and the "presents" being articles of art, prestige or ceremonial splendour which the Emperor could very easily afford. A further purpose was to keep the Navy in active service, engaged in long voyages which developed the skill of its personnel and increased the knowledge of navigation. The defence uses of such a programme of extensive training are obvious. In some ways the Ming voyages almost foreshadow the naval training of modern fleets. Finally the choice of eunuchs, and of Cheng Ho in particular, can be justified by the evident success which they achieved, and explained by the fact that as servants of the Palace they were men better known personally to a ruler who was a shrewd and able judge of talent. The ordinary channels of official life in China provided for the civil official, who passed into the imperial service by taking stiff examinations based on classical learning; there were also the army officers, very often promoted for bravery or resource from the ranks. They had their own specialities, but neither the one nor the other were familiar with naval operations, navigation, nor, indeed with diplomatic missions of a partly commercial character in far-off countries. The Emperor needed men who could be trusted with great power, were able to conduct complicated operations of diplomacy and trade far from Court supervision, and were wholly dependent on himself for their careers and even for their lives. The eunuchs fulfilled these conditions; it is not easy to see what other group of imperial servants could have done so.

The Emperor Yung Lo, after dethroning his nephew in a brief but violent civil war in 1399, the year following the death of the founder of the dynasty, moved the capital from Nanking, devastated in the war, to Peking, where he ordered the construction of the present imperial palace, or Forbidden City. This shift to his old headquarters in the north did not mean that the new Emperor had lost interest in the south, nor in the control of the seas. He had for years been the commander-in-chief of the northern armies which guarded the country against any resurgence of Mongol power; his personal following were men who had lived long in Peking, but the imperial family came from central China, and Nanking still remained the second capital. There was also the fact that the dethroned boy emperor had disappeared on the night that Nanking was stormed and the palace set on fire. His body had not been discovered in the ashes, and the suspicion that he might have escaped with his life remained. Yung Lo could truly fear that opposition might gather round him as the legitimate Emperor if he remained at large. That he might take refuge overseas was possible, and the risk that he might rally a fleet, or bring over the existing fleet, based on the southern ports constituted a danger. These considerations were no doubt one motive for commissioning Cheng Ho to set forth on the first of the great maritime expeditions in 1405, only two years after Yung Lo had formally ascended the throne. As an historical fact Yung Lo's fears were in part justified; in one of the very few authentic cases of the world-wide popular stories of missing princes miraculously preserved, the boy Emperor Chien Wen had not perished in the fire: he was saved by faithful eunuchs, conducted to a secret hiding-place, and disguised as a Buddhist monk. For the next forty years and more he wandered over China, a begging monk, and only in old age was he detected, arrested and sent to Peking, where his identity was confirmed by an aged eunuch. Yung Lo had long been dead; his great-grandson, a boy of thirteen, was then on the throne, and the whole problem was half-forgotten. The aged monk-emperor was allowed to live out his remaining years in the solitude of a monastery near the capital. Chien Wen never went overseas, neither he nor his followers ever attempted any restoration or uprising.

Cheng Ho held the post of San Pao T'ai Chien, "Grand Eunuch of the Three Jewels" from which his popular name in the dialects of south China "Sam Po" (San Pao) derives. He was a native of Yünnan and a

Muslim by religion. Yünnan is far from the sea, and Cheng Ho cannot have had any early experience of maritime life; the fact that he was a Muslim might suggest that he was not wholly of Chinese descent, since most of the Yünnan Muslims are descendants of the mercenary central Asian troops whom the Mongols had brought into that province; but alien origin is nowhere alleged. Muslims converted children whom they adopted, or bought, from the poor parents unable to support large families. Such may well have been Cheng Ho's origin. On the voyage, in addition to overall command, Cheng Ho had diplomatic duties and the status of an envoy of the Emperor. There were sixty-two of the great ships and they carried a force of about 30,000 men. Sailing south along the coast of China and then across the South China Sea the fleet made its immediate base at Malacca, a city which had only recently (1403) thrown off its allegiance to the kingdom of Majapahit, based on Sumatra. The new king of Malacca, still Buddhist, welcomed the Chinese and paid tribute. Thereafter he based his policy on reliance upon Chinese protection. In return Yung Lo recognised him as king of Malacca. He proved a faithful follower: in 1411, again in 1414 and finally in 1419 the king travelled to Peking, accompanied by his family, to have audience with the Emperor, staying a considerable time in the new Chinese capital. He became converted to Islam, the first of his line to become Muslim, but this change does not seem to have in any way affected his relations with the Chinese. The Ming, like other Chinese dynasties, paid very little attention to the religions which their subjects might profess, so long as they remained loyal subjects.

From Malacca the fleet proceeded across the straits to Palembang in Sumatra. This city long known to the Chinese, and in the fifth and sixth centuries A.D. described by them as a centre of Buddhism, had fallen into the hands of Chinese adventurers with the decline of the kingdom of Majapahit. In 1377, already thirty years before Cheng Ho's fleet arrived, a certain Liang Tao-ming, a native of Nanhai in Kuangtung province, and a pirate leader, had seized the city with his strong following of Chinese. This is one of the first indications of large numbers of Chinese in Indonesia or Malaya, although earlier, in 1349, the Chinese writer Wang Ta-yüan mentions a resident Chinese colony at Tumasik, the old name for modern Singapore. The pirate ruler of Palembang when the Ming fleet arrived was a certain Ch'en Tsu-yi, who not only proved unwilling to submit, but offered resistance. He was attacked, defeated and captured. Cheng Ho then installed as ruler another resident Chinese, Che Tsing-ch'ing. In so doing he nominally acted in the name of the king of Majapahit, and Yung Lo rejected the claims of the king of Malacca to Palembang. These decisions are interesting. Malacca was a faithful ally, but Majapahit a larger kingdom even if one in full decline. It was presumably thought better to keep on good terms with its ruler, since Malacca, with many enemies around it, had little choice but to rely on China. As for Palembang, the local Chinese were clearly in control, and it was practical to choose one among them as ruler of the city, so long as he was properly subservient. Effective Majapahit authority was not restored, nor was direct Chinese imperial rule imposed; Palembang did not become an imperial Ming colony. Yet it is recorded that it remained under the control of the local Chinese for nearly two hundred years.

After dealing with the affairs of Sumatra the fleet crossed the eastern Indian Ocean to Calicut in south India, then a very important port. It remained there for several months, returning to China by the same route in the following year. The Ming fleet, like all other navigators of the period, sailed south and west in the winter months when the north-east monsoon blows, and returned northwards and eastwards in the summer with the south-west monsoon. This pattern explains the dates of the great voyages, and their normal two-year intervals; the fleet sailed south in 1405, returned to China in 1406, set out again in 1407, returned in 1408, and departed once more on the third expedition in 1409. From the third expedition the intervals are longer, because the destinations of the fleet were ever more remote and it took more than a two-year cycle to go and return. The second expedition included in addition to Java and the Indian ports and countries of Calicut and Cochin, Siam (Thailand) whose king also paid his tribute. Some of the commodities received for this purpose included such obviously useful commercial imports as copper, timber, sulphur and spices. The large imports of copper are believed to have supplied the raw material for the fine brass industry which arose in Ming China. The timber is also known to have entered largely into the manufacture of the best furniture, many pieces of which, of Ming date, still survive in use. The voyages were paying off in the terms of the imperial concept, and the third expedition was planned to include new countries. It reached Ceylon (as well as the Indian ports) but found that King Alagakkonam was recalcitrant. He refused tribute and "treacherously" attempted some attack upon the fleet. Cheng Ho landed his force, defeated and captured the King, who was sent back a prisoner to Peking, another monarch being installed in his place, who was willing enough to pay tribute. King Alagakkonam was later pardoned and released, but it is not at all clear that he ever regained his throne. This incident, with that at Palembang, are almost the only cases in which the Ming fleets used their military strength upon recalcitrant kings. Perhaps no further need arose; the examples would be widely reported, and the advantages of "tribute" and "presents" soon appreciated. The restraint exercised on both occasions, where all that happened was the deposition of the contumelious monarch and the enthronement of a more accommodating alternative without any continuing or direct Chinese rule, is clear proof that territorial acquisition was no part of Yung Lo's policy. Prestige, suzerainty, and the imperial-style trade were the purposes he sought to achieve.

Up to and including the third expedition of 1409 the voyages of Cheng Ho's fleet had not gone further afield than ports of call long familiar to Chinese navigators. Ibn Batuta, the Arab traveller whose home was on the Mediterranean coast of Morocco, was in India in 1330 and mentions seeing thirteen Chinese ships in the port of Calicut, some of which were large, with four decks, cabins and saloons for the passengers. It would seem likely that they were official vessels, part of the Mongol fleet, for Ibn Batuta says that they carried 1,000 men, 400 sailors and 600 soldiers, and that their commander was like a "great Emir". When he landed he was accompanied by a bodyguard of archers, who went before him with spears, swords and musical instruments. He calls some of these bodyguards "Abyssinians" which may mean Negro slaves. Marco Polo, fifty years before, had ended his service with Kubilai Khan by escorting a Mongol princess to Persia by the sea route, presumably in a ship of this type. Thus the Chinese Navy, at least, was familiar with the route to the Persian Gulf, but it does not seem that apart from a special mission, such as that of Polo, Chinese shipping went beyond India. The prosperity of the south Indian cities was in part due to the fact that they were the meeting-place for Arab ships coming from the West and Chinese ships from the East.

The fourth expedition of Cheng Ho was directed to cross the Indian Ocean to Hormuz, in the Persian Gulf, after visiting the Indonesian countries and south India. It made this long voyage and also visited Aden at the entrance to the Red Sea. Clearly this was a change of plan from that followed on the earlier voyages. Persia and even Aden were too far away to pay tribute or admit suzerainty in any realistic meaning of those words. The produce collected and brought home as "tribute" and the "presents" given in return were nothing more than official trading operations politely disguised to suit Chinese terminology and susceptibilities as "tribute offered to a suzerain". The countries on the western side of the Indian Ocean were Muslim, and often fanatically so. Cheng Ho was a Muslim too, and a very suitable envoy to be sent to such places, but he was certainly not presenting any military threat to them. If his fleet were ever to return it must be revictualled in these far-off ports, and spend many months waiting for the monsoon. Yung Lo was surely aware of these facts and cannot have entertained any territorial ambitions in Arabia. On the other hand the Chinese trade was valuable to the Arab rulers and their products welcome in China. There is no hint that relations were ever anything but harmonious. These considerations apply still more strongly to the destinations of the fifth and sixth expeditions, of 1417 and 1421 respectively. They also went by India to Hormuz, and then on to Aden, but extending to the north-east coast of Africa, the city of Mogadishu, today capital of Somalia.

The evidence of coins, pottery and other artifacts of Chinese origin and varying dates found along the coasts of Somalia and Kenya prove that in reality some commerce with China had been continuing for many years before Cheng Ho arrived on the African coast. But it cannot be proved that these objects had been brought to Africa by Chinese merchants, nor in Chinese ships. They may very well have been brought by the Arabs who then ruled along the coast, and traded with China via India, as they had done for a long period. It would seem most probable that this trade which was lucrative, and included products unobtainable in China, attracted the attention of the Court, after hearing reports made by the commander of the fleet following the Aden and Hormuz expeditions. The Chinese who left records of Cheng Ho's visits to Africa all describe the extreme aridity of the country (possibly, it is conjectured, because they arrived during a long drought) and the poverty and "savagery" of most of the inhabitants. They claim that their kings welcomed the Chinese, paid "tribute" and were given "presents"—in other words gladly entered into official trading relations. Court interest in the country was also stimulated because it was known to be the home of strange animals, the giraffe and the ostrich among others. A giraffe, presented by the king of Bengal, had been sent to Peking several years earlier, where it was received with high ceremony, being equated by scholars with the Chi Lin, a mythical animal only supposed to appear when a Sage occupied the throne. Yung Lo, that old soldier, is said to have brushed aside the suggestion that he was a Sage. The Chinese knew that this giraffe (whose portrait was painted and is still extant) had not really originated in Bengal, but came from Africa. Ostriches had in earlier times been brought back to China also, as is proved by the excellent representation of one in sculpture at the tomb of the seventh-century T'ang emperor Kao Tsung, near Ch'angan in Shensi province. Nevertheless the feat of bringing back live giraffes and ostriches across the Indian Ocean and China Sea in the ships of that period must have required considerable care and organisation.

Yung Lo died in 1425, and his son, Hung Hsi, only lived to reign ten months. The throne passed to the grandson of Yung Lo, Hsüan Te, and it was under his auspices that after an interval of ten years the seventh and last expedition sailed in 1431, also to the coasts of Africa. It did not return until 1433, and there is reason to believe that Cheng Ho himself died very soon after the fleet reached Nanking, if not, as some scholars have suggested, during the return voyage while still at sea. In either case the death of the great navigator was perhaps timely; Court politics were changing, and the successors of Yung Lo were about to abandon the expeditions, and indeed, to allow the Navy to fall into decline and decay. The reasons for this momentous alteration in policy, which unwittingly opened the road to the intrusion of European sea power into the Eastern seas, deserve separate treatment.

CHAPTER SIX

THE DECLINE OF CHINESE SEA POWER

The Emperor Hung Hsi, on the very day of his accession on the death of the great Yung Lo (1425), decreed the abandonment of the overseas maritime expeditions, the sixth of which had only returned home four years earlier. It is therefore probable that had Hung Hsi reigned for long the decline of Chinese sea power would have been swifter and more complete than it was to be for another ten years. But Hung Hsi, already a very sick man, only lived for ten months after his accession. His son, the Emperor Hsuan Te, was still young when called to the throne, and no immediate reversal of his father's policy was ordered. However five years later, in 1431, the last, seventh, expedition set out and as before visited Africa as well as South-East Asian countries. This last expedition was officially justified as being needed to inform the kings of the far-off lands that Hsuan Te had succeeded to the throne, perhaps to reassure them that the rapid succession of rulers did not portend a decline in Ming power. In fact this was precisely the danger the empire ran, and which it was soon to encounter. Hsuan Te only reigned a mere ten years, and at his death the throne passed to a child of eight, his son, Cheng T'ung. This of course meant a regency; thus within twelve years of Yung Lo's death the power of the absolute emperor was to be wielded by women and eunuchs in the name of his great-grandson. The monarchical institutions of the Chinese empire were never secure in these circumstances, and minority rule has almost at all periods meant weak government.

The succession changes were not the only political factor which operated against the maintenance of sea power in any form. The civil service had never been a warm partisan of these enterprises, and senior ministers, censors and other officials had voiced criticisms—somewhat more freely after the death of Yung Lo. There can be little doubt that Hung Hsi, the brief successor of Yung Lo, had been strongly influenced by the critics. His death was a setback to them, and enabled the party in favour of sea operations to regain sufficient influence to send out the seventh and last expedition. The power of the palace eunuchs had been under the strict control of Yung Lo, who used these servants for his purposes, but was certainly never under their influence. It was different when the monarch was no longer a famous warrior, experienced administrator and mature statesman. Young men, then a boy, the next generations of emperors, had been bred in the palace, served by eunuchs since their earliest childhood; they had no personal knowledge of the outer world, no experience of war and very little practical training in government. They came easily under the influence of the faithful servants whom they had known so long. Eunuchs, given administrative authority under Yung Lo in certain limited fields, acquired political influence, and thus power, under his successors.

It was a very old tradition of Chinese political life, dating back to the disasters which precipitated the fall of the Han dynasty in the late second century A.D., that the scholar official class should oppose and fear eunuch power. They had to admit the necessity of eunuchs, a view which was then universal, since the continuation of the imperial line was the first priority of any régime, and to secure this against any hazard, the monarch must have the largest possible number of sons. To expect that one wife, the Empress, would always meet this requirement was unrealistic; so concubines were needed, and inevitably became more numerous than was biologically necessary. To guard against illegitimacy these women must not be served by men, nor must men inhabit the palace in any capacity. Eunuchs supplied the answer. It might be thought that women servants would have done as well; it does not seem that the Chinese ever accepted this alternative, perhaps because eunuchs could perform some heavy labour of which women were not believed to be capable.

Eunuchs were a fact of imperial life and the monarchy; but the scholars held very strongly to the view that their place and function was entirely within the inner female apartments of the palace, and that their duties should be strictly menial. Throughout the centuries, under dynasty after dynasty, this view was held; sometimes with a degree of success, more often ignored by monarchs who knew their own eunuchs too well and did not know their ministers on any such terms of intimacy. Thus the early Ming officials were strictly following a long precedent in denouncing the use of eunuchs on outside duties, and their acquisition of administrative authority. It was a misfortune for China that the employment of eunuchs in the sea service, however brilliantly a man such as Cheng Ho had acquitted himself, made the maintenance of naval power and over-seas expeditions the principal target for scholar-official criticism of eunuchs' influence.

When eunuchs, under a regency and the reign of a young emperor, almost inevitably began to acquire direct political influence at the very centre of the government, the criticism of the scholar-officials was enhanced. They were now not merely disapproving, they were alarmed.

No one had foreseen such rapid changes of monarch, so early a development of the type of situation which was well recorded as the prelude to the domination of the eunuchs in the late Han dynasty and the consequent ruin of that empire. It became essential to reduce the power of eunuchs while there was yet time. They could not be removed from their intimate association with a young ruler, not yet exercising his power, but they could be deprived of the potentially very dangerous instrument of a powerful navy commanded by their own members and looking back to the great Cheng Ho with loyalty and deep respect.

If these were the real motives of the opposition, it was clearly not possible to state them too plainly. It was much better to employ two time-honoured arguments to which no ruler could take exception: the first, that the naval expeditions (and thus the Navy itself) was excessively costly and drained the treasury. The second, that the promotion of trade, which was well known to be the foundation and real purpose of the expeditions, was contrary to the duty of an emperor and the traditional philosophy of government. Thus the naval expeditions were portrayed as extravagant excesses inspired by eunuch cupidity pandering to the vanity of Court ladies. It was said that they were sent out to collect useless curios, baubles and novelties to satisfy the idle curiosity of concubines. The claim that the great ships were excessively costly was simply not true. Figures have survived which show that their real cost was assessed as 1,000 piculs of rice, the equivalent of 350 taels (ounces) of silver. This is a very small sum for such a construction. Even if somewhat under-stated it makes it highly improbable that the great ships were so expensive that they constituted a drain on the national resources. But "eunuch extravagance" was a traditional, and well-documented story; the young emperor was certainly not learned enough to refute it on historical evidence, nor experienced enough to deny its validity in the case of the Navy. Moreover, there is reason to think that the source of funds over which the civil service had no supervision nor control, the sale of the former hunting lands of the Mongol emperors, had now dried up. The Court had to use ordinary revenue for the Navy, but ordinary revenue for an institution controlled by eunuchs was a red rag to the official bull.

The ideological argument was also one which a Confucian-educated emperor must find hard to answer. "The scholar does not take account of gain or loss." Trade was for merchants, ranked as third down the social scale (scholar, farmer, merchant and artisan). The duty of an emperor was to encourage learning among the educated and promote agriculture among the people. Trade was not his business, was derogatory to his dignity and harmful to his moral standing. It was also an evil to be tolerated rather than an activity to be encouraged. Scholar officials came from landowning families; they despised traders, they did not (at this time) gain from their profits, and they disliked the concomitant rise of men, such as eunuchs and other naval personnel who were not members of their own class and profession. By the reign of Hsuan Te the generation of soldiers, adventurers of poor and obscure origin like the first Ming emperor himself, had passed away. These men were not scholars, some were hardly literate, but they were practical, able, and did not share scholar prejudices any more than they shared their learning. The young ruler was educated by scholars, even if he was waited upon by eunuchs. There were now few of the old hard-bitten generation to offer him advice contrary to that of his learned tutors and ministers. Trade and its possibilities was not a subject put before him for study. So Hsuan Te can hardly be blamed for taking the advice of the most influential ministers at his Court and feeling that if the eunuchs and the palace ladies would have liked more of the overseas expeditions, their motives for supporting them were not really respectable.

There was also at this time an important shift in the economic support for naval power. As it was not proper for the Emperor to engage in trade, even if he disguised the fact as Yung Lo had, then it would be best, since some trade was really necessary, to leave it to merchants. Private trade overseas was now authorised, and as public, official or imperial trade ceased with the seventh expedition, it became very profitable. Those who knew its value hastened to invest in private trading with the lands beyond the sea. None knew the value better than the eunuchs who had conducted the imperial trade. They had no doubt made plenty of money on the side for themselves. Imperial favour kept them wealthy, and investment in private trade was clearly a proper activity for a class who could not own land. The eunuchs became the backers of private enterprise, among others. They had the Court influence, and it was now directed against revival of the imperial trade, which aroused so much official opposition and thus endangered the position of the eunuchs who supported that policy. It was safer, and perhaps more profitable, to swim with the tide, mouth Confucian criticisms of imperial trade, and engage in lucrative private trade oneself. No one objected to that; dirty trade was just the fitting occupation for mere eunuchs. Economic self-interest combined with political fears and pressures destroyed the support for the imperial trade, and thus the foundation on which Chinese sea power had rested. The decay of the Navy was the inevitable result of the collapse of the system of imperial trade. A Court already prejudiced against the nature of the naval power could not foresee that the loss of it would inevitably create a power vacuum, to be filled by hostile forces, which would in turn ruin the private trade which they believed they were promoting.

Yet another factor in this general turn around of opinion and influence was the military situation of the empire. The naval expeditions had themselves all too clearly proved that China had no dangers to face from the south. Everywhere the Ming emperor was acknowledged, nowhere was he seriously opposed, no ambitious local state challenged nor menaced China. This was not the case to the north. Half a century after their expulsion from China, the Mongols, back in their native environment, were recovering the strength and virility which decadent Court life in China had undermined. Before very long the Ming were to find this danger real once more, and the more so as their capital at Peking was so close to the hostile border. Yung Lo had built Peking for this very reason, to be able to deal swiftly with any Mongol resurgence. But Yung Lo was a great soldier. His successors were palace-bred princes, who had eunuch favourites. The danger these were to cause was before long to be all too plain.

The Emperor Cheng T'ung, great-grandson of Yung Lo, came of age in 1443. He had been nominally on the throne since the age of eight, and was devoted to his eunuch attendants who had ministered to his whims since childhood. Once in power he gave his full confidence to one of them, Wang Chin, who soon exercised an influence greater than that of any minister, and far more noxious. Wang Chin was a native of the region just beyond the Inner Great Wall, near the town of Huai Lai. In 1450 he persuaded his young master to undertake an expedition against a minor Mongol chief who had been raiding the border. The purpose was to bring the Emperor and army to Wang Chin's native place where he planned to entertain the monarch and so secure enormous prestige and "face". Not only did Cheng T'ung undertake this campaign which could perfectly well have been left to the regular frontier army and its experienced generals, but to make matters worse he made the eunuch Wang Chin commander-in-chief, an action which deeply offended the senior officers of the army. The campaign under such amateur and ignorant leadership was disastrous; even when retreat was essential Wang Chin would not give up his plan to entertain the Emperor in his native village. Thus the army was cut off near Huai Lai without adequate water or provisions, and overwhelmed. Wang Chin and many able officers were slain, the Emperor himself taken prisoner.

The relevance of this catastrophe in the north to Chinese policy in the south and to naval policy is that it finally ended the Ming supremacy over the Mongols, and thus reopened the northern border problem. Not that the Mongols were then, or ever again to be, strong enough to conquer China, but they were close to the capital, Peking, and could raid the environs if a chance offered—as they did after Huai Lai. This meant that the government became preoccupied with questions of what were really local defence and frontier warfare. Had the British government of India been established in Rawalpindi, a similar preoccupation with the problems of the North-West Frontier would have been even more prominent in the minds of the Viceroys than they actually were. The Mongols later released Cheng T'ung, who regained his throne, and replaced a brother who had occupied it during his captivity. He was one of those figures in history who seem to survive every check and disgrace and come back with undiminished authority and even support. But he took no interest in the southern trade nor in naval matters; the navy was now virtually out of service.

Cheng T'ung died in 1465 and under his successor, Ch'eng Hua, there was a brief revival of interest in the maritime expeditions. It seems that the new Emperor toyed with the idea of resuming such activity. He called for the archives and documents relating to the great voyages of the Yung Lo era. They could not be found; not even (or perhaps, particularly) the sailing directions and other technical information. They had been "lost". Since there had been no major disaster in the capital, it is clear that they had not been destroyed by a natural calamity, nor lost in a sack and fire. They had been suppressed by a bureaucracy which was determined to put a stop to naval expansion for ever, to remove a potential source of more eunuch power, and a diversion of funds which would equally be outside the control of the regular civil service. With eunuch influence growing at Court it cannot be said that these fears were groundless. A revived navy would have been placed under eunuch control, and it is far from certain that its commanders might not have been men of the stamp of Wang Chin rather than that of Cheng Ho. It is due to this background of political intrigue and administrative manipulation that the dynastic history of the Ming (*Ming Shih*) makes such brief and slight mention of the great voyages of Cheng Ho, does not reveal their real character nor true purpose, and thus led to their significance being completely underrated and the record of their achievement virtually forgotten, most of all in China. In modern times it was really European scholarship which rediscovered the story, traced the subsidiary documents which fill out the scanty official mention, and finally has produced a reasoned explanation of aspects which seemed baffling to early research.

One further factor in the decline of sea power can be taken into account. The Ming dynasty was of southern (Yangtze valley) origin: its first two sovereigns ruled from Nanking. But Yung Lo, who displaced his young nephew, had for years been the commander-in-chief in the north, with headquarters at Peking, the former Mongol capital. After usurping the throne he moved the capital to Peking, rebuilt the city and built the existing imperial palace (Forbidden City). His successors were born and bred in the north; they never visited the south, not even Nanking. Imperial progresses meaning a vast displacement of the machinery of government, now so centralised on the monarch, were very expensive, inconvenient and unwelcome to the bureaucracy, so the once southern dynasty of the Ming became northern in habitat, outlook and in some respects also in the personnel of its government. Officials were chosen after passing the stiff civil service examinations, and advantages of wealth and opportunities for higher education gave the lower Yangtze provinces, Kiangsu, Anhui and Chekiang, a much higher proportion of successful candidates, and therefore of officials than was normal from other parts of the Empire. But the eunuchs were exclusively northerners. This had been the case, perhaps since Mongol times if not still earlier, and it was to remain the rule until the end of the Chinese monarchy. Probably it arose because the Mongols at first ruled in the north but not over the Sung southern empire. Eunuchs, always Chinese (it was not regarded as an honourable occupation, and no family of standing would contribute an eunuch) came from the poor country folk. As time went on certain districts gradually established a monopoly for supplying the palace with eunuchs. Some families regularly contributed a son to this service for generations on end. The need to support families of relatives who were not rich landowners was a major incentive to eunuch corruption.

The later Ming emperors, palace-bred, were attended by these eunuchs, all northern country folk in origin. They were the only intimate companions, other than the palace ladies, whom the Emperor encountered in his daily life. His ministers and high officials were more often of southern, or Yangtze province origin, but these men were only seen by him at regular formal audiences, devoted to the discussion of state business and high policy. The absolutism and aloof character of the Ming monarchy seems to have precluded the more familiar contact which in the T'ang period at least permitted the monarch to visit the house of one of his great ministers on social occasions. But then such great officers in the T'ang period were aristocrats of imperial lineage or connected by marriage with the imperial family. In Ming times this kind of society had passed away. Consequently the Emperor did not have contact with men from the real south, except the few who were high officials, and with these his relations were formal, official and confined to state business. For the impressions which he would receive in early life of the world beyond the palace and the relative importance of the differing parts of the empire, the opinions and conversation of eunuchs were the sources.

These northern men of slight education had no personal knowledge of the south, the sea, or indeed of any region of China other than their native place and the palace at Peking. Inevitably the emperors became northern-minded, if not in reality provincial northern-minded men. The south did not usually demand the Emperor's attention even on state business; there were no dangerous enemies to guard against down there, but near at hand, within a few hours' ride from the capital itself, were the Mongols: a nuisance rather than a danger, but a constant nuisance none the less. Pre-occupation with northern local questions, conditioning to northern ways and outlook from early childhood, lack of any incentive to involve policy in any major southern enterprise, the inconvenience, expense and time needed to travel to the southern provinces (up to two thousand miles from the capital), these factors constantly reinforced the northern character of the Ming dynasty and led to the steady neglect of naval power, southern trade interests, and the influence of southerners not themselves high officials long resident in the capital or elsewhere, men who were in any case largely expatriate in outlook and wholly so in their careers and ambitions. The naval power of China had come to birth under a dynasty established in the south, the Southern Sung, it was maintained by the Mongols whose ambitions reached far beyond China, it was kept alive by the rebels in the south against Mongol power, enhanced to its highest degree by the early Ming, and then steadily declined as the Ming dynasty became northern-minded, preoccupied with northern land frontiers and increasingly uninterested in the south and the sea.

Before many years had passed the adverse consequences of this neglect became apparent. Trade with Japan had been carried on through the Chinese port of Ningpo, in Chekiang province. It was, in Chinese eyes, nominally on the "tribute" basis. That is to say the Japanese sent what were in fact trading missions, which the Chinese chose to regard for official purposes as tribute missions. But as at this time Japan had no uni-fied government under the purely ceremonial rule of the secluded emperors in Kyoto, such missions were in practice organised and dis-patched by the leading feudal lords—Daimyo—of the western provinces of Japan. The Chinese officials in charge at Ningpo took the stand that only one mission could represent the tribute-sending state, and they soon began to pick and choose between rival missions. Those that had the more desirable goods, or paid the largest bribe, received recognition and the right to trade, the others were turned away. Since the feudal lords at home were often antagonistic to each other this treatment transferred to the China coast the animosities of Japan. The rejected missions refused—or did not dare—to return empty-handed to their lords; they turned to smuggling instead, and found willing collaboration from the Chinese merchants who also suffered from official extortion. Rival missions

E

established clandestine bases in the many islands off the coast, such as the Chusan archipelago, and the absence of Ming sea power made them virtually secure. Rival groups engaged in mutual attacks, and resorted to piracy when it seemed more profitable than trade of any sort. The Ming government in 1430—when it still had some sea power left—limited all trade with Japan to one mission every ten years in the hope of reducing the nuisance. But as in the succeeding years the Chinese Navy was allowed to decline to impotence, this action proved worse than the previous inaction.

Smuggling continued on an increasing scale, competition for the lucrative ten-year trade mission became more intense, and the reaction of the unsuccessful competitors more violent. In 1523 a major clash occurred in Ningpo city, caused by the open preference which the Chinese official in charge of trade, a Court eunuch, showed to one mission and the violent resistance of the mission which had been, in effect, unjustly rejected. The city was seriously damaged by fire and looting. The Court then decided that trade with Japan was merely an unnecessary source of trouble, and with bland indifference to realities and economic forces, imposed a total ban on all trade with that country "now and forever".

The result was to make all trade illegal, and therefore to make smuggling, protected by piratical power, the only opening left to the traders of both countries. As the Ming government refused to see any connection between their own neglect of naval power and the rise of smuggling and piracy, they in effect left the field wide open to the latter. The evil became swiftly very serious. For more than forty years the coasts of China were harried by pirate smugglers, not only, or even it would seem mainly, Japanese, but combined forces of Japanese and Chinese from the coastal provinces. The latter in fact outnumbered the Japanese, but often seem to have enlisted in Japanese bands. They not only plundered and ravaged the coastal region, but often struck inland on prolonged forays in the manner of the Viking raids in north-western Europe. In some cases they had the co-operation of powerful local landlords, or of corrupt officials in the cities. The land forces of the government were either too weak, or too badly-led to hinder them. The final reaction of the Ming government was to order the evacuation of a wide coastal strip in the affected provinces, in which lawful citizens were forbidden to live except in garrisoned cities. This was intended to deny food and provisions to the pirates. It is possible that this costly and harsh measure was a contributory cause to the decline of piracy and smuggling after 1564, but it is at least equally probable that the changes occurring in those years in Japan were as important. The long period of anarchy in Japan was coming to an end, and the rule first of Oda Nobunaga, then Hideyoshi, and finally of

Ieyasu Tokugawa (1568–1603) established an authoritarian central government in control of all parts of the country.

Already before the decline of the joint piratical power of the Japanese and south coast Chinese, the first Western navigators had arrived in China. The Portuguese captured Malacca, the former ally and base city of the Ming expeditions, in 1511. In 1517 their ships reached the south coast of China, and some of their commanders were sent up to Peking, being treated as a tribute mission. The mission was not a success; the newcomers did not understand their rôle, and behaved in Chinese eyes disgracefully. They were sent off and forbidden to return. Not unnaturally the Portuguese, observing the chaotic conditions on the China coast and the absence of effective Chinese sea power, joined in the game themselves. Since every trader needed to be a smuggler at best, he might as well be a pirate when such activity seemed more profitable. The Portuguese occupation of the island of Macao in 1557—with the connivance of local Chinese officials—was only a slightly more legal establishment than those of the Sino-Japanese pirates in the Chusan islands. It may also be regarded as highly probable that the advent of the Portuguese contributed to the decline of the Sino-Japanese pirates. Portuguese ships were built to perform the very long voyage from Europe round the Cape of Good Hope, across the Indian Ocean and the South China Sea. They needed to be as strong and seaworthy as the shipbuilding art of that age could make them. Chinese ships, since the Ming government had abandoned its naval policy, were smaller, lighter, and designed for short voyages; so were those of Japan. The great ships of Cheng Ho's fleet were no longer built either by the government, nor by private merchants, who would have been unable to command the necessary resources, and highly suspect of prospective piracy if they had tried to obtain them. Portuguese ships could be built openly, in government or in private yards. Inevitably the Portuguese vessels were superior both in their sailing qualities and as men-of-war. Any clash would go against the Chinese or Japanese ships, and the tendency to avoid such a risk equally diminished the opportunities for lucrative smuggling.

Early in the next century the entry of the Dutch into the South China Sea produced a new factor. The Dutch were Protestant, the Portuguese Catholic; no love was lost between the two nations. Portuguese influence —and bribery—secured a Chinese prohibition of Dutch trade (1607), and then the Dutch, like the Japanese and Portuguese before them, promptly turned to smuggling and piracy. They felt free to prey on all alike, Asians and Portuguese. The latter had always felt that piracy against pagans was no sin, an inheritance from the ethos of the Barbary Coast. The Dutch felt no more compunction in regard to Roman Catholics.

Failing to get permission to trade or use any islands near the coast as bases, the Dutch in 1623 occupied the ports of the large island of Taiwan, and in effect made it their colony. The Portuguese had also used Taiwanese ports, and named the island Formosa—"Beautiful". The loss of this fertile island highlights the baneful results of the later Ming neglect of sea power. It had been incorporated in the Chinese empire, at first rather nominally, ever since the Sui and T'ang periods (seventh century A.D.). Gradually migrants from the mainland, the adjoining province of Fukien, had crossed the strait and settled, until by the early seventeenth century they had occupied most of the western fertile plains, confining the native inhabitants, a non-Chinese people, to the eastern mountain chain. Taiwan was supposed to be a prefecture of the province of Fukien. Since the Ming no longer had an effective navy their control over the province was becoming purely nominal well before the Dutch took it over. Pirates of all nationalities had long resorted to this safe refuge.

The Dutch could not be dislodged; they remained in possession for forty years and their rule seems to have been quite acceptable to the immigrant Chinese; order was kept, other pirates were excluded, taxation was lighter than in Ming China. Chinese migration rapidly increased. In these ways the Dutch occupation of Taiwan is a curious forerunner of the later Dutch empire in South-East Asia. Their rule brought benefits to a simple peasantry, but denied any share of power to the educated, or commercial classes. So long as no local sea power arose to challenge them they remained in secure possession, but when such a force appeared, they could not defend so distant a colony. Had this challenge not come as early as the second half of the seventeenth century, it is more than possible that the Dutch would have remained masters of Taiwan until modern times. The Ming dynasty was, by 1623, far gone in decline, within twenty years of its collapse. The Manchus were not a seafaring people. It is improbable that they could have ejected the Dutch, very possibly they would never have made the attempt.

The loss of Taiwan by the Dutch was the result of an unexpected resurgence of Chinese sea power, not instituted by any change of policy in the declining central government, but a result, on the contrary, of the collapse of that power. After the Manchu entry into China in 1644, and the occupation of Peking, Ming resistance in the south was organised successively at Nanking, Foochow, Canton and then driven into the inland south-western provinces. Fatally, but consistently, the Ming pretenders failed to raise naval forces which might have stemmed the Manchu conquest of the south, perhaps resulting in a new division between north and south. The Manchus conquered the south of China by land, aided by Chinese leaders who had forsaken the Ming dynasty. It was one man, who, disgusted by the inept policy of the Ming generals and ministers, set himself to recreate naval power on behalf of the failing dynasty.

Cheng Ch'eng-kung became known to the West through the Portuguese and Dutch, by the strange and un-Chinese sounding name of Koxinga. It derives from his title; after he had successfully created a fleet and scored some notable victories over the invader, the Ming Pretender conferred upon him the distinction of the Imperial Surname (Chu), thus adopting him into the imperial family. He was then known as Lord of the Imperial Surname, in northern Chinese *Kuo Hsing Yeh*, in the dialect of his native Fukien, *Kok Sing Ya*, which latter version was turned by Portuguese tongues into Koxinga. Cheng, born in 1624, was the son of a former pirate, who had submitted, been pardoned, and become a Ming official in charge of coastal defence in Fukien, a career which was typical in the age when Sino-Japanese piracy was in decline. When the Manchu invasion spread to Fukien, the elder Cheng decided that the Ming were finished and surrendered to the conquerors. Not so his son; Cheng Ch'eng-kung repudiated his father's submission and seizing a few ships set out with a small following to make war on the invading Manchus. It was the year 1651, seven years after the Manchu occupation of Peking, when their authority in the south, beyond Nanking, was mainly dependent on the loyalty of the Chinese generals who had joined them when the Ming fell.

For the next eight years Cheng Ch'eng-kung demonstrated what the Ming might have done had they put their war effort into naval power. He soon raised a considerable force, and his fleet dominated the south-east coasts. Cheng found no difficulty in recruiting the hardy seafarers of Fukien and Kuangtung. Chinese naval power was, for the last time for centuries, once more a major factor. If Cheng had found any adequate co-operation from the armies still loyal to the Ming he might have achieved much more than he did. In 1659 he entered the Yangtze and sailed up to Chenkiang, the junction of the Grand Canal and the Yangtze River. This is a vital strategic point; if cut, the tribute or tax grain from the south cannot be sent up to Peking. Cheng Ch'eng-kung captured Chenkiang, and then sailing upstream besieged Nanking itself, the southern capital of the Empire, and the main base of the Manchu invasion of the south. Had he been able to take and hold this city, while commanding the waters of the Yangtze, the Manchu invasion of the south would have been halted. But Cheng's forces were not strong enough by land for these objectives, and his naval power could not in itself enable him to seize a very large city. He had to abandon the siege, and Chenkiang also, and withdrew down the coast to Amoy in Fukien, his main base.

When this city was threatened by the continued Manchu land invasion Cheng turned to Taiwan, and in 1661 drove out the Dutch and established himself as virtually the sovereign in that island. The Ming pretenders were soon to lose contact with the coast. Cheng Ch'eng-kung, secure in Taiwan, dominating the southern sea, and having proved his fleet capable of challenging the European ships, and winning, had shown that Chinese sea power could play a very significant rôle if maintained and intelligently applied. He died the next year, 1662, undisputed ruler of Taiwan. His son succeeded him and was later, when the Ming cause was finally lost, to be recognised as King—or Emperor—in Taiwan, which he ruled for twenty years. Just as U.S. sea power had denied Taiwan to the Chinese Peoples' Republic in our time, the Cheng family's sea power in the seventeenth century denied the island to the Manchu dynasty.

In 1683 the Manchu government, aided by the troubles which broke out among the grandsons of Cheng Ch'eng-kung after their father's death, found their chance to occupy Taiwan and remove the last stronghold of Chinese opposition. In this task, being weak at sea, they obtained the assistance of the Dutch, who were rewarded by being granted four ports at which they could trade on the Chinese coast. One of these ports was Canton, and the concession to the Dutch was the beginning of the later monopoly of foreign trade conferred on that city. In later years also, the Manchus abolished the trading rights at all other ports, and from 1757 onward all foreign trade was confined to the one city of Canton. In adopting this restrictive policy the Manchus were not so much opposing trade in itself as aiming to control it at a point far removed from the northern provinces, and at the same time nearest to the countries from which the foreigners came. By making Canton the sole port, there was no reason for foreign shipping to move further up the coast, and contacts with potential dissidents could be minimised. At the same time all Chinese subjects of the emperor were forbidden on pain of death to travel outside the empire for any purpose. The Manchus thus consciously tried to put an end to Chinese expansion by sea, whether demographic, commercial or even political, and they were only too successful. Some of the South-East Asian kingdoms continued to be nominally tributary to China, but this status was only realistic in the case of Vietnam (the Empire of Annam) and Burma, which were contiguous by land.

Manchu policy was firmly opposed to the creation or expansion of naval forces. They adopted the policy expressed by the phrase "coastal defence, but no battles at sea". This meant that such armed ships as the government equipped were only short-range vessels designed to police estuaries and harbours. Long-range seagoing vessels were not built. As it was an offence to voyage over the seas the Chinese merchants dared not build any such ships, and the government's policy precluded any such activity. Foreign commerce was left to the foreign shipping, Portuguese (a diminishing force), Dutch, French and British. The Napoleonic Wars which left Britain as the master of the oceans swept all other competitors from the scene, except for the small beginnings of American trade, the first ship under the U.S. flag to visit Canton arriving in 1784. Thus although the Manchu empire remained until the end of the eighteenth century a mighty land power, with which no foreign state cared to meddle, it was already totally ineffective by sea. This meant that beyond the reach of Manchu armies advancing by land, there could be no continuing Chinese political influence. The abdication of all sea power by both Japan, following the seclusion policy adopted by the Tokugawa Shoguns, and then by China under the Manchu dynasty was the origin of the Western ascendancy in the Far East. When Japan abandoned that policy the West was soon faced with the consequences, which were disastrous to their colonial empires. The result of the Second World War brought the U.S. into the Western Pacific as the new dominant sea power, Japan having been eliminated in this respect. China, up until modern times, has not yet seriously attempted the revival of her early sea power, but there is no apparent insuperable obstacle to her doing so.

The deplorable consequences, for China, of Manchu policy, were all too clear throughout the nineteenth century. The Opium War, in which the British (1842) employed only very small land forces, was a coastal war in which the absence of Chinese naval power gave the British complete freedom of action to choose their objectives. The same situation prevailed twenty years later in the "Arrow" or Second Opium War (1858–60); and when the Manchus belatedly learned the lesson of these two defeats, and began, in the seventies, to build a modern fleet with foreign assistance and technical advice, it was still too weak to withstand the French in the Franco-Chinese War of 1883–5. The Manchu government once more built a modern fleet, of no great size, and this force was destroyed by the Japanese Navy at the battle of the Yalu in the brief Sino-Japanese War of 1895. It had been left with virtually no ammunition, and it was stated with good evidence that the funds with which the Navy should have been provided had been diverted by the Empress Dowager Tz'u Hsi to build the Summer Palace near Peking.

Manchu conversion to the necessity for naval power was late and never wholehearted, nor effective. Basically the reason was distrust of the southern Chinese, who provided both ratings and officers. It was certainly true that such naval forces as had been restored by 1911, when the Revolution against the Manchus broke out, made no attempt to defend the monarchy, but went over, like the southern provinces as a whole, to the Republican side without a shot fired. It might have been thought that as the Navy was clearly so attached to the new régime, it would at last receive the support and patronage of the government. In theory this may have been so; in practice the weakness, disorder and military domination of the early republican governments made any heavy investment in naval building, or even in maintenance, out of the question. The Chinese Navy was quite unable to meet the Japanese in the early period of the Second World War which began, for China, in July 1937 and ended with the Japanese Surrender in August 1945. After the loss of all ports in 1938 the Navy ceased to exist except for a few light vessels which had withdrawn to the upper reaches of the Yangtze. In 1949 the Nationalist régime did not have the naval power to prevent the Chinese Communists crossing the narrow strait and seizing the island of Hainan; aided by America, and the presence of the Seventh Fleet after 1950, they have been able to deny Taiwan to the Communist Peoples' Republic; but this is the operation of American sea power, not Chinese.

There is evidence that since they took power in 1949 the Communist government has set about the restoration of the Chinese Navy. The direction of this effort appears to be towards providing effective short-range vessels for coastal defence, and above all to frustrating Nationalist forays upon the coast from Taiwan. Submarines for more distant operations have been launched, but their numbers and size do not yet suggest any commitment to a navy on a large scale capable of supporting an overseas expedition or presenting a real challenge to the present domination of the Pacific Ocean by the U.S.A. It may be that the contemporary rulers of China have understood the folly of their Manchu predecessors, but they certainly have not yet adopted the policies of the early Ming emperors. If this is so, it is not from fear of the southern Chinese, who are far from dissident to the Communist régime. It is at least as probable that the traditional preoccupation with the northern danger, characteristic of Chinese régimes centred on northern capitals, is once more potent. The northern danger is not now the nomadic peoples of the steppe, but the U.S.S.R. It may seem to the Chinese Communist leadership that a powerful navy would not greatly increase their defensive strength in relation to Russia, which has a common land frontier of immense length with the Peoples' Republic. It may also seem probable that with the changing technology of modern war, and the incalculable factors of inter-continental ballistic missiles and nuclear bombs, that the Chinese do not see clearly what rôle the Navy could play at the present time.

The historical fact is that since the Ming Court abandoned the upkeep and employment of naval power in the mid-fifteenth century, China has never exercised this power no matter what changes of régime have followed. The reasons for Ming indifference, Manchu aversion, republican weakness or Communist caution have been various and sometimes contradictory, but the outcome has been that the naval power of China, potentially great, has remained undeveloped and insignificant. The consequences have been that the Chinese drive to the south, the expansion of Chinese influence, settlement and commerce into the south-east of Asia have not for five hundred years been supported by the power of the Chinese state, and if they have none the less spread and consolidated in many of these countries, it has been due to other factors operating without the sanction of the state, or often, in defiance of its commands.

By the Sung dynasty (tenth century), it had become clear that very real obstacles had arisen in the path of Chinese expansion by land. Vietnam had grown strong, and developed a fierce national identity: Yünnan, which the Mongols, not the Chinese Sung, conquered and incorporated in the empire, was the limit of profitable advance to the south-west; Burma, for climatic reasons and prior settlement, offered only restricted opportunities. The movement turned with the development of Sung overseas commerce to the sea, and the countries reached by sea. The Mongols inherited this trend, and sought to use it to expand their empire. The Ming took up their policy in a more sophisticated form, and, had they maintained their effort, would in all probability have set up a Chinese overseas empire by the end of the fifteenth century. They abandoned their naval policy, and thereby aborted the southward expansion of the Chinese empire, which, under the Peoples' Republic today, remains within the same southern land frontiers as the Ming took over from the Mongol empire. Vague claims to suzerainty further south were maintained by Ming and Manchu emperors, but there was no force behind them beyond the reach of land armies.

Had all Chinese expansion to the south ended with the Ming Navy it could be assumed that this event marked the end of a great historical and demographic movement which had continued from prehistoric times through some two thousand years of recorded history. But it is well known that the end of Chinese state power overseas did not, in spite of many obstacles and difficulties, bring the southward expansion of Chinese culture, commerce and settlement to a stop. It has been suggested on the evidence relating to the early Chinese migration and cultural penetration of the southern borderlands reached by land, that the action, or inaction, of the distant central Chinese government was rarely a major factor in this process; and when it operated at all, it was late, long after the demographic and cultural penetration had made a much greater contribution towards changing the original condition and circumstances of the countries concerned. There seems to be reason to see a similar situation in respect of the expansion by sea; it began as a commercial, and also (in its earliest days of Buddhist pilgrimage) as a cultural movement. Early state promotion and intervention was strikingly evident for a time, but faded away. Much the same is true of the land expansion. After the T'ang, the Sung virtually renounced any ambition in Vietnam and positively refused to meddle in Yünnan. Nearly five hundred years passed before, as a result of the intrusion of the Mongols, an alien people, the landward pressure resumed and Yünnan was finally fully incorporated as a province of China, an event which by that time provoked hardly any serious opposition from the people of Yünnan, who, five hundred years earlier in the T'ang period, had successfully and fiercely defended their kingdom of Nanchao.

It is also at the present time about five hundred years since the end of the Ming naval power, and during that long period China has not expanded across the southern seas, any more than from T'ang to Mongol she expanded across the southern frontiers. The catalyst which disrupted this long pause in the thirteenth century was the invasion of an alien world power, the empire of Ghenghiz Khan and his successors. It may be too soon to reject the idea that the catalyst which may put an end to China's long abstention from naval power and direct state intervention in the southern lands is the intrusion into the area of another alien world power, the U.S.A. Should China be stirred to resume her southern movement, or to profit, as the Ming did in Yünnan, from the changed situation which an alien invasion has brought about, she will certainly find that in these countries the prior stage of Chinese settlement, cultural and commercial penetration has, as in Yünnan, already paved the way.

CHAPTER SEVEN

CHINESE ART AND CULTURE IN
SOUTH-EAST ASIA

The influence of Chinese art and Chinese culture in a broader sense in South-East Asia is ancient and has been continuous, but uneven both in the areas where it operated and in the periods in which it was stronger or weaker. Nor was it all an outflow from China; the Chinese civilisation received many and important traits from the lands to the south, but this inward influence has usually been better documented and recorded by foreign and Chinese scholars than the outward movement of motifs and ideas. This is largely because so much that China drew from the Nanyang was connected with Buddhism, while what she gave was either secular or less directly related to religion. One important part of what China received at an early date, records and information concerning the southern countries, has in the long course of time been repaid by supplying for these countries the only historical evidence of their beginnings and development for nearly the first thousand years of their history. Cambodia apart, without Chinese historical record and notices we would know next to nothing of the history of South-East Asia before the end of the first millennium A.D. The cultural relationship has been one of give and take, but both in the different regions and in the different centuries this process has been uneven.

The region of the south divides in cultural as in political matters into two major parts. Yünnan and Vietnam are the countries where Chinese culture was to dominate; the rest of mainland South-East Asia, Cambodia, Laos, Thailand, Burma and Malaya, received their first advanced civilisation from India and have in one way or another retained this cultural heritage to modern times. The island region, in so far as it was in touch with the mainland of Asia, also received the Indian influence; the outer islands of Indonesia, including Borneo, and the Philippines were not touched by any culture from the mainland until long after the Indian influence had declined; it was the Muslim religion, and in the Philippines and in parts of Celebes Christian missionary activity, which first planted the seeds of later civilisation. Direct Chinese contact was in the early centuries slight, and when the massive immigration of Chinese occurred in recent times—the nineteenth century onward—the cultural effects were very largely confined to the immigrants themselves.

The most obvious example of this difference between the areas under Chinese influence and those which were originally affected by India is the form of the script in use. Until the modern introduction of the system of writing Vietnamese in the Latin alphabet (called *Quoc Ngu*) the Chinese ideographic script was the medium of literature in Vietnam, and it has of course remained so in Yünnan, not only since the incorporation of the old kingdom of Nanchao within the Chinese empire, but also during the Nanchao period itself. Sanskrit, as in China, was restricted to religious texts and inscriptions, much as Latin might be used in modern Europe. Beyond these two countries the Chinese ideographic script was neither used nor understood except by the small number of Chinese merchants of sufficient education to be literate. Although much valuable information regarding their own past remained on record in Chinese dynastic histories, this information was unknown to the peoples of South-East Asia until modern Western scholarship made it available.

The second area, the further countries of the mainland and the islands, wrote their languages in scripts derived from Sanskrit through the medium of later Indian variations. No one form is common to all these countries, except the classical Sanskrit itself, which is not the medium of current literature. The forms vary, and are not mutually intelligible, producing a situation not unlike that of the ancient classical world of the Mediterranean, where Greek, Latin and Punic scripts co-existed, dissimilar, but originally derived from a Phoenician original. It is an interesting and significant fact that the co-relation between script and art in all the Nanyang is very close. There is no country which uses an Indian-derived script and has a Chinese art; there is no country using the Chinese ideographs, either in ancient or modern times, which expresses its art in the Indian form. The division between the two regions of culture is sharp in other respects also. Although the Chinese and Vietnamese are Buddhist, their form is the Mahayana, while that of the formerly Hinduised kingdoms, Cambodia, Thailand, Laos and Burma is Theravada (Hinayana). The island regions, with the exception of Bali, which retains its ancient Hindu religion, came under Muslim influence since the thirteenth and fourteenth centuries, although in art the influence of the former Hindu culture is still conspicuous. The Indian heritage is so dominant in the great art of Cambodia, and in the later and derivative art of Thailand and Burma, that the presence of any Chinese influence at all has usually been ignored or denied. It is possible that this is a mistaken view; in certain less obvious manifestations there is reason to think that contact with China had significant results.

The variation in periods is almost as marked as the division between regions. The once uniform Hindu influence throughout the lands south of Yünnan and Vietnam was first overthrown by the conversion to Islam of Malaya, Sumatra and Java, and the Muslim colonisation of North Borneo. Later the European influence, especially the Christian religion, has contributed a new element to some of the older cultures, and dominated the more recently civilised countries such as the Philippines. Chinese culture, absent in the early Hindu kingdoms, or only a lesser contributory influence, has been firmly planted wherever the Chinese resident community is large and economically strong, as it is in many of the countries of the south. As the overseas Chinese steadily become predominantly native born, and immigration ceases, the level of transplanted Chinese culture has risen, not fallen, so that communities which were mainly illiterate only a century and less ago, are now steeped in the culture of their ancestral homeland, and unwilling to forego this heritage. This development is relatively very recent; the resident Chinese communities were small until the middle of the nineteenth century, their cultural level was low, and their influence on the peoples among whom they lived very slight. At the present time in areas of strong and proportionately large Chinese population the use of Chinese as the language of commerce, business and also in education and professional activities is very prominent, and in so far as it is challenged by any other tongue, it is not by the native languages but by English (or in some countries French), which provides an alternative medium. Chinese draws from the vast reservoir of China itself, where the adoption of new terms to meet new needs and skills, new learning and ideas, had taken place several decades ago and constantly continues. The languages of South-East Asia had no such advantage; they were overborne in modern usage by the strength of the alien speech of their colonial masters; they must now create the modern terminology which is in constant use if they are to meet modern needs.

The interchange of cultural influences in the past has thus been diverse, but also restricted to certain fields. No country which had not experienced direct Chinese rule adopted, or had imposed upon it, the Chinese ideographic script; no country beyond the Chinese sphere adopted Mahayana Buddhism permanently; all remained either Hindu, or, later, Hinayana (Theravada) Buddhist. In consequence the literature of the Indian sphere and later Muslim sphere is without significant Chinese content, and very little indeed outside Buddhism has reached China from the Hinduised kingdoms of the south. One of the few examples of a cultural borrowing from the Nanyang which China received and has adopted, if only on a limited scale, both illustrates the exceptional and perhaps meagre content of such contact and the need to modify even that which was taken. In Peking there is a popular art, which when on the point of extinction was revived by the present government after it came to power. It is locally known as "*Luanchou Ying Hsi*", "Shadow plays of Luanchou". It is quite recognisably the Indonesian *wayang klitik*, a very well-known popular art in Java. The art consists of projecting from behind a lit screen the shadows of cut-out figures, gaily painted, which can be manipulated by sticks and threads attached to their movable limbs. A vivid and lifelike puppet show of shadows is created which serves as the medium for heroic tales; in Indonesia these are taken from the Hindu epic the Ramayama, but not so in China. There the subjects of the plays are drawn from Chinese folk legend, some Buddhist, some secular. The Chinese figures are made, as in Indonesia, from skins, and painted, decorated and designed in very close reproduction of the Indonesian types. The style is pure Javanese, not at all Chinese. Luanchou is a city of north China, in Hopei province, some hundred and fifty miles north-east of Peking, not far from the border of the Manchurian province of Liaoning. It is not a seaport, although, being on a river not far upstream from its mouth, it may have been a port in earlier times when ships of shallow draught could have reached it. It would seem very probable that the art was introduced in the early Ming period, when Peking was already the capital, and probably as a by-product of the voyages of Cheng Ho and the great fleets. But there is no adequate record of its origin; being popular, not scholarly, and, still worse, foreign, it is not mentioned in official records. It does not seem to have spread in China beyond the capital, and it survived there in the hands of no more than three families until it was given the accolade of being a "Peoples' art" (which it was) by the present régime. Then its continuance was assured.

This art illustrates both the rather minimal impact of South-East Asian culture on China, and the need even when it was accepted, to change the content of the plays to matters which would be familiar to the Chinese audience. The cohesive Chinese culture was not able to digest a truly foreign art, religion, or idea until it had gone through this process of metamorphosis. Buddhism, the great importation, went through a similar transformation. Mahayana Buddhism originated in India; but it did not win a lasting place in either its land of birth nor in the South-East Asian countries which adopted Buddhism after their Hindu culture had been long established. They took the Theravada form, which prevailed in Ceylon. No Theravada cult ever established an enduring hold in China, although in the early period there were monks and scholars who preached it. China equally did not produce an art form which appealed to the peoples of the south, nor did her own peculiar religions make any im-

pression beyond the confines of countries once ruled by China as provinces, such as Vietnam, or later incorporated in the empire, such as
Yünnan. Objects of trade produced in China were acceptable and won a
wide market, notably porcelain; but manners and customs, ideas and art
remained untouched.

Centuries of contact and in more recent periods close contact with
Chinese migrants made virtually no impact upon such matters as dress,
furniture or ways of living. Neither did the Chinese modify their habits
from contact with the Nanyang. The Chinese adopted the chair and gave
up the mat in the tenth and eleventh centuries A.D. The invention owed
nothing to overseas contact, although it did have some relation to contact
by land with the chair-sitting peoples of eastern Europe—very much
further away than the peoples of South-East Asia. The southern peoples
continued to use mats and sit on the floor for the next thousand years until
European influence began to introduce the use of chairs, which the
Chinese had then employed for all of that long period. The southern
peoples use variant forms of the *sarong*, under different names, as their
basic garment. They did not wear trousers. The Chinese never adopted
the *sarong*, although in south China it would be very comfortable, and
when as a result of contact with the northern nomadic peoples they
gradually added trousers to their traditional flowing robes, neither the
one nor the other was accepted beyond the area of Vietnamese population. Only in modern times when the trouser-wearing Europeans came to
reinforce the habit of the trouser-wearing Chinese, did the new fashion
begin to make any deep impression. One consequence of this is that in art
the postures of subjects are markedly different. Balinese, Indonesian or
Malay, Thai or Burmese and Cambodian postures are quite unlike those
portrayed in Chinese art. People who sit on mats do not sit in the manner
of chair-users, their costumes are different, and even the standing posture
in art is distinctive.

It has been observed that the culinary art in the Nanyang has clear
and close affinities to Chinese cooking, and that the Chinese of the
southern lands have also for their part adopted the curry as one of their
dishes. But the non-Chinese people did not use chopsticks, eating with
their hands in the Indian manner; the Chinese never abandoned their
chopsticks. It is indeed rather uncertain how far the apparent influence of
Chinese cooking is a real cultural influence rather than due to the economic domination of Chinese in the restaurant as in so many other fields of
business. Muslim religious rules impose limitations on the use of certain
foods and forbid others; the Chinese have no such rules nor prohibitions.
You can eat anything which the cook is skilful enough to prepare in a
palatable form. This gives the Chinese restaurateur a great advantage.

Chinese cooks and Chinese food became popular, the effect being probably more to inhibit the widespread use and development of native dishes than to improve them. One may compare the example of French cooking in Europe, particularly in north-western Europe. In South-East Asia today it always seems in effect to be Chinese food that is offered, even if it is eaten with a spoon and fork, and the traveller in search of the real native cooking has a hard time finding it in a public restaurant. The cause is more probably due to the domination of Chinese in the industry than to the changed taste of the non-Chinese inhabitants. Buddhist avoidance of meat, hardly taken seriously in China except by monks, is a much more effective rule among the Buddhists of the Nanyang countries.

Very few Chinese words seem to have won lasting acceptance in the languages of the south; the rare exception strikes the ear at once. The Thais call the motorised rickshaw, or "trishaw", a *samlor*. The word is a corruption of Chinese *san lun*, in southern dialects *sam lun*, and with the Chinese diminutive "erh" added and elided with the last word; it means "three wheels". Foreign and colonial rulers brought in some Chinese words which seamen had adopted. "Typhoon", "junk", "sampan" are examples, but it would seem doubtful if these terms were used before the advent of the Europeans. Notably, the titles of grandees and royalty are never words of Chinese origin, nor are the terms used for "city", "temple" or "palace". This is in marked contrast to the relationship between words of these meanings in almost every European language. The Chinese for their part seem to have borrowed very little indeed from the vocabularies of the Nanyang languages. Their language has a genius for translation rather than transcription, and foreign words of any origin, ancient or modern, are remarkably rare. The Javanese shadow plays, although foreign in style, are not known by any variant or corruption of their Javanese name. Perhaps the twin Chinese pronunciations of the word for "tea", "*ch'a*" (or "*ch'ai*") in northern speech, "*tay*" in southern dialects are the best-known examples of Chinese words which have become naturalised abroad, but not only in the southern borderlands of China; these words have entered into every language in all parts of the world; originally the form depended on whether tea was obtained by land caravan from north China (*ch'a*) or by seaborne commerce from the southern ports (*tay*).

China did not succeed in exporting her own religions beyond the zone of direct Chinese rule. Confucianism was adopted and respected by the ruling class of Vietnam, but not beyond that country; Taoism, the Chinese popular polytheism, based in part on an ancient quietist philosophy, never made any impact beyond Vietnam, and even in that country its presence was much less prominent than the scholarly Confucianism.

The Vietnamese had their own popular religion of spirits and mountain gods, similar to, but distinct from the Chinese form. When Chinese moved into the Nanyang as migrants they brought their cults with them, particularly the popular unofficial sects concerned with specialised deities, not infrequently the patrons of some secret society. These cults did not touch the non-Chinese peoples, and their shrines are exclusively used by Chinese. It must be remembered that official China considered the adoption of Confucianism as the state ethic and the teaching of its doctrine as tantamount to acceptance of Chinese suzerainty, although it was never made a condition which all tributaries must accept. Consequently those kings who did not feel themselves directly dependent upon the goodwill of the Chinese emperor had no incentive to adopt Confucian rites which would have conflicted with their own beliefs if Buddhist, and still more had they been Muslims. Equally the Chinese did not thrust their religions upon others. The Sultan of Malacca, a firm ally of the Ming emperor Yung Lo, three times made the long journey to Peking to pay homage; he began his reign as a Buddhist and then converted to Islam. He did not become a Confucianist, and his changes of religion seem to have made no difference to his friendly relations with the Emperor of China, who also confided his fleet to the command of a Muslim eunuch. With so little evangelical zeal it is hardly surprising that the Chinese religions made no headway beyond their empire.

It is thus in the sphere of the material rather than in the linguistic or the spiritual that Chinese cultural influence in South-East Asia must be sought. The effects of trade were probably more significant in this respect than the missions of diplomats or the wanderings of pilgrims.

It has often been remarked that Chinese architecture has two styles, the Northern and Southern. The two are exemplified by the Forbidden City (Imperial Palace) style in Peking, the northern building *par excellence*, and by many well-known temples in south China, which lacking palaces, can only be known through Buddhist and Taoist temples and other edifices of quasi-religious significance, such as memorial arches, family shrines and tombs. The characteristic of Chinese architecture as a whole is the roof, walls being subordinate, and in fact not supporting the roof, which rests on columns. Walls are mere filling. The roof is the principal feature, and in it or on it, is concentrated much of the decoration and characteristic style of a Chinese building. The roof is built in sweeping curves, coming down to the eaves in an unbroken line, and the ends where the angles of the walls meet are turned up in a kind of horn-like form. In the northern style this upturn is slight, not departing from the main sweep of the curved roof itself; in the southern style it is much more pronounced, and the decoration placed upon this feature is much more elaborate than the

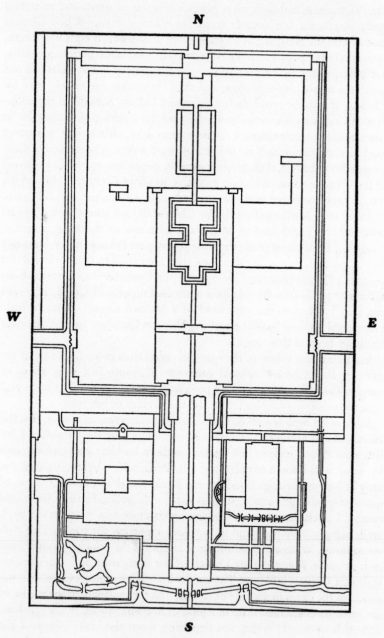

Plan of Imperial Palace, Pekin

rather restrained style used in the north. It is uncertain when and why this difference emerged; ancient paintings (of the twelfth century A.D. onwards) give no convincing answer since the buildings depicted are in any case the imaginative works of the artist, and may be intended to represent northern or southern buildings. Ancient clay models of the Han period are equally ambivalent sources, since on some there is no perceptible curve at all, probably due to the limitations of the potter's skill, whereas in others it can be seen either as a crude attempt to portray one or other style. There are very few buildings now standing in China older than the tenth century A.D., and only an exceedingly scanty number which are so old. These as it happens are all in north China, except for some pagodas of the eighth century, notably the great pagoda at Tali, capital of Nanchao, which, when it was built, was an independent state by no means wholly under Chinese cultural influence.

There is no generally accepted functional explanation for the upturn of the ends of a roof; the curve of the main structure of the roof certainly does serve a functional purpose, that of cutting off the high summer sun from direct contact with walls and windows, but admitting the low winter sun to warm the rooms by day. The value of this device is more apparent in north China, with a cold winter and a hot summer, than in the far south where if summer is hot, winter is not really cold. However there is another problem; the southern type of upturn at roof angles is clearly related to the characteristic style of much architecture in South-East Asia, particularly in the continental countries. In Thai, modern Cambodian, and Burmese buildings, temples or palaces, the upturn at roof angles is very pronounced, becomes a major feature and is multiplied into several superimposed horns on the roof-tree of the angle. This feature is not apparent in the stone temples of the Angkorian period in Cambodia, where architecture is entirely Indian in inspiration and decoration if not entirely in planning. No wooden buildings of the early ages of South-East Asia survive, nor have we any pictorial representation of them. Those shown on the bas-relief friezes at Angkor represent shops and small private houses, not palaces and temples. It is not therefore possible to say whether lighter constructions such as the palace of the kings at Angkor is known to have been from its foundations, were, or were not, in the style of their later and modern successors.

Modern palaces, or those of recent date such as the royal palace at Phnom Penh, and the Grand Palace at Bangkok, are striking examples of the style of architecture which prevailed in all countries which had received the Khmer culture, but it is not possible to say with any certainty whether this later style, which is not found in the classical stone structures of Angkor and elsewhere in Cambodia, was contemporary

Ta Yen T'a Pagoda, Ch'angan (7th Century)

with them for buildings of a secular character, or developed later. It can be observed that contemporary or recent temples in these countries do use the upturned horn at the angles of roofs, and in general conform more nearly to the south Chinese style in architecture than to classical Khmer. The possibility that this later style in the Buddhist countries of South-East Asia may have been developed under the inspiration of south China buildings, with which the peoples of the Nanyang would be much more familiar than with those of north China, cannot be ignored.

There is also another possibility; there is no present knowledge of how the south Chinese style evolved, nor why it should show such clear difference from the northern style. It is at least equally possible that the south China style was ancient, local, and related to the art of the southern countries, and in particular to the style of simple architectures which they may be presumed to have developed before the Hindu influence arrived.

Such a style could have remained in use during the period when temple architecture was under strong Hindu influence, since the materials used were different (brick, wood and tile, as opposed to cut stone, with no use of wood, and roofing with stone slabs). The stone buildings of the Khmer are always and exclusively religious; no secular building, not even the royal palace at Angkor, was built with these materials; only the terrace on which the palace stood, and the stone bases of the columns which supported its buildings now remain. It is at least very possible that when in existence it resembled in style the present royal palace at Phnom Penh.

There is clearly a family resemblance between south Chinese architecture and that of Buddhist South-East Asia today, but no connection between classical Khmer religious architecture and any Chinese style. Influence from south China could have reached the ancient kingdoms of Indo-China before the Hindu contact, remaining as the style for the secular buildings, and only much later, when stone construction was too expensive for the reduced resources of the Cambodian kingdom, becoming adopted also for religious constructions. On the whole the time factor favours this hypothesis. South China was incorporated into the Chinese empire of the Han dynasty in the first century B.C., and had already been under strong influence from China for a century before that. Chinese records of contact with the kingdoms of Funan and those then established in what is now South Vietnam mention that Brahmans were already active as advisers at the courts of these kings. The Hindu influence was present by this period, the first and second centuries A.D. But we have no direct evidence for the earliest contact with India, and no knowledge of what style of architecture prevailed before the Hindu travellers arrived. Hindu architectural style appears with the beginning of stone temples, the oldest of which so far known dates from the mid-seventh century A.D. The first contacts with India would seem to have been (on archaeological evidence) in the first century A.D. Chinese records concerning the kingdom of Funan, the first phase of Cambodian civilisation, state that the royal palace was built of fine wood and magnificently decorated; another Chinese record tells us that the palaces in the kingdom of Lankasuka, in the northern part of the modern Malay state of Perak, then a Hinduised kingdom, were also built of wood with tiered roofs, a feature which seems to have persisted in some buildings in the present Buddhist countries down to modern times.

These indications at least suggest that a secular style existed which differed from that of the Hindu-inspired stone and brick architecture which was to attain its apogee at Angkor. There is thus a possibility that alongside the Hindu temple architecture there was another tradition, which had links with the architectural styles of south China, and which may very well have been earlier than the Hindu influence. By the second century A.D. when these Chinese notices of such buildings, scanty though they are, appear, it was already more than three hundred years since Chinese, that is northern Chinese, domination had been imposed first by the Ch'in and then by the Han dynasty on the far south of China. The Han conquerors may have found in south China an architectural style somewhat different from, although obviously closely related to their own, and this style may have already influenced the southern countries. It would not seem probable that the influence could have come the other way round, since there is no doubt that the advanced techniques of building and the political systems which made the building of elaborate and costly palaces possible had arisen in China several centuries earlier than in the south.

The possibility that Chinese examples had an influence upon the styles of lay architecture in the early period of the southern civilisations, which later also were adopted in religious architecture after the Khmer classical period, is not the only instance of Chinese architectural influence in the style of Cambodian and related art. It has been observed by all who have specialised in the study of the classical Khmer art and architecture, that although the form and the religious inspiration derive exclusively from Indian art and legend, these great buildings are more magnificent than any found in India and represent the rare phenomenon in art of the pupil excelling the master. By the great period of Khmer architecture, the Indian origin had been absorbed; it was no longer directly copying Indian examples, and had expanded into a glorious achievement unrivalled in the country from which its distant inspiration had come. It has been said that the Khmer and the French of the seventeenth and eighteenth centuries alone understood the "architecture of space".* It is possible that this is not quite so sure. If the "architecture of space" implies the use of wide-open areas not covered with buildings in order to offset the magnificence of the main structure, the symmetry of the grand design and the regularity of its proportions, the use of broad moats to enhance the beauty of great walls, all these features are found in still existing Chinese palaces, and they were ancient and traditional, as literary descriptions and plans attest.

There was a religious explanation for the form of Khmer temples. They were orientated by the four points of the compass, with as their central feature the pyramidical structure which symbolised the sacred mountain, Meru, the centre of the Hindu universe and abode of the gods. The sanctuary faced east, and was surrounded by a rectangular wall. Chinese temples and palaces also are surrounded by a rectangular wall,

* B. P. Groslier. *Indo-China* Art of the World Series. Methuen 1962. P. 98.

orientated by the points of the compass, but face south, which to the Chinese was the aspect which royalty and power required. "To face south" meant to rule. The form of a Chinese city, when terrain permitted, was always rectangular, surrounded by wide water-filled moats, and entered by four gates placed in the four walls, with four main streets leading to a central building, the palace, chief magistracy, or a tower which controlled all four roadways. This plan is that of Angkor Thom, the city, with addition of an extra gate retained when the city was rebuilt, because it had an historical relationship to the earlier capital and its palace. In Angkor Thom it is the Bayon, the royal temple, which occupies the central point. In the Chinese capitals it was the imperial palace enclosure.

The use of space, wide avenues, great open courtyards, buildings raised on terraces and in perfect harmonious relationship to the spaces before them are the features of the great Chinese palaces of which that in present-

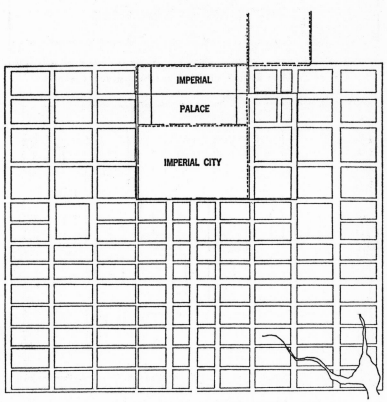

Plan of Ch'angan in the T'ang Period

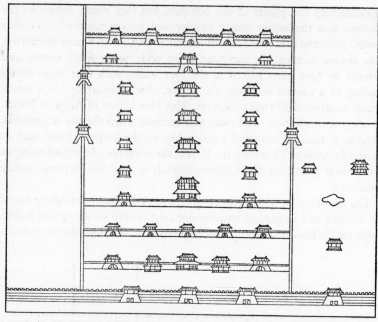

Plan of Ta Ming Kung T'ang Place at Cha'ngan (7th Century)

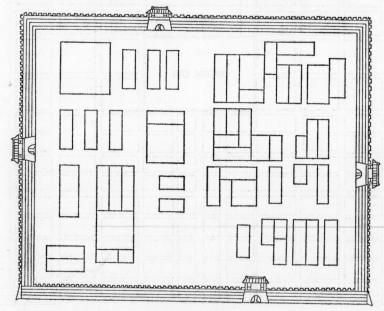

Plan of the Imperial Palace Ch'angan, T'ang Period

day Peking, built by the Ming emperor Yung Lo between 1405 and 1410, is the last example. The outer courts and ceremonial halls of the imperial tombs, including that of Yung Lo himself, near Peking, exhibit the same features, as do many smaller temples, minor palaces and official buildings of the old empire. The surviving plans of the cities of Ch'angan and Loyang, and their palaces when they were the capitals of the T'ang empire from the seventh to tenth centuries A.D., exhibit exactly the same features, and from the excavations recently carried out at Ch'angan it is known that the plans were strictly correct representations of the shape and distribution of the buildings of which only the terraces now remain. Thus it was certainly not only the Khmer who in the Middle Ages knew the value of the architecture of space, which they had not learned from their original Indian mentors. The Chinese had been practising this style of architectural planning for more than a thousand years before the final form of Angkor Thom took shape, or Angkor Vat was built.

This last, the greatest and most magnificent realisation of Khmer architectural genius, is in design, purpose and decoration purely Indian inspired, but adapted to a scale which only the Cambodians ever applied to Hindu religious architecture. However its ground plan, that of wide moats, rectangular walled enclosure, four gates, and raised approach causeway to the principal building, here the temple itself, is extremely close to that of the imperial palaces of China. In the palaces the central building on its high terrace is the Throne Hall (Tai Ho Tien in Peking), and it is approached by a raised causeway above the level of the wide courtyard which stretches before the great hall. This is just the plan of Angkor Vat. But it is the plan, not the architecture which appears so familiar to observers who are from China, and it is this plan, the architecture of space, which is not Hindu, and which is the mark of classical Khmer architecture. The question can therefore be asked, did the Khmer invent their architecture of space in the ninth–thirteenth centuries A.D., or did they derive some inspiration from the models which then existed in China, in Ch'angan and Loyang, the capitals of the great T'ang empire, with which the Cambodian kings were in diplomatic relations, and which inspired at this same period the Japanese to plan their new capital at Heian on the exact lines of Ch'angan?

The Khmer political system, derived from Indian example and Brahman teaching, made the king the centre of the realm in a spiritual as well as a temporal character. He was the force which related men to the gods, and by his sacrifices and rites ensured the prosperity of the kingdom. Consequently the monuments of the Khmer are primarily royal, funerary temples, such as Angkor Vat itself, or representations of Mount Meru on which the king performed the rites which identified him as a devoted

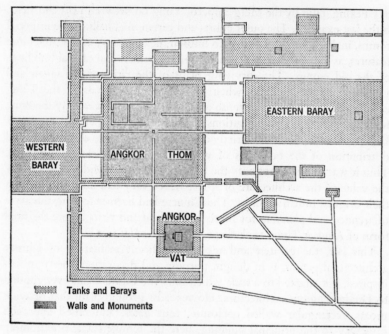

Tanks and Barays

Walls and Monuments

Plan of Angkor

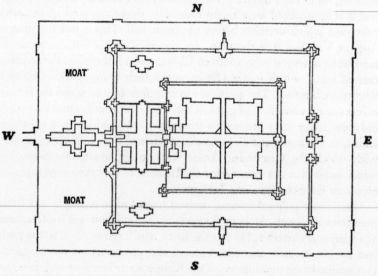

Plan of Angkor Vat

servant and chosen representative of the gods. The Emperor of China was also the mediator between gods and men; he was the Son of Heaven, that is to say the man chosen to relate his fellow humans to the supreme deity of the ancient Chinese world. His annual rite of ploughing the soil and his worship at the Temple of the Year (the so-called "Temple of Heaven") symbolised his power to ensure the fertility of the soil and the growth of the crops. He was the centrepiece of the empire, and the very ideograph for "kingdom" in one form is a simple rectangle enclosing the character for king; the monarch at the heart of the kingdom. Chinese styles for cities and capitals, palaces and monuments can thus hardly have been alien to the thinking of the Cambodian rulers. They had their own religion, differing from that of China: but the ideas, especially the political ideas, which emanated from these religions were very similar in purpose and conception. The style in which Chinese imperial royalty lived was then the model for all the Eastern world—by virtue of the size, antiquity, splendour and power of the Chinese empire, no matter what dynasty ruled it. It would seem strange that these features of the political realities of their time should have been ignored by the Cambodian kings as they attained to their own widespread, but still much more restricted imperial authority. The Chinese emperor and his way of life was a splendid example of how to be a monarch; the plan of his capital and palace, with its generous and magnificent use of space and proportion, was there to be observed, reproduced and modified to suit the religion of Cambodia, but also to enhance the grandeur of its edifices and the glory of their royal builder.

There is no remaining documentary or inscribed evidence of who designed the great Khmer temples of the Angkorian age; it has been accepted that the architects were men of great skill, imagination and enterprise. Required by their royal master to create monuments of the scale of Angkor Vat or cities of the size and design of Angkor Thom, it would seem probable that such men would not have been ignorant of the greatest contemporary cities in their part of the world, nor of the plans of their famous palaces. They were not concerned with the architecture as such, but the use of space, proportion and arrangement on a very grand scale was their objective, and they had their models.

If there is some reason to conjecture that in the ground plans of the great buildings of Angkor some influence from China is present, there is almost conclusive evidence from the observations of the Chinese envoy, Chou Ta-kuan himself, that in government and the style of Court life, the Khmer did not receive any significant institutions or fashions from the great contemporary dynasties, the T'ang and the Sung. Chou describes the public appearances of the king of Cambodia as a magnificent spectacle, with the monarch progressing standing upright on a caparisoned elephant, attended by female guards, and watched by the public—albeit from a prostrate position. When the king appeared at public audiences in a pavilion on the terrace wall of the palace, the silken curtains which concealed him were drawn back by four girls, and in general women attendants played as prominent a part in secular ceremonies as in religion, as the Angkor sculptures so well attest. All this is not at all Chinese: the emperor very rarely went beyond the palace, principally to carry out religious rites at the Altar of Heaven, or at the imperial tombs of his predecessors. Only the dynastic founders and their immediate heirs, men bred outside Court life, led armies in battle. Hunting was an imperial pastime, but carried on in vast private parks, into which no ordinary person dared intrude. When the emperor did go forth, the public were forbidden to appear on the streets through which he passed, and the intersections were closed with palisades so that no distant glimpse of the monarch was vouchsafed to his subjects. Even pictorial representations of the capital showed the palace as an idealised abode half wrapped in swirling mist.

The Chinese emperors were attended by eunuchs, in large numbers, who performed all the services of the palace which Chou Ta-kuan saw done by girls at Angkor. The emperor had many concubines, organised in several ranks, but these were not servants; on the contrary, they were ladies of aristocratic or at least of official families, and if the lower ranks had some duties to carry out in respect of the empress, they were more those of a lady-in-waiting than of a maidservant. The idea of girl guards armed like soldiers would have seemed very improper to the Chinese, indeed positively indecent. There is no suggestion in Khmer records that the officials of the kingdom were recruited by public examinations, the great and characteristic Chinese institution which was in the long course of time to be copied by all modern bureaucracies. In Vietnam this institution flourished, and produced its natural flower, an élite class of scholar officials—the "Mandarins" as the Westerners were to call them. Korea, and even Japan were to borrow this Chinese system, with some variations, but it made no recorded impact on the kingdoms of the south. There seems no doubt that in government the ancient Hindu model was retained. The kings of the Hinduised states of the south were advised by learned Brahmans, but these scholars were priests rather than officials, their learning was religious, not secular, and they did not gain the royal confidence by entering an organised civil service recruited by open public examinations. Beyond Vietnam the influence of Chinese ideas and methods of administration seems to have been almost non-existent.

On the other hand the absence of the caste system in the Hinduised countries of South-East Asia, and still more the decline and disappearance of caste as a social institution among the modern Indian population in Malaysia, may perhaps be related on the one hand to the basic social customs of the southern peoples before Hindu influence arrived, and on the other to the example of the Chinese population in the modern communities. The influence of Buddhism had indeed caused some discrimination against butchers in imperial China, with the result that this trade was largely left to Chinese Muslims, who were unaffected by beliefs in the sanctity of animal life. On the whole, the social distinctions of the Chinese were based on descent, wealth, landed property and official office—the latter being virtually identical with academic distinction. When this last upper class was absent, as among the migrant communities of the Nanyang, and the origin of all families was obscure and humble, wealth remained the only effective class determinant, and any man of enterprise and skill could acquire riches in the rapidly expanding economies of the nineteenth-century Nanyang countries. This social mobility cannot have failed to impress the Indians of low caste who came to Malaya, and since their foreign rulers had no wish to enforce caste rules, the Indian population had every inducement to abandon a discriminatory system from which they themselves were the only sufferers.

Without question the principal impact of Chinese culture on the southern world was through trade; it was the manufactures of China, her artifacts rather than her art, which made the appeal, and these material imports far outweighed the importance of Chinese thought which could only be appreciated by means of Chinese literature, which beyond Vietnam was a sealed book. Even paper, which the Chinese had been making and using since the first century B.C., and printing, which they had invented in the ninth century A.D., remained unknown, or at least not used, by the southern peoples before the European occupation. However, silk was imported into the south at an early age, and as Chou Ta-kuan testifies, was in use at the Court of Angkor; the climate of the south is not one which requires much clothing of any kind, and it is natural that the Nanyang peoples should never have taken to the heavy embroideries and long robes of earlier China—nor did silk preserve well in damp climates before the age of refrigeration. It remained a Court luxury.

Tea was originally a medicinal preparation in China; it began to spread as a beverage in the eighth century A.D. and by the ninth was sufficiently popular to attract the attention of the tax-gatherer. It is unlikely that it had been exported to the southern world very much earlier than the Southern Sung dynasty, when trade increased with the Nanyang due to improvements in shipbuilding and navigation techniques. The conversion of the Malays and the majority peoples of Indonesia to Islam at a slightly later date must certainly have stimulated the tea trade; Muslims may not use alcohol. Even if this prohibition was largely ignored, the local forms of alcoholic drinks are not very well adapted to constant use in a hot climate. Tea was the answer for Muslims and pagans alike, easily prepared, healthy and refreshing. The need to boil water when making tea has undoubtedly had direct and beneficial results not only in China, where it is believed to have been one of the underlying causes of the late centuries' great rise in the population by eliminating many infections, but also in the southern countries where water sources are easily polluted. Tea comes mainly from the south-eastern provinces of China, and these are the home countries of the overseas Chinese of the Nanyang. The introduction of tea to the south was therefore natural, easy and profitable. Many years later tea was to be grown in Ceylon and in India, but this development did not occur until after the European domination had been long established.

Porcelain, the third great Chinese export of the old economy, was developed in China from the sixth century onwards, arising out of ever more refined glazed pottery. T'ang porcelain has been found all over the south-east of Asia, and as far west as Iraq (the site of Samara) and also on the African coast. This trade must therefore have spread very soon after the perfection of the new technique in China itself, and made an immediate appeal to the peoples of the south-east. The beauty and pleasing character of porcelain is only the most obvious factor in this preference; porcelain is clean, and can be cleaned more effectively than coarser pottery or wooden ware. The people who used it may not have known that this fact contributes to their health by avoiding the risk of small particles of decaying food remaining in the cooking or eating vessels, but they must certainly have appreciated the comparative immunity to staining which is the mark of glazed porcelain. In the Southern Sung period, if not somewhat earlier, Chinese porcelain was being exported in large quantities throughout the Nanyang, and even reached the primitive peoples of North Borneo, where Chinese vessels were preserved from generation to generation for religious rites. As far west as Malacca the Chinese seem to have had a monopoly of this trade, and the wares of Persia and of India are hardly found in the countries east of Malaysia. The Chinese cultivated this market with designs calculated to meet the taste of their customers. In Ming times porcelain for the Muslim market could be decorated with verses or lines from the Koran, and the human figure was left out in deference to the dogmas of Islam. Before long the widespread demand for porcelain stimulated the rulers of the southern kingdoms to start their own industries.

Vietnam, under strong Chinese cultural influence, was among the first

CHINESE ART AND CULTURE IN SOUTH-EAST ASIA   137

to do so. In the Yüan (Mongol) period of the thirteenth century A.D. kilns in Vietnam were producing not only for the home market, but for export also. In the fourteenth century Thailand followed suit, and it is believed that Chinese potters were specially imported to teach native workers their skill. These local industries continued to flourish for a long period, and that of Vietnam not only produced magnificent examples in the Middle Ages, but has endured until modern times. Yet these local efforts seem hardly to have made any real competition injurious to the Chinese trade. The enormous size of the imperial industry in itself, apart from the many local and unofficial kilns, assured an ever-expanding market, until "China" became synonymous with porcelain. Fine porcelain was sent in large quantities as presents to distant rulers, as the collections in the palaces of Turkey and Persia still attest, but it was not until comparatively late that any Chinese porcelain seems to have reached western Europe. The earliest examples, in themselves nothing very exceptional, were the treasured possessions of great princes until after the Portuguese had opened the sea route across the Indian Ocean.

Although much Chinese export porcelain was decorated to the taste of the customer, this was not invariably the case. Those countries which did not have Islamic prejudices against the representation of the human figure were ready to buy Chinese wares decorated in the traditional patterns; scenes of mountains or rivers, bamboo and flowers, often including human figures, and sometimes associated with Chinese folklore or history in a way which must have been quite unintelligible to the non-Chinese purchaser. It is not apparent that this decorative side to Chinese porcelain export wares was copied or reproduced as an influence in the artistic styles and fashions of any South-East Asian people beyond Vietnam. The Thais were to find an unique use for pot sherds of Chinese and local porcelain, as a surface decoration for the walls of pagodas and temples, using the multi-coloured fragments to form a gay and glittering façade. Bangkok, a late city of the end of the eighteenth century, has also in the courtyards to the royal palace (the Grand Palace) several large-scale Chinese statues of warriors such as were placed along the approach avenue of important Chinese tombs. This form of sculpture is in China exclusively associated with funerary art; no such statues adorn the palaces or mansions of the living. The kings who founded Bangkok and wished to decorate its new palace with symbols of power and might seem to have been imposed upon by some astute Chinese merchant who supplied them with these pieces of traditional Chinese funerary statuary without disclosing the use to which they would have been put in China itself.

Perhaps this trifling example may stand as the model of all relations in art between China and the peoples of the Nanyang beyond the sphere of former Chinese direct rule. Chinese artifacts were admired, even copied, but rarely was their true purpose or symbolic meaning understood. There was between the two cultures an impenetrable barrier, which was based on the mutual ignorance of languages and literature. There is nothing other than Sanskrit Buddhist literature, which came from India, rather than from the Nanyang, which penetrated China. The history and literature of the south were known to the Chinese only by their own observation, never, it would seem, by knowledge of native sources. Consequently they knew something of the history, but little or nothing of the literature. Even what was known was the prerogative of scholars who could read the style of the dynastic histories and pay attention to the rather short and comparatively scanty mention of foreign countries, whose names, rendered in Chinese ideographs, would have been sounded in ways totally alien to the native speech. It would seem that until modern times very few Chinese scholars paid more than cursory attention to this source of information, nor did they collate the entries in differing dynastic histories to make a continuous intelligible story of their empire's relations with the lands of the south.

Equally, nothing in South-East Asian literature suggests any knowledge of the history of China, save when, exceptionally, Chinese military invasion, such as the expeditions of the Mongols, had a direct impact on the country concerned. The great Ming expeditions for the most part did not have this character, and are consequently no better remembered in such countries as Indonesia than they were in China after Ming indifference to the south had turned all interest away from the subject. The contact between Chinese and southern peoples has thus a strangely exclusive character; it was, indeed, "all or nothing". For Yünnan and to a very large degree for Vietnam, it was all; the non-Chinese elements of their original art and culture were virtually obliterated. The very realisation that in the Middle Ages Yünnan, as the kingdom of Nanchao, was not only non-Chinese, but actively hostile to China and a strong obstacle to further southward expansion, has been almost wholly forgotten in Yünnan itself, and is only known to historians in China. Elsewhere the Chinese impact, except for trade in articles of convenience such as porcelain and tea, or of luxury such as silk, is hard to trace, remains largely conjectural, and would be little known but for the occasional references and observations of Chinese writers and travellers.

On the other hand the Chinese themselves, wherever they have settled, have brought with them their own culture, at first in simple forms suited to a mainly illiterate migrant population, but as the level of their wealth and standard of living rose, they turned without hesitation to the more sophisticated art and literature of their ancestral land. The modern art of the Chinese of the Nanyang may seem to be popular and out of touch with much classical tradition, but it is the art form and culture of the modern southern Chinese as exemplified in Hong Kong, the greatest concentration of Chinese wealth and economic power outside the bounds of the Peoples' Republic. The Chinese of the Nanyang are not today under the direct influence of the contemporary culture of China itself; they look to Hong Kong for their music, their films, their theatre and for much of their popular literature. This art and culture is readily absorbed by all overseas Chinese, for its roots in south China are common to all; but it remains just as alien to the other peoples of the Nanyang as the older imperial and classical culture of China which originated in and was exemplified in the capitals of the north. Not only have the Chinese proved to be resistant to the cultures of the south, but the southern peoples make very little contact with the civilisation and ways of their Chinese co-citizens. Culturally and artistically the two worlds remain almost as much apart as they did in the days of the Hinduised kingdoms and Chinese dominated Vietnam.

Demographic assimilation is hardly more conspicuous than cultural interaction. Very few of the overseas Chinese communities, the Baba Chinese being the most obvious exception, have either assimilated with non-Chinese peoples or borrowed anything of significance from other peoples. Muslims do not marry "infidels" and Chinese Muslims come from parts of China which have had no relations with the Nanyang. When some years ago it was suggested that Chinese Muslims who had left China rather than live under the Communist régime should be allowed to migrate to Malaya, and should be welcome there, the idea was very coldly received; Chinese were Chinese; their religion was clearly not a factor strong enough to alter this basic character. When Chinese women were few among the early migrants and merchants, the Chinese married girls from the peoples among whom they lived; but in most cases their children were regarded as Chinese, and brought up to be Chinese in thought and outlook. In Thailand and in Cambodia, Buddhist countries, this situation was modified, and some real assimilation did take place before the great influx of Chinese migrants, soon followed by their women, in the late nineteenth century. This influx created a Chinese community more cohesive than the earlier immigrants had been; and this new strength and Chinese character of the community in turn provoked Thai nationalist reaction which has checked if not wholly arrested the earlier process of assimilation.

When the Chinese were few, or are still a small minority as in Burma, their cultural influence was negligible: when they became numerous and strong they brought and cultivated their own civilisation and it remains confined to them alone. In so far as there has been interaction in modern times in art or literature it is through the common alien influence of European civilisation, which epitomises the fashions of modernity that appeal to Chinese and non-Chinese alike. It may be that this is the course of future development; a new mixed culture drawing from both local and Chinese sources, but filtered through the European and American media, may one day dominate the art life of the Nanyang as once the Hindu influence ruled supreme. There are difficulties in the way of any such change, and among them are the nature of the Chinese written language, which is unlikely to be changed for linguistic reasons, apart from others, and the new pride of the former colonial subject peoples in their reviving national cultures.

It is apparent from the survey of China's relations with the countries beyond her southern frontiers, whether ancient or modern, that the motive of the southward expansion of the Chinese has not been cultural colonisation but physical possession of the soil, or commercial domination of the economy. Only in Yünnan and Vietnam, where the rule of China was once, or later became direct, did the political fact of domination lead to cultural conquest also. In Yünnan certainly this last development was associated with massive immigration continuing over a long period; in Vietnam the immigration was much less, but the political domination at a formative period much stronger, and incidentally longer, than has yet been the case in Yünnan. The Chinese ruled Vietnam for more than one thousand years; they have incorporated Yünnan in their country for just over five hundred years. The large Chinese communities in the Nanyang are at the very most three hundred years old, but substantially they date from the mid-nineteenth century. In some countries and in several cities they are none the less a major element in the life of the whole community and have developed their own distinctive Chinese variation of the civilisation of the ancient homeland; but they have not deeply influenced the peoples among whom they have settled.

CHAPTER EIGHT

EUROPEAN COLONIAL EXPANSION AND CHINESE IMMIGRATION

The decision of the Ming government to abandon its naval policy and leave the great fleet to rot away preceded in time by only little more than a half-century the coming of European sea power to the Eastern seas. In 1497 Vasco da Gama, the Portuguese navigator, rounded the Cape of Good Hope and sailed across the Indian Ocean. By the year 1510 Albuquerque, the Portuguese viceroy in the East, had captured Goa in southwest India, and only two years later he also captured Malacca, the city state which had been the close ally and client of Emperor Yung Lo and had provided the main overseas base for the expeditions of the great fleets. The Ming Court, one century after these expeditions, remained quite indifferent to the changing situation in the south. There was no Chinese opposition to the penetration of the Portuguese. By 1521 these hardy strangers had taken control over the Moluccas, the Spice Islands, in what is now eastern Indonesia. This gave them for a time a world monopoly of what was then a most valuable article of commerce. There can be no doubt that Chinese trade with these regions suffered, since Chinese ships had no protection from their own government, and the Portuguese were very apt to combine plain piracy with trade.

The power of Spain, then the dominant European power, was also now felt in the Far East. Magellan had found the Philippine Islands on his round the world voyage in 1511; but it was not until half a century later, in 1565, that the Spanish founded their first permanent settlement in the islands, at Cebu. Five years later they occupied the large island of Luzon and founded the city of Manila which became, and has remained, the capital. Spain was debarred, by the papal ruling which in 1493 had divided the undiscovered world between Spain and Portugal on the line 370 leagues west of the Cape Verde Islands, from moving into what is now Indonesia; the lure of the Spice Islands did indeed lead to breaches of the partition, but the Spanish made no sustained attempt to move west. Characteristically in this age, while the Chinese empire claimed the overlordship of mankind, but did not try to make any such claim good, the

141

Pope felt himself entitled to dispose of the globe in favour of two of the more faithful Catholic powers. The assumptions of right of conquest, of racial superiority and European dominance thus take root in the religious attitudes and beliefs of the European fifteenth and sixteenth centuries.

Portuguese power was thinly spread along the sea route to the Cape. The Portuguese were never strong enough to occupy or to administer large territories far from the sea. They relied on ports which acted as bases controlling the strategic sea lanes; Malacca in that period fulfilling the function which later fell to Singapore. This fact may be one reason why Portuguese operations did not provoke the hostility of the larger powers of the south-east. These kingdoms, Burma, Thailand, Cambodia or Vietnam did not have their capitals upon the coast, nor did the sultanates of Java depend mainly upon their coastal cities. They did not feel themselves threatened as they would have been by large-scale conquests on land. It was not until more than a century later that other nations, now more powerful than the Portuguese, began to move inland and to annex large areas. The exception was the Spanish colony of the Philippines; but these islands were in other ways different from the rest of the region. No local power had arisen in the Philippines; most of the tribes were small and fragmented, only in the south-western islands had Muslim sultanates, mostly small and weak, imposed the rudimentary beginnings of state organisation. They could not effectively oppose the power of Spain, and in a relatively short time the whole of the main island group came under Spanish rule. Since no prior higher culture had developed, it was Spanish civilisation which formed the future Filipino people. Catholic in religion, and for education, Spanish in language; administered with a form of European feudal tenure, the Philippines became and has largely remained an European outpost in Asia, inhabited by people mainly of native stock, close to the Malays in ethnic origin, but essentially European in their culture.

The heyday of Portuguese domination was not of long duration: before the end of the century (sixteenth) they were being challenged by the Dutch, who first entered the area in 1595, forming their Netherlands East India Company in 1602, and seizing upon the Javanese port of Jacatra (later named by them Batavia, and now renamed Jakarta by the Indonesians) in 1619. The Portuguese were soon ousted from the lucrative Spice Islands (Moluccas) and in 1641 lost their main far eastern base, Malacca, to the Dutch. Even before that it had been a tenuous holding. Between 1570 and 1575 the Portuguese had had to sustain determined Malay attacks and sieges. From the loss of Malacca onwards Portugal's power declined. Some of the old bases such as Goa remained to her, but the establishment of the Dutch in South Africa, and then in Ceylon, gave the newcomers the control of the great sea route to the East. The Dutch had other advantages. Protestant, they did not burn with fiery missionary zeal to convert all the heathen. They found it therefore easier to deal with Muslim Sultans. The Portuguese had hoped to convert as well as to conquer, but the Dutch were almost exclusively interested in trade and the naval power which could protect it. Thus, although possessed of Malacca by the middle of the seventeenth century, they did not proceed to conquer the relatively weak sultanates among whom the Malay peninsula was divided. Malacca controlled the straits, and that was enough. Even in Java they were slow to extend their authority beyond the coast. They had taken the Celebes in 1667, but it was not until late in the century that their domination of Java, not its outright annexation, was established from 1682 onwards. Thereafter their expansion into the outer islands was slow and long retarded, especially in northern Sumatra, by the strong resistance of warlike Muslim states.

The English, who came next, were relatively late-comers. Sir Francis Drake had, on his round the world voyage, touched at the Moluccas in 1578, and the English East India Company was founded in 1600. But it was India itself which for a long period interested the English. Their intrusion into the region of South East Asia was not significant until the second half of the eighteenth century, when in 1786, Captain Light founded Penang. Originally intended as a naval base to protect the route to China, which was becoming more important for trade, it did not prove very suitable for this purpose, but did develop as a trading entrepôt for the Malayan peninsula. The Napoleonic Wars destroyed the Dutch supremacy; Holland was occupied by the French. The Eastern colonies were placed by the fugitive government under British protection, and Java was occupied and administered by Sir Stamford Raffles for ten years. When the wars ended, the British returned Java to the Dutch, but in 1824 obtained Malacca, in return for the cession to Holland of the small port of Bencoolen on the west coast of Sumatra. In 1819 Raffles had obtained from the Sultan of Johore the island of Singapore, then almost uninhabited, although at an earlier period it had been a flourishing city named Tumasik. For fifty years the British were content with the three ports of Penang, Malacca (which was silting up) and Singapore, which was becoming a major port. Then the increasing disorders in Malaya forced a rather reluctant home government to authorise the governor of the Straits Settlements, as they were called, to intervene. At the island of Pangkor, off the coast of western Malaya, Sir Andrew Clarke obtained the agreement of the warring sultans to a settlement which placed British residents at each court, whose "advice and counsel, except in matters of Malay religion and custom, must be asked for and acted upon". This formula virtually ended independence and set up a British protectorate throughout the country.

In 1895, twenty-one years later, the four sultanates of Perak, Negri Sembilan, Selangor and Pahang were combined into a federation, leaving Johore and the northern states out, and this new body became to all intents and purposes a directly ruled British colony. In 1909 the king of Siam (Thailand) was induced, in return for the abandonment of extra-territorial jurisdiction by the British, to cede his suzerainty over the four northern sultanates of Malaya. Thus the British had done what neither the Portuguese nor the Dutch had seriously attempted to do, annex for all practical purposes the whole of the Malay peninsula. In 1841 a British adventurer, Brook, had given valuable service to the Sultan of Sarawak. He made Brook his heir, and thus the "White Rajahs" came to rule this north Borneo region, and under British protection continued to do so until the Second World War. British protection was also extended to Brunei, and then to modern Sabah (the British North Borneo Company's concession area) mainly to put an end to the activity of pirates. The fact that some of these places were to prove rich in oil was as yet unknown, and would not have been seen as a valuable asset in an age which had not yet invented the combustion engine nor developed the technology of oil extraction.

The British may have acquired both their standing in Malaya and in North Borneo rather unwillingly, in response to local disorders—for rubber was not yet cultivated in Malaya, and there was no great market for this commodity before the age of the motor car—but their intrusion into Burma, and ultimate conquest of the whole country was a more planned and calculated imperialist expansion. Burma lay close to India. The Burmese king, early in the nineteenth century had made claims upon Assam, not yet ruled by the British, but within what they deemed to be "India". Piracy and maltreatment of sailors and traders in Burmese Arakan, a province bordering the sea, and only recently conquered by the king of Burma, led to the first Burmese War, which ended with the British taking possession of that province and also of Tenasserim, the long southern projection of Burma which reaches down towards the isthmus of Kra. Forty years later a war, started on very slight pretext, gave Britain the control of the rich rice delta of the Irrawaddy, and the great port city of Rangoon. In 1885, following the misgovernment of King Thebaw, and still more the fear that he would make France his ally and protector, Britain invaded the rest of Burma and annexed the whole country as a province of the Indian Empire.

The last steps in the European colonial domination of South-East Asia, China's southern neighbours, were taken by France in the second half of the nineteenth century. The empire of Annam was successively assailed in 1859, when Saigon was taken, in 1862, when the Mekong Delta—most of which is now called South Vietnam—was annexed and renamed Cochin-China, and in 1864 a protectorate over Cambodia was accepted by its hard-pressed king. It was not until after the Franco-Prussian War that France resumed her pressure upon what was left of Vietnam, establishing a protectorate over it following the war with China of 1882. The northern province of Tongking passed, in effect, under direct French rule; the centre remained under the emperor of Annam, but his power was virtually nominal and ceremonial. Laos was brought under French control in 1890, and Siam was forced, in 1907, to cede back to Cambodia the provinces of Siem Reap and Battambang, which had been taken from the declining kingdom when it was still independent. Siem Reap contains the ruins of the former capital of the Khmer empire, Angkor.

France and Britain had therefore abandoned the more limited aims of the Portuguese and Dutch; they did not only seek naval bases and entrepôt ports, but came to rule directly over large territories and to suppress or control the ancient kingdoms of the region. The Dutch had rounded off their position in the Indonesian archipelago by imposing direct rule on Java, Borneo and Sumatra, with the lesser outer islands also. Only Siam remained independent. This vast transformation had not interested the late Ming government, nor did it provoke any reaction from the Manchus when they took power. Most of the European expansion was in fact contemporary with the Manchu dynasty, and all the more significant expansions occurred when that régime was ruling China. Ch'ien Lung might take a lofty tone with the British king's envoy, Lord Macartney, but he made no attempt to challenge the expansion of British power in the areas where once the Ming had claimed suzerainty. Late in the course of European expansion, when France made it plain that she intended to occupy northern as well as southern Vietnam, the Chinese had reacted, in the war of 1882, and although winning some victories on land, had been defeated at sea, and then compelled to renounce China's ancient interest in Vietnam. It was hardly surprising that to the Europeans, China, whether under the strong rule of the early Manchu emperors, or under the weak and vacillating policy of their nineteenth century successors, was no longer regarded as a factor in the politics of the south-east of Asia. She had renounced her latent sea power, and the course of history since Vasco da Gama rounded the Cape had proved conclusively that sea power was the foundation of empire in the whole vast region of South-East Asia.

But if the Chinese government had lost interest, the Chinese people, and particularly those of the south, remained very much involved. The connection was old, it was to grow stronger under the rule of the colonial powers than it had ever been before. In search of personal wealth and security thousands of migrants were to create a Chinese presence in the borderlands of the south while Peking slumbered.

When the Ming withdrew from South-East Asia, there were certainly Chinese settlements in Sumatra, notably Palembang, and probably at a number of other ports. They had acquired considerable local power and influence, and seem to have retained it for many years. But the history of these communities is not known with any certainty until Dutch rule was established. It is certain that a considerable proportion of the Chinese community in Indonesia descends from families which have been there more than three centuries, and perhaps longer still than that. Chinese women among them were few; after the later Ming prohibited private travel abroad, a prohibition maintained by the Manchu dynasty, it was very difficult for men who left their country as adventurers to take wives with them. They went by stealth, and they might never return. So the migrant Chinese tended to marry locally, a custom already recorded by Chou Ta-kuan in Cambodia in the late thirteenth century. In Indonesia at least, and probably in all the countries of Muslim faith, the children were none the less counted as Chinese, taking the father's line as deter-minant of nationality or ethnic affiliation. The sons of "infidels" (i.e. non-Muslims) could not be other than foreigners; thus it came about that very many of the "Chinese" in these countries are in fact of mixed descent.

The constraints imposed upon free emigration by the Chinese authori-ties at home had also the effect of making this way of life difficult or too dangerous for all those who were not forced into it by fear of starvation and poverty, or so located that escape was easy. This has resulted in a curiously sharp pattern of local origin in China among the Chinese over-seas. The great centres of emigration, apparently both before and after the legalisation of travel abroad, were the southern half of the coast of Fukien province, the whole of the Kuangtung coast, and some of the com-munities of non-local origin, such as the Hakkas, who are not always found on the coasts. Hardly any Chinese from the Yangtze area, or from the northern provinces, and virtually none at all from the west or south-west went overseas. The migrants, who spoke differing dialects in the home provinces, the region where extreme differences in speech are most prominent, tended to flock together and go to the same region, or port, where their fellow provincials would make them welcome, find them work, and understand their language. The south coast of Fukien has few wide river valleys, and these are heavily populated. Much of the coast is mountainous with poor agricultural opportunities. The same is true of a long part of the coast of Kuangtung. Only the West River delta near Canton, an area very heavily populated, provides a wide extent of good farming country. The people of these areas had nowhere to go when increase made it no longer possible to live off the small family holding. The interior is barred off by high mountains, and the provinces beyond them, Hunan and Kiangsi, are inhabited by people who do not speak the dialects of the coast. Moreover they were already thickly inhabited. The coastal people turned to the sea, as a long tradition suggested. They had, probably from before the Christian era, moved south across the sea, along the coast, to Hainan Island and then to Vietnam. Now they could go further, and probably fare better.

The pattern of Chinese emigration therefore settled, at a time which has not been fully recorded, into a shape which it retained until modern times. The Hokkien speakers, from the region of Amoy, whose name means simply "Fukien" in their dialect, went to Java and later to the eastern outer islands, and also to Malaya. Teochiu, who come from the port of Swatow in northern Kuangtung (taking their name from the city of Chaochou, which they pronounce as "Teochiu") went to Siam (Thailand), to Malaya later, and to Sumatra. Cantonese tended to settle wherever the prospects of trade were good, for they came from a more sophisticated area, and were able to adapt to new conditions more easily. The Hakkas, also found in many parts of South-East Asia, went at first in large numbers to Borneo, which others shunned, and from the middle of the eighteenth century, before Dutch rule had been established in the island, the Hakka community had become large and locally powerful. In their relative isolation both from other Chinese settlers and from strong native rulers, they developed a very unusual form of political organisation which was called "Kongsi", a word (in Standard Speech Kungssu) which in modern times is used to render "company". The Hakka Kongsi obtained from small local rulers the right to open mines and farm uncultivated land, of which in jungle-covered Borneo there was more than enough. They paid the local ruler a tribute, or rent, and were left to govern themselves. They had no hereditary leaders, the Kongsi was a sort of communal organisation, both social and political, and thus very much unlike the traditional forms of government prevalent in China itself. It could almost be called a miniature republic. This idea was certainly unknown to the Hakka settlers of the mid-eighteenth century. They created their Kongsi to meet the needs of a large and growing community in a new, wild country; and as among them there were no men of ancient lineage or established social prestige they developed a system which reflected the social equality of a pioneer people.

In Malaya, or Thailand, where the local government of sultans or the king was more effective, the Chinese settlers did not follow the Kongsi type of social organisation. In Thailand, a Buddhist country, there were few obstacles at that time to assimilation with the native inhabitants. Chinese tended to intermarry, but also to retain their Chinese character. They sought preferment from the king, or served him in business matters, but did not try to create political movements or organisations of their own. In later times, especially after the Manchu conquest, which in south China was not effective until nearly the end of the seventeenth century, the overseas Chinese were often permeated by the secret societies, which took their origin in south China as resistance movements against Manchu conquest. Abroad, where many of their adepts fled, they organised the migrants, protected them, and exacted contributions from them. They formed the only organisation conducted by his own people to which the migrant could turn, and they became very powerful and constituted a secret, unofficial but potent social control over the migrant people.

This migration of Chinese into the "Nanyang" (Southern Ocean), as it is called in Chinese, was received with varying degrees of welcome or opposition by the newly come colonial rulers. On the one hand the Chinese facilitated trade. They acted as the middle men, collecting the country produce and bringing it to markets at the ports. This made it unnecessary for the colonial rulers to extend so much direct control over the hinterland as they might otherwise have found desirable. Secondly the Chinese distributed the imports brought by the foreigners to up-country markets, often far beyond the control of the colonial authority. The Chinese trader in his small boat stocked with trinkets and imported goods made his way far up the wild rivers of Borneo and traded with people who were normally hostile to all strangers. In this activity they were an exact parallel to their countrymen in the jungles of northern Burma and the Assam borderlands, who trade in this way with the head-hunting tribes. How often such traders met with disaster remains unrecorded; that most did not is proved by the steady penetration of the trade over many years. It is indeed uncertain how long it may not have gone on well before there was any Western presence in the region.

The Chinese had gone to Borneo for timber, used in the fine furniture which was made from Sung times onward, and also for the beaks of the hornbill, a curio much valued and carved into ingenious shapes. They also seem to have collected birds' nests for the famous delicacy, bird's nest soup, the origin of which is lost in time, but sustained an active trade with parts of North Borneo, where this sea bird nests in caves. The nest is made from the regurgitated bones of the fish on which these birds live. When treated and boiled down it becomes a jelly of delicate flavour. The inland tribes of Borneo, the Dyaks and others, obtained from the Chinese trader porcelain vessels, which they treasured as objects used in funerary rites, and which have been found in quite large numbers in their districts. Some of these porcelain pots date from Sung times, indicating that the trade was ancient by South-East Asian standards. This type of trade, in special commodities which had a high price in China, or which could be disposed of at a high price in the Nanyang, but were in themselves neither bulky nor difficult to ship, seems to have been the pattern of Chinese economic activity before the age of the steamship and plantation agriculture.

When Sir Stamford Raffles founded Singapore in 1819 the island was hardly inhabited except for a small number of Malay fisherfolk. Within a year or so Chinese began to arrive and settle, greatly to the delight of Sir Stamford. As this immigration continued year by year, he was even better pleased, for he equated the settlement of Chinese with the future growth and prosperity of his new colony. Raffles was perhaps the most intelligent and far-sighted of the colonial founders of the early nineteenth century; he realised that these countries would never become the permanent home of large numbers of European settlers; the climatic conditions, with malaria then uncontrolled, were heavily against any such development. He foresaw the future of places such as Singapore as naval bases and commercial entrepôts, and for the latter development, if not in supplying labour for the former, Chinese settlement was essential and highly desirable. It is quite evident that Sir Stamford had no qualms about future political complications; the interest, if any, of the distant Chinese government, nor the inherent problems of building up a multi-racial community. To his age and outlook it was an unquestioned assumption that where the British flag had been hoisted, Britain would continue to rule. The Asian inhabitants of every race would have a part to play; the Malays would grow the crops, the Chinese would conduct trade on their own behalf and as the intermediaries of the European merchant. Later, when plantation agriculture was introduced, his successors equally confidently imported many thousands of south Indians to work on these plantations.

But in Malaya itself, beyond the still narrow bounds of British rule, confined to Penang, Malacca and Singapore, the Chinese were busy in another occupation, which had much more political content. Tin mining had been operated by Chinese from the late eighteenth century, or perhaps somewhat earlier, and had become a Chinese monopoly, attracting ever larger numbers of immigrants. They came mainly from the districts around Canton, known locally as the Si Yap (Ssu Yi) or Four Towns. This is an agricultural area lying in the delta of the West River. Mining is not a local industry. It is therefore obscure how it came about that the people of the Si Yap should have become miners overseas and developed in that occupation a specialty which was to carry them to many far-off countries. In later times it was from this area of China that the miners employed in the U.S.A. set out, and they were followed very shortly after by those who went to Australia. The American and Australian Chinese communities descend from these miner immigrants, and in those countries very few of the Chinese from other parts, Teochiu, Hakka or Hokkien are to be found. The names by which California (San Francisco) and Australia (Melbourne), are still commonly known in Chinese reflect this fact. Chiu Chin Shan (Kao Kum Shan in Cantonese), the Old Gold Mountain, is San Francisco; Hsin Chin Shan (Sim Kum Shan), the New Gold Mountain, is Melbourne. Gold was the metal they came to seek; "mountain" means in colloquial Cantonese "island" also, because off the Kuangtung coast, a submerged plain, all the islands are in fact mountains large or small. Any overseas place thus became in popular speech a "mountain", or "island".

In Malaya the Cantonese miners concentrated in the western Sultanates, where they dredge-mined tin in the rivers flowing into the Malacca Straits. The work was hard, but profitable; and the local Sultans and Malay rulers of lesser rank gained a valuable revenue from it, a revenue far in excess of what could be gathered from their other resources, for the country as a whole was sparsely inhabited, and only settled along the river valleys. The Chinese miners conducted their own affairs with very little interference from the Malay rulers, but also with a high degree of independence from their control. Rival secret societies among them led to disputes, and to armed clashes. Rival hopes of rich revenue from mines inspired the enmity of different Malay rulers. The conditions grew more chaotic, the Chinese mining communities were well armed, numerous, and led by men of courage, enterprise and ability. It seemed likely that unless some order was imposed upon the country as a whole it would dissolve into a confusion of warring small states, Chinese and Malay, in constant conflict. Already, by the middle of the century such towns as Kuala Lumpur, Taiping and Ipoh, founded by the Chinese, had become their strongholds.

The Chinese merchant class of the English-ruled Straits Settlements had also prospered and grown wealthy, expanding their business interests beyond retail trade to the marketing of tin and the supply of the mining communities. They had become deeply involved in the economic situation of the peninsula, and were increasingly worried lest the anarchy which was developing would destroy their investments. The pressure which they thus exercised upon the British colonial authorities was at least as powerful a factor as any imperialist ambitions among the British administrators. The British on the spot could foresee an economic crisis

which would impinge directly upon the prosperity of the Straits Settlements, which could not now be disengaged from the economy of Malaya
as a whole. There was another factor. The Chinese of Penang and Malacca,
to a lesser extent of Singapore also, were the longest settled part of the
Chinese in Malaya. They had come to Penang with the British in the late
eighteenth century, and they had been in Malacca under the Dutch and
probably the Portuguese also long before the British acquired that city.
In Malacca, which had been the Ming base in the early fifteenth century,
it is possible, but uncertain, that a Chinese community had existed ever
since that period.

One of the principal sights of Malacca is the old Chinese temple which
is dedicated to the spirit of the great navigator Cheng Ho (known locally
by the southern pronunciation of his official title "Sam Po Kung") and it
is claimed that this temple was founded in the Ming dynasty. It is probable
that the existing building, at least, is rather later, but certainly precedes
British rule. The Chinese of this old settlement were for long periods
unable to bring women of their own race from China, and intermarried
with the Malays. They form a special section of the Chinese in Malaya
known as Baba Chinese, and in customs and dress have adopted some
fashions from the Malays, yet remain in essence a different community,
still counted as Chinese. This assimilation in the past has little parallel
with any such development in later times; it would now be rare indeed
for a Chinese to be able to marry a Malay girl. The religious barrier
between Muslim and non-Muslim is very strictly maintained. Some
Chinese girls have been taken into the establishments of Malay aristocrats,
but the reverse process hardly ever occurs. It is therefore remarkable that
at an earlier period it should have been sufficiently widespread to create
and maintain a rather numerous community of mixed descent. It is, of
course, true that Malacca was a port, a resort of people from all over the
archipelagoes of South-East Asia; the Malay population of the city, under
the Portuguese and the Dutch, were not in any sense a ruling group, but
rather an underprivileged one, and suspect to their European masters.
The interior of Malaya, where the Sultans ruled, was very lightly inhabited. It would seem therefore probable that the Baba Chinese do not
descend on their maternal side from Malays from the countryside, but
from the urban people of Malacca, drawn from many parts of the South-
East Asian region, whereas the Malays of the peninsula are very largely
descended from relatively recent immigrants from Sumatra, a strongly
Muslim region.

The majority of the Chinese merchant class in Penang and in Singapore
were also not of the same origin as the miners. They were largely, but
not entirely, Cantonese, but from the city itself, or from families of

merchant background, not peasants from the Si Yap. These reasons made it difficult for a cohesive Chinese national outlook to grow up among the immigrant community. The Baba may indeed have felt Malacca (or Singapore when many moved there) to be their only home, but they certainly saw the later immigrants as a very different people with whom they had few ties. The Cantonese, Hokkien and Teochiu could not understand each other's speech, and literates were still rare among them. Early, established settlers of these groups also regarded the newcomers, "Sinkeh", as somewhat alien, and in any case poor and inferior. Social prestige in a new country was rated mainly by material prosperity. Thus no national feelings entered into the outlook of Chinese financiers from the Straits who feared the too warlike activity of their fellow countrymen, the miners inland. They were all for the imposition of British control and laws, under which they themselves had grown rich, while in no way partaking in the framing or administration of this legal government.

These aspects of the psychology and traditions of the Chinese overseas are important, for they tended to have a great influence upon the nature and development of the communities. China as a national state exercised in this period no influence of a political nature whatsoever. The Ming dynasty fell in the middle of the seventeenth century, before the British had effectively entered the area, and when the Dutch were still in the early stages of building up their empire: the Portuguese were in full decline. Thus it was from Manchu-ruled China that the Chinese community for the most part had emigrated. Only relatively small groups descended from earlier migrations. The Manchu government for long regarded them as criminals subject to severe penalties, even death, if they returned home. They did nothing for them abroad, and did not care what others might do to them. The colonial rulers were well content that this situation prevailed. They were not inhibited in their policy towards the Chinese by worrying about possible hostile reactions from a distant, but powerful motherland. The Chinese must rely on themselves, trust to the impartiality, or the tolerance of governments over which they exercised no direct influence at all, were indeed remote across distant seas, and could only be moved by the manifest economic advantage of employing Chinese and profiting from their skills and enterprise. This situation put a very strong emphasis on the value of material prosperity, and devalued all other forms of activity, including intellectual pursuits.

Unlike the settlers who at much the same time were leaving Britain and Europe for Canada, the U.S.A., Australia and New Zealand, the Chinese left their homeland without encouragement (indeed in the face of risk or arrest) and came to countries where their own government had no power, and seemed to have no interest. They did not come to lands already under free institutions, but to the colonies of distant imperial powers administered by civil servants drawn from the home country who remained only for the length of their active careers. The Chinese had no rights, political nor social, only toleration. This did not prove to be so disadvantageous a position as it may appear today. As the Chinese had no political backing from their home country, they did not appear to be any sort of political threat to the rule of the colonial power. They showed no aspirations to acquire political power in the countries of their settlement, and were not associated, at first nor for a long period, with any of the local movements of opposition to colonial rule which in any case did not develop until the early twentieth century. They were, usually, good and well-behaved citizens. Their only fault was the rather infrequent but violent faction fights which broke out among them when two secret societies engaged in a secret power struggle. For a long period the colonial authorities were content to suppress these disturbances without attempting to explore their causes or origin.

The Philippines is a country which differs in most respects as to its history from all other parts of South-East Asia, and the history of its Chinese community shares this characteristic. Firstly, when the Spaniards took the islands they were in the pre-literate stage of culture, except for some of the southern islands which had recently been conquered and settled by Muslim Malays from the western islands. There were no other states or organised kingdoms in the Philippines, and the Spaniards were able to introduce their own type of feudal land-holding and European administration of the early sixteenth century without significant resistance or conflict with existing institutions. In effect the natives became the agricultural serfs of the Spanish landowning gentry. The Church was also given unfettered power to convert the population to the Christian faith, and not being resisted, except in the southern Muslim islands, by any organised higher religion, the Church was able to carry out this task in the greater part of the country. The Muslim islands were never effectively reduced to Spanish obedience, and even when the Americans succeeded the Spaniards they had a hard task to impose their authority.

Christian, feudal and Spanish-speaking, the Philippines lacked certain essential features of a viable economy until the Chinese came to supply them. There were no traders beneath the official overseas trade carried on with Mexico and the South American coast, which was the avenue of communication with distant Spain. There were no artisans, no craftsmen, nor skilled workmen. All these occupations had to be filled with Chinese, since the natives had not these skills and the Spanish settlers, few and proud, would not demean themselves with manual work of this kind. So the Chinese community came in to provide the basic needs of everyday life; bricklayers, masons, carpenters, smiths, shopkeepers and restaurant keepers; at every turn it was a Chinese who provided these services. But the Spanish official attitude to them was hostile and suspicious. The Chinese would not easily convert to Christianity; they came from a great country, which was rather closer to the Philippines than to any other overseas part of South-East Asia, and in the seventeenth century China, under the early Manchu emperors, was clearly a great power in the Far East: but not a maritime power, and Spanish fears were thus ill-founded.

The Chinese numbers increased; it was for them a land of opportunity, and the oppressions under which they suffered not seriously worse than those they had experienced at home. They were all from the southern provinces, and these were never favoured by the Manchus. The Spanish population remained small, even the number of troops was very inadequate to the control of such a large area if it had been actively hostile. Making little or no attempt to communicate with these useful aliens, and deeply suspicious of their strength and potential hostility, the Spanish governors heaped more and more restrictions and exactions upon the Chinese until, in 1603, the Chinese made a desperate protest. Believing that this was the long-feared rising and rebellion, the Spanish authorities resorted to wholesale attack upon the Chinese, and massacred almost the entire community in Manila, about twenty thousand men, women and children. The result was to deprive the country of the entire skilled working class and small traders. The Chinese had to be permitted to settle once more, but the Spaniards had learned little. As suspicious as before, they practised the same oppressions, provoked the Chinese to a desperate resistance, and in 1639 again resorted to unrestricted massacre, this time estimated to total twenty-four thousand people. All Chinese settlement ceased, but, as before, the economy of the country ran into immediate disaster. It was necessary to re-admit the Chinese. They settled once more. In 1662, the Ming loyalist Koxinga (Ch'eng Cheng-kung), who was by then master of Taiwan (Formosa) and had briefly revived Chinese sea power, sent an ultimatum to the Spanish Governor-General demanding his submission. A third massacre of all resident Chinese was averted by the intervention of the Governor himself, backed by the Archbishop of Manila, and when Koxinga died the next year, this fear of Chinese intervention passed away.

The Spaniards in the Philippines now realised that they must accept Chinese settlement, but the authorities in Madrid did not yet understand the facts. In 1762 the British had occupied Manila for a brief period, and the Chinese had found the new rulers much more to their liking. When, by the peace treaty which ended this war, Britain gave Manila back in 1764, the Chinese were seen as collaborators with the enemy, and a third, but less extensive massacre took place. Madrid now decided that the Philippines should do without any Chinese. In 1776 all Chinese were ordered to leave the country. Two years later the disastrous consequences forced the Spanish king to revoke this order, and the Chinese returned, soon in large numbers. In 1778 fresh orders for their expulsion were issued, but had to be cancelled before they were actually enforced, when the impending ruin of the economy led to vociferous protests from the local authorities. There is no certainty concerning the size of the Chinese community, when from the latter part of the eighteenth century, they were allowed to survive. By 1850, a century or so later, they were estimated to number fifty thousand, which is probably too low. In 1939, on the eve of the Second World War, the numbers given in the census of that year were 117,000.

Perhaps no other overseas Chinese community suffered so much from the oppression of the colonial rulers, nor occupied such a key position in the economy of the country to which they had migrated. The home government did nothing to alleviate their lot, and took no interest in their fate. Yet they survived, increased and grew to be the most wealthy group in the country, dominating its commerce and industry. The argument that had China exercised her latent power and founded colonies herself, the oppressive rule of the imperial bureaucracy would have hindered their development and inhibited the prosperity of the immigrants, an argument which might have some validity in comparison to the government of Malaya or to the Dutch rule in Indonesia, can certainly not apply to the Philippines. No régime would have oppressed the Chinese more than that of Spain, nor slaughtered them more often. Chinese rule under Ming or Manchu governors might have been corrupt, slack and arbitrary, but it would not have been designed to hamper the growth of the Chinese community and destroy it if possible. The consequences of the abdication of sea power by the Ming, when they had actually reached the point when a Chinese administration could have been set up in the Philippines, unresisted, is the most striking example of the failure of later Chinese governments to take advantage of opportunities which were open to them.

The emphasis on overseas emigration which marks the later phase of Chinese expansion into the southern borderlands is in marked contrast with the comparatively small-scale migration into countries which were in land contact with China itself. The Chinese in Burma went mostly to Rangoon, by sea, not across the land frontier from Yünnan. The end of the great caravan road across Yünnan to Ssuchuan and the Yangtze was Bhamo, in northern Burma, whence goods were shipped down the Irrawaddy to Rangoon and thence across the oceans. But in Bhamo there was only a rather small Chinese settlement of merchants engaged in the furnishing of caravans, and the provision of lodging for muleteers in transit. There was no settlement of Chinese in the countryside, and the small trade and shopkeeping was more in Indian hands than in Chinese. China was only some sixty miles away, but the proximity of Yünnan was only significant for the caravan trade. By this route Yünnan imported some foreign manufactures, mainly cotton yarn, and also some tobacco. China exported mainly raw silk from Ssuchuan, which was shipped down to Rangoon and thence to Calcutta. Burma was merely part of the route taken by this freight, not its destination. The economic impact of Yünnan on Burma was thus very slight, and the reverse was also true. Most of the caravans returning to China carried freight well below the load capacity of their mules. To hire mules going east was easy and cheap; to join a caravan going to Burma was much more difficult and the hire of beasts far higher. Northern Burma was not annexed to the British Indian Empire until 1885, one of the last large areas to come under direct colonial rule. It is not apparent that this political change made any significant difference to the trade between the two countries, nor led to any marked increase in Chinese settlement. It would rather appear that long before the British established their rule the ancient pressure upon the western borders of Yünnan had largely eased and come to stability. British rule in Burma may have stabilised the Burmese side of the line, but did not really impose a barrier to Chinese expansion which had not been there before.

Southern Burma, including Rangoon, had been a British colony for much longer, since 1852. The rather larger Chinese community which then grew up in the capital of the country was not of Yünnan nor west China origin, but formed by immigration by sea from the southern Chinese provinces, just as were all other overseas communities of Chinese. Rangoon was the port beyond Penang; British rule had increased its trade and given the area stable administration. These factors drew Chinese to Rangoon as they had drawn them to Singapore and other newly-developed port cities. The Rangoon Chinese had little to do with the caravans of Yünnan, whose freight was not destined for the Burmese market. In Burma, also, the Chinese found themselves in strong competition, not so much with Burmese as with Indians, who flocked into the country when British rule was established, and had the advantages of knowing the ways of British administration, its legal forms, and sometimes the language of the rulers as well. The Burmese had no great love for either immigrant people. The Chinese skill in trade, and their control of money was, as elsewhere, a source of envy and dislike. The Indians occupied so many of the clerical posts in the administration and in business that Burmese were often a minority in such institutions. Thus the

Indians became a political factor in the later stages of British rule in Burma, whereas the Chinese never had this rôle, and were not numerous enough to create any political minority problem.

The same situation as in Burma arose in Vietnam. Saigon grew into a great city under French rule, from 1859 onwards. Chinese, who do not seem to have been more than a small community in South Vietnam before this, increased rapidly, settling in the almost exclusively Chinese suburb of Cholon, across the river from Saigon proper. This settlement became a very wealthy one, with a large part in the economy of the country, but it was in numbers comparatively small compared with the Vietnamese population, and like other port communities, drawn there by the sea route from south China, not by land across the frontiers. Cambodia had also its Chinese immigration, which was the continuation of a very ancient pattern, noticed in the early fourteenth century by the envoy Chou Ta-kuan. The numbers of Chinese increased under French protection, especially in the cities, although the Vietnamese immigrants always greatly exceeded the numbers of Chinese.

In Cambodia, as in Vietnam, Thailand and also Burma, all Buddhist countries, there was no religious barrier to intermarriage and assimilation, unlike the countries of Muslim faith or, to some extent, the Christian Philippines also. In all these Buddhist countries, with the exception of Burma, where Chinese are relatively few, there has been in the past much intermarriage and assimilation. In Vietnam the Chinese were so outnumbered by the Vietnamese, and the cultural relationship was so close, that assimilation is not easily traced. Chinese who by marriage or circumstances became closely related to Vietnamese simply merged in the larger community.

In Cambodia, where the distinct character of the Khmer language defines personal names much more sharply than between Vietnamese and south China dialects, and in Thailand where the same is true, the large number of surnames which are of Chinese origin even though the people concerned now consider themselves fully Thai, or Khmer, is conspicuous; and in Thailand at least, it is not uncommon to find families who have two sets of names, one Chinese, the other Thai. Families are also quite often divided into branches, headed by different brothers, one of which in business, retains its Chinese name, character and associations, the other, in government service, adopts a Thai name and assimilates to Thai custom. The real number of ethnic Chinese in the country is therefore very hard to calculate, and depends very much on what criteria are used. It is clear that for a long period neither of the two kingdoms felt any prejudice against the Chinese immigrants. They came, undertook the development of resources, increased trade and thus revenue, and were accordingly welcome or at worst easily tolerated by the royal government. Yet it is also evident that although there had been Chinese settlers in Thailand and in Cambodia in the earlier periods, the great influx only followed the development of international trade which in itself was a product of the colonial régimes then arising in the adjoining parts of South-East Asia. The modern Chinese settlers in Thailand, as in Cambodia, are urban, came by sea or up the Mekong from Saigon, and are from the south Chinese provinces like the immigrants elsewhere. The colonial empires were thus everywhere the incentive which brought the great Chinese migration of the nineteenth century into existence. Before they were created trade and commerce were limited, public order was often insecure, the seas were beset with pirates.

Whether alien ruled or native kingdoms the South-East Asian régimes of the nineteenth century welcomed, or accepted Chinese immigration; in most countries it provided an essential ingredient for a developing economy, in almost all it came to control small-scale commerce and later to take a dominant rôle in the learned professions and in industry. Without it this development would have been hindered or never achieved. The climate of the region prohibited any prospect of permanent large-scale settlement by people of European stock, and the traditions and inclinations of the majority race in most of these countries were not directed to the occupations which the Chinese undertook. The Chinese received from their home government no help at all, but every type of interference with their planned emigration, and every range of danger to those who came home again. Yet they persevered, and built up very large overseas colonies of settlers. It was perhaps natural that when the movements for national independence began to stir among the colonial peoples of South-East Asia, they saw with alarm that even with these handicaps, and often others imposed by the colonial rulers, the Chinese had won a dominating place in the economy of their countries, and were also in some areas coming close to a parity in numbers with the native inhabitants. If the Chinese could achieve this despite home neglect, overseas indifference or even hostility, what might not happen if China herself resumed an imperial rôle and backed the possible aspirations of her overseas sons with a new power?

These apprehensions were not at the time as yet very real, but just when the native nationalist movements began to arise, so the Chinese overseas, who had for so long been quite apolitical in their outlook, now became roused by the cause of reform at home. They had always been anti-Manchu in sentiment, remembering the oppressions and neglect their ancestral provinces had suffered under the "alien" dynasty. Now they turned to the republican movement with enthusiasm. Before long, at the turn of the century, Dr. Sun and his colleagues were to discover among the overseas Chinese the ardour and the money to sustain a long series of abortive revolts and conspiracies. The Chinese abroad took as yet no part and had no interest in the politics—such as they were—of the colonies in which they lived: but they did take an increasingly active interest in the politics of their motherland, which all could easily see was now approaching that critical point which seemed to foreshadow the fall of the dynasty. With what it should be replaced was now the real question, and the overseas Chinese were quickly won to the republican cause and belief in its value as the real means of restoring the power of China.

This was a strange development; no overseas Chinese enjoyed any political rights in any of these countries, unless as assimilated Thais or Cambodians they held some office in the royal governments of those countries. Democratic policies were not current in any colony, neither Chinese nor natives had a vote for any assembly. The Chinese abroad had no more experience of democracy nor republican government than their relatives at home. Yet they were readily persuaded that these forms of government were essential for China, and would lead to her recovery and renewed power. But they did not then argue that, if this were so, they themselves should have similar rights in the lands they lived in. Their interest was wholly orientated to the affairs of China.

At that time the colonial authorities were not concerned to suppress the new interest in Chinese politics manifested by their resident Chinese. So long as the Chinese concerned themselves with China, and did not break the peace, nor engage in acts which were openly and actively hostile to a power with which the colonial authorities had normal diplomatic relations, they had no objection to the Chinese subscribing money for a revolutionary party, nor publicising its aims and purposes. With some of these they themselves in part at least agreed. No one was a real friend to the Manchu dynasty—especially after the Boxer outbreak of 1900. Most Europeans, in so far as they worried about China at all, would have agreed that the dynasty should be reformed or replaced by a more modern government. That Chinese in their own colonies took this view and seemed to support democratic reforms was also rather flattering; it suggested that the example of the British (or the Dutch, or the French) way of life was impressing the Chinese, as it should of course, and leading them to appreciate the blessings of European manners of government. That these blessings were at second-hand, and that however democratic the institutions of Britain, Holland or France might be at home, they did not export these practices to the colonies, seems rarely to have been given any attention.

In retrospect it is possible to see that the interest of the Chinese in their homeland politics and their tendency to support liberal or democratic solutions for China's institutional problems was but a prelude to a later interest in their own situation abroad in the future context of independent states when the colonies had passed away. What was right for Chinese in China must, inevitably, be seen as also right for Chinese abroad. The reason for this growth in political awareness, by stages, was the changing condition of the overseas Chinese, both in material circumstances and in intellectual opportunities. The community which had grown up in all these countries from a narrow base of long settled merchants, and enormously expanded through the immigration of illiterate poor, but enduring and industrious peasants, had now become in part well educated, wealthy and sophisticated. It may be that to the Chinese scholar from China itself the overseas Chinese seemed still *nouveaux riches*, brash, uncultivated and provincial; but they were creating an intellectual élite, motivated more by interests in the sciences and professions than in Confucian learning, but for that very reason more in tune with the movement of thought among the young in China than bound by the traditional learning of the past.

At this same time the fall of the dynasty and the Revolution of 1911-12 brought a Chinese government, at first weak and distracted, back into the field of power politics in South-East Asia after an interval of more than three hundred years. At first its activity was marginal and ineffective, but if it long remained so in the political arena, it was otherwise in the sphere of culture, education and national sentiment.

CHAPTER NINE

THE DEVELOPMENT OF THE CHINESE OVERSEAS COMMUNITIES IN SOUTH-EAST ASIA

One consequence of the establishment in the nineteenth century of the European colonial régimes in South-East Asia was perhaps unexpected, and probably unintended. It was to impose still further an artificial separation on a region already divided between opposing cultures and peoples. After the Muslim conversion of most of the Indonesian peoples and the continental Malays (thirteenth–fifteenth centuries), the region of the southern countries with which China had so long been in touch was divided between countries which still retained their Buddhist–Hindu culture, such as Burma, Thailand (Siam), Cambodia, Laos and the isolated island of Bali, which resisted Muslim conversion and has remained Hindu in religion. Vietnam was also Buddhist, but here the form of that religion was Mahayana, as in China and in Japan, whereas the form practised in the other countries of the region is Theravada (Hinayana). Malaya, Java and Sumatra and the Malay settlements along the coast of Borneo and in the southern Philippine islands had been converted to Islam. This division meant more than a change of faith: the Buddhist–Hindu culture retained Sanskrit as a sacred language, and used derivatives of Sanskrit for the script in common use, even though these derivatives differed from each other substantially in each country. The Muslim lands used at that time and until the recent spread of the Latin alphabet a form of Arabic for their script. Thus the division reached into all aspects of the culture, not only the languages were mutually unintelligible but the written forms had become widely different from each other. The Buddhist–Hindu countries still retained much in common in the forms of their art and the common heritage of Hindu myth and legend. On the other hand, the Muslim lands lost all but vestigial remains of their pre-Islamic culture, and became orientated more to Arabia and the Middle East than to India.

European conquest and rule brought new divisions. The various European colonial authorities were under the direction and control of their home governments, and had no independence of action or permanent diplomatic relations with the neighbouring colonial régime under another power. Such relations were conducted, when need arose, between the home governments in London, Paris, The Hague or Madrid. Colonial governors very rarely visited each other, no continuing forms of collaboration existed between one country and its neighbour, even trade was in most cases restricted to the nationals of the ruling colonial power and to shipping under their flag. The educational system and the legal system reflected those of the home countries; internal policies were various and independently evolved. Although sometimes actually sharing a common border, or separated only by a narrow strait, there was less communication between such countries under colonial rule than had they been distant some thousands of miles from each other. Newspapers rarely reported any news from the next country, unless it was truly sensational, and had been already mentioned in the home country journals. Correspondents were not maintained in neighbouring colonies of another power. Above all, when in the later nineteenth century the youth of the subject peoples began to go to Europe for higher education they went as a matter of course to the capitals and universities of the ruling colonial power. Young Indonesians went to Holland, the Vietnamese to Paris, the Burmese, Malays and also Chinese from Malaya and Singapore, to London, Oxford or Cambridge. They returned with a view of European civilisation formed only on these models.

Consequently, the local educational systems became geared to producing students who could profit from higher education in the "home" country, or, by virtue of their knowledge of the language of the ruling colonial people, could be usefully employed in the clerical services of government and business. There was no sense for a young Malay to learn Thai, nor for a Burmese to learn Malay; no Indonesian youth thought of studying the languages of the continental colonies. The schools did not teach these tongues, nor the history of the countries concerned, nor anything else about them. They were in every real sense foreign; there were neither official nor business reasons for learning about their affairs or their culture. Divisions which history and dynastic rivalries had created were accentuated by a complete divorce between the neighbouring countries under colonial rule, not only when these were under separate European governments. Burma was a province of the Indian Empire (treatment which the Burmese continued to resent bitterly), and as such its governor looked to New Delhi for instructions, and its colonial policy, educational system and legal code were those of India. It had no relations with Malaya, although the distance between the southern part of Burma and the northern states of Malaya is very short. British North Borneo and the more or less independent régime of the "White Rajahs" (the Brook family) in Sarawak, although in part inhabited by Malays, came under the

Colonial Office, and had no connections with British Malaya other than trade. The rest of Borneo was Dutch, and therefore "foreign".

It is a curious fact that although, to the modern observer, this artificial division of the region of South-East Asia in this strange way seems to be one of the least desirable inheritances of the colonial era, and one which has done more harm to the unity of these peoples and their political co-operation than any other single factor, it is the feature of the colonial age which is least resented, and indeed actually perpetuated by the new independent successor régimes. The languages of their neighbours, their history and their culture are not taught in the schools nor even in the universities of South-East Asian countries. English, French, even still Dutch, remain the languages of higher education in all these countries. It is still to Europe that their students prefer to go if they cannot get to the U.S.A. Nationalism is apparently stronger than anti-colonialism in this case; it might be thought that with the determined effort to root out European business and government, which has prevailed in many of the newly independent former colonies, there would go a revival of interest in the common heritage which many of them shared, and in which all had some part, before the European conquest. It is not very obvious that this is so to any significant extent. There is attention paid to the local national language and its literature, not to that of neighbours with which it is often intimately connected. The culture of the former dominant colonial power remains in high esteem (as no doubt it should) but this respect is not extended to the similar European influence in the next country. Malays and Indonesians do not learn French; Cambodians and Vietnamese do not (or did not before the Vietnam War) know English. The intellectual division imposed by the form of education established in the colonial period remains intact.

To all this there was one very significant exception: the Chinese. In all the countries of South-East Asia there were Chinese communities, great or small, mostly growing rapidly in the nineteenth and early twentieth centuries. These people were migrants, some of long standing, others very recent, and they came from one or two provinces, although they spoke several distinct dialects. Thus as a people, the Chinese formed the only ethnic group common to all the colonial countries and to independent Thailand. They were not only ethnically distinct from the autochthonous peoples, they had a common culture of their own. They did not become Muslims, nor adopt the local forms of Buddhism, but retained their own religious practices. In the early period they were very largely an illiterate community of small traders and "coolie" labour. But they prospered, and as they became wealthy they at once began to educate their own children in the Chinese traditional method, and in Chinese language and literature.

They advanced to more modern methods of teaching learned from contact with the colonial rulers, but they retained and intensified the Chinese cultural content of the education itself. A young Chinese might learn some Malay to get on with his customers, but he had been taught to read and write in Chinese, kept his accounts in that language, and read a Chinese newspaper. So did his fellow countryman in the next colonial country, and in all the others. Dialects might differ, but the written word in China is above and independent of speech and thus unaffected by dialect pronunciation. Chinese newspapers published in Singapore or Batavia (Jakarta) could be freely read in either country, and far beyond. This gave the Chinese in the whole region a sense of unity, of common interests and of common problems, which was totally foreign to the native peoples, or indeed to their colonial rulers, who had no such common vehicles of information and communication.

The rapid rise to wealth and economic power which the Chinese achieved in these countries during this century (later nineteenth and first thirty years of the twentieth centuries) aroused the envy and even the hostility of the native peoples, and the doubts as well as the admiration of the colonial ruling peoples. It was attributed, no doubt with truth, to the qualities of hard work, patience, endurance, temperance and austerity of the Chinese migrant. It was admitted that he was prone to the vice of gambling by which the fruits of these good qualities were often cast away; but it was always assumed that he had some innate characteristic which made him, commercially at least, inevitably superior to the native peoples, and this must be accepted as a fact of nature. It was compensated for, in the view of many of the early colonial authorities and writers, by the fact that the Chinese were unwarlike, indeed "cowardly". The Chinese would thus always come out on top in a bargain, but never be a serious challenge to political authority. It was a strangely limited view, and one which characteristically showed not only almost complete ignorance of China and Chinese history, but even of local history too. The Chinese who fought each other and Malays in the tin miners' wars of mid-nineteenth century Malaya were not cowards, nor, in the view of those they encountered, unwarlike. Many millions of Chinese in China had always lived in poverty and had no "innate" key to commercial success and economic power. Indeed the classes who had some success in these activities did so against a constant weight of imperial and official contempt and disapprobation, laced with persecution, confiscation and spoliation. There were few if any Chinese millionaires in China when they were already numbered by the score in Malaya, Java and Singapore.

It never seems to have occurred to observers of the Chinese in the "Nanyang" that they had a new advantage, not prominent in the home country, and not shared by the natives of the lands they had come to. In China it was no great advantage to be literate in Chinese, since all Chinese who were literate used only the Chinese language and its ideographic script. Moreover such a high value was placed on scholarly learning that mere commercial literacy was not much esteemed. But in South-East Asia, the Chinese found that their language and their script alone had currency in all the countries in which they settled, among their own folk, forming a kind of exclusive code which no others could, nor for the most part even tried to break. Commercial intelligence could be published in a Java newspaper and read in Singapore, Bangkok or Rangoon—by Chinese, and only by Chinese.

The value of teaching Chinese boys (later girls also) to read the Chinese language rather than that of the people among whom they lived may have seemed chauvinistic and doubtful. But it was overlooked that this acquisition meant that the Teochiu could communicate with the Cantonese, or the Hokkien and the Hakka, and with all the literates whose spoken dialects were less well known than these. Inter-communication between Chinese in different countries, of different provincial origin and spoken dialect was not only possible but easy and natural. The Chinese community became to some degree an inter-colonial community, passing freely from country to country, corresponding on business with distant customers or merchants, learning from its Press the varying conditions of the markets in other colonies. Raffles and other founders of British colonies were often surprised at the speed with which the news of Singapore's foundation, for example, seemed to have spread among the Chinese, who soon resorted to the new entrepôt. This, too, was still in the age when only a few Chinese merchants in the Nanyang were literate. More than a century later some enterprising London brokers who tried, and nearly succeeded, in making a world corner in pepper, were undone at the last moment by a Chinese combine in South-East Asia, who with its intimate local knowledge of the trade and production in these countries, had watched the market and made their own arrangements. One of the secrets of Chinese commercial and economic success in the region of South-East Asia was simply the fact that, with or without the qualities for which they were praised, they possessed an inbuilt advantage in the pervasiveness of their community, its common language and its readiness to use these assets for intercommunication and information.

The Chinese thus became the one ethnic group at home in all the countries of South-East Asia and the best informed about the market and economic conditions prevailing in them at any given time. Yet they remained under the rule of colonial authorities who followed different policies, some more, some less, inimical to the interests of the Chinese, but which they were in any case quite unable to influence or to change. They had no political power; they were very often not regarded as citizens, or as subjects; their own home government did nothing for them, seemed indeed, for a long period, to be positively hostile to them. The Chinese had some admirers, but few friends. In more than one respect this situation did not differ from that encountered many centuries earlier by the first Chinese to push into Yünnan; the pattern of the seaborne expansion was in certain ways related to that which the land migrants had formerly established. The adventurer, the merchant, the pirate, the miner, were among the first; the men of education among the very last to arrive.

The period during which the main overseas Chinese communities in South-East Asia came into being lasted just over one hundred years. Before the early nineteenth century there were older Chinese settlements at a few places, but it was only after the establishment of the colonial empires that conditions were created which favoured large-scale migration. In 1936, following upon the Great Depression of the early thirties, Malaya restricted and then stopped all Chinese immigration: within a very few years the Japanese invasions of all the countries concerned brought further immigration to an end, and since these countries gained their independence after the war their own economic and demographic policies, and in addition the fact that Chinese immigrants would now come from a Communist-ruled state, has prevented any resumption of the movement. Apart from natural growth the Chinese communities were formed as they now are by the middle of the 1930s, which is now a full generation past. It is therefore possible to treat their development during the period of expansion as a chapter which is now over, and complete in itself.

There are very few reliable historical records of the size or location of Chinese settlements before the coming of the Europeans. The Chinese writer Wang Ta-yüan records that at Tumasik, the predecessor of Singapore, there was a Chinese community in 1349. It certainly did not survive the disappearance of the ancient city, for when Sir Stamford Raffles occupied Singapore island in 1819 there were only 120 Malays and 30 Chinese living in the obscure fishing village which was all that remained of fallen Tumasik. But in 1821, only two years later, he recorded with pleasure the rapid growth of the population which now included 1,159 Chinese, some of whom had come by sea direct from Amoy in Fukien province of China, although most had moved in from Malacca. From such small beginnings the Chinese population of Singapore was to rise in just one century to 423,000 in 1921. It is today nearly 2,000,000. The growth of a city such as Singapore in this century is closely paralleled by the growth to similar size of many of the large industrial cities of Britain, the U.S.A., Canada and Australia in almost exactly the same period, and is thus not so much an exclusive function of Chinese enterprise and migration as a feature of the development of modern economies in the age of industrial technology. None the less Singapore became and has remained the main centre of Chinese settlement in the Nanyang, one of the few places where the Chinese form the clear majority, and as such different in character and destiny from most of the other centres and regions of South-East Asia.

Malacca was an older city than Singapore, and had been settled by Chinese possibly as early as the fifteenth century, the period of the great Ming maritime expeditions, but it did not have so peaceful a history. The Portuguese do not seem to have favoured Chinese settlement, and practised a restrictive trade policy. Local records of the population during their period of rule from 1511 to the Dutch conquest in 1641 are lacking, but when the Dutch took the city, which was largely ruined and depopulated in the siege, they found only 2,150 inhabitants of which only 300–400 were Chinese. Dutch rule does not seem to have been conducive to rapid growth either; by 1678 there were only 852 Chinese out of a total population which was still very small, 4,884. One hundred years later the Chinese had increased to 2,161 in 1750. Another century, and under British rule since 1821 the Chinese had grown to about 10,000 and the total population to 67,000. By that time the prosperity of Malacca as a port had passed away; the harbour was silted and too shallow for modern steamers, and its trade, as also, it would seem, many of its Chinese inhabitants, had passed on to Singapore. Malacca remains, however, the oldest centre of Chinese settlement of which there is continuous record for the past four hundred years. It is the home of the Baba Chinese, a race descended on the paternal side from the early Chinese settlers, who took Malay or at least, non-Chinese wives, and who now form a distinctive group speaking a form of Malay which differs widely from the standard language. The formation of this group can be dated at least as far back as the third quarter of the seventeenth century, when Dutch writers noticed the practice of Chinese taking non-Chinese wives. At the last census of 1961 the Chinese formed 41% of the total population of the state of Malacca, but were the strong majority in the city itself, Chinese 53,000, Malays 9,000, but slightly outnumbered by the Malays in the state as a whole (Chinese 120,000, Malays 143,000).

Penang, the first British settlement in South-East Asia, was leased from the Sultan of Kedah by Captain Light in 1785. The island was then uninhabited, or if there were any residents, too few to attract the notice of the founder. Chinese immigration began at once, probably largely from Malacca, down the coast and still under the Dutch. In nine years their number had grown to 3,000 (1794) and Light, like Raffles, welcomed the Chinese migrants as a proof of the coming prosperity of his colony. In Penang also the Chinese did not have women of their own race and inter-married with others; here also, a Baba Chinese population, partly originating in Malacca, developed. Later migration changed this early pattern. Penang became like Singapore an overwhelmingly Chinese city, in 1961 with 171,000 Chinese to 26,000 Malays, while in the state of Penang as a whole, which includes some mainland agricultural territory, the Chinese are also a clear majority; 327,000 to 165,000 Malays. Unlike Singapore, Penang is a state of the Federation of Malaysia, but like Singa-pore a city and region of predominantly Chinese population.

The three cities of Singapore, Malacca and Penang with some mainland territory, the former Province Wellesley, formed for most of the period under consideration the Straits Settlements, and were not politically identified with the Malay sultanates. It was not until 1871 that the British took the mainland peninsula under protection, and the process was not complete until suzerainty over the three northern states was yielded by Thailand to Britain in 1908. The Straits Settlements were thus enclaves of majority Chinese population in a country which was until the later nineteenth century still sparsely inhabited, mainly by Malays. The establishment of British Protection over first some, and later all of the Malay states was both caused by and a condition of a great influx of Chinese migrants, who had come to the country as miners. Before con-sidering the varied history of the Chinese in these states, the general extent of the migration and its consequences can be assessed. It is known from the voyages of Cheng Ho in early Ming times that there were some, probably small, settlements of merchants in Malay port cities. Johore seems to have been the most important and in the late seventeenth century was regarded as the main centre of Chinese trade and settlement in Malaya. There were estimated to be "1,000 families" of Chinese settled there. Chinese influence was still apparent in many ways, dating from the Ming period. In 1783 a British observer noted that the royal guard of the Sultan of Perak was dressed and armed in Chinese style, and the Ming imperial yellow colour was highly honoured. The soldiers were, pre-sumably, none the less Malays, not Chinese. Early in the nineteenth century, still many years before British Protection was established, Chinese miners began to move into Malaya wherever the prospects of tin seemed good.

In Johore, which was one of the last of the Malay states to accept full British Protection (1914), the Chinese from 1830 onward had begun to settle on the rivers of the interior of the state, both for trading and mining purposes, and were recognised by the Sultan, whose revenues they swelled by their activity. These settlements were placed under the headship in each case of a "*Kangchu*", i.e. in Standard Chinese, *Chiang Chu*, "River Lord" who controlled his fellow countrymen and was answerable to the Sultan for peace and order. This system, which continued as late as 1917, seems to have met the need rather better than anything devised in the western states where Chinese mining was soon to become a disruptive factor and lead to serious disorders. As a result of the long continued and relatively harmonious relations which grew up in Johore this state and city became one of the largest centres of Chinese settlement. In the city of Johore itself the Chinese outnumbered the Malays (76,000 Chinese to 54,000 Malays) and in the state as a whole the Malay majority was small (Malays 445,000, Chinese 392,000).

The main Chinese immigration was caused in the first place by the prospect of tin mining, and was therefore concentrated on Johore, and the three western Malay states, Negri Sembilan, Selangor and Perak. The eastern states were not the objective of Chinese migration to any great extent, since they lacked these resources. Negri Sembilan in the early nineteenth century was not one state, but several small ones, usually hostile to each other, and in any case sparsely inhabited. After British Protection was imposed the states were combined to form one sultanate and it is probable that already at that time the Chinese, mainly miners in origin, constituted a very large part of the small population. By the census of 1961 they were the majority in the capital, Seremban (68,000 Chinese to 31,000 Malays) and in the state as a whole almost exactly equal in numbers to the Malays (Chinese 150,000, Malays 151,000). In neighbouring Selangor, which had also been from the early nineteenth century a main centre of Chinese mining activity, the country was slightly populated at the beginning of the century, but from 1850 onwards received a great influx of Chinese. Kuala Lumpur, the capital, and now the capital of the Malaysian Federation, was virtually founded by the Chinese miners and has remained a city of predominantly Chinese population (Chinese 300,000, Malays, 75,000) and in the state of Selangor itself the Chinese, with 488,000 outnumber the 291,000 Malays. It is a pattern which is also found in Perak, the next state to the north, and a major centre of tin mining. In Kinta, the state capital, the Chinese were 244,000 and the Malays 65,000: in the state as a whole the Chinese population of 539,000 had a large majority over the Malays with 484,000.

Thus Chinese settlement had made the western states very largely and in some cases predominantly Chinese in race; in the central state of Pahang the numbers were not far from equal; Chinese 108,000, Malays 179,000, but in the east and north this picture is completely reversed. In these four states, Perlis and Kedah in the north, Trengganu and Kelantan on the east coast, the Malays are a clear and mostly a very large majority out of a population which is smaller than that of the south-western states. In Perlis, a small state, the Malays number 71,000, the Chinese only 15,000; in Kedah the Malays have 475,000, the Chinese 143,000, while in the two eastern states the Malay majorities are very large; Kelantan, Malays 463,000, Chinese 28,000, and in Trengganu, Malays 265,000, Chinese 18,000. In these two states the Chinese communities are small but long established, being traders rather than miners, and Hakka rather than Teochiu or Hokkien.

The consequences of the great Chinese influx into Malaya in the nineteenth and early twentieth centuries were thus to create a new and massive overseas settlement in the former Straits Settlements (Singapore, Malacca and Penang), where the Chinese are in a large majority, and also in the southern and western states of the peninsula, Johore, Negri Sembilan, Selangor and Perak, where the Chinese are an overall majority and in the principal cities this is especially conspicuous. On the other hand the north and eastern part of the country remains predominantly Malay. As it is the area heavily settled by Chinese which is the most developed and the richer, this imbalance has today very significant political importance, and is the source of many of the problems confronting the Federation. Singapore and Penang were virtually uninhabited islands when the British took possession, consequently it is less exacerbating to Malay nationalists to find these places now predominantly Chinese; Malacca had not been in Malay hands for more than three hundred years when Britain took it over from the Dutch; the Chinese, few in number as were the Malay inhabitants also, increased until the two races are now at almost equal strength in the state, although the Chinese are the large majority in the city. Here, too, is a situation which does not represent Chinese infiltration of an old Malay state so much as the development of a former colonial possession: but in the four sultanates of Johore, Negri Sembilan, Selangor and Perak the Chinese influx is relatively more recent, mainly in the second half of the nineteenth century, and was accompanied by wars and disorders on a large scale which were the prelude to British Protection.

Coming from an under-privileged area of China, constantly suspected by the Manchu government of subversion and disloyalty, the Chinese from Fukien and Kuangtung had long been accustomed to look to their own secret societies for protection against official persecution. The secret societies had been originally formed as anti-Manchu resistance organisations; they had had to accept the Manchu conquest, but they did not do so with any goodwill, and became institutions protecting all those who were dissident, engaged in illegal or disloyal activities, and therefore the societies themselves developed this character. The migrants to Malaya brought the societies with them, and in the new land they flourished. No Malay ruler understood Chinese, nor knew anything of Chinese law and custom. The immigrant looked to his society for help, support and protection. As the immigrants were from various districts, so the societies they belonged to tended to become to some degree identified with these regions and their dialect groups.

In the mining states, Negri Sembilan, Selangor and Perak, the Cantonese from the Four Districts (Si Yap) counties close to Canton, were the dominant group and their society was known as the Ghee Hin. Their rivals were Hakka, also from Kuangtung for the most part, and were organised by the Thian Ti (Heaven and Earth Society). This allegiance was more important even than ethnic group and kinship, although, in China, the Cantonese of the original population, known as Punti ("natives") were not at all friendly to the Hakka ("guests" or immigrants) who had come into the country as refugees from the Tartar and Mongol invasions in the thirteenth century. The old enmity lingered, and was exacerbated by rival society allegiance and conflicting economic ambitions. During the decade before 1871 several violent conflicts known as the Larut Wars, since they centred on this mining town, occurred between the two groups. The British, not yet in control, tended to favour the Ghee Hin, Cantonese in the majority, possibly because this group had close business connections with the Chinese merchant communities in the Straits Settlements. The Ghee Hin had the best of the struggle in the early stage, but when it became complicated by disputed successions among the Malay rulers, first in Selangor and later in Perak (Negri Sembilan was not yet an unified state) the rival claimants bid for the support of the warlike Chinese miners, and the two societies tended to back opposite sides.

In Selangor the war which began in 1860 dragged on virtually until British Protection was imposed ten years later, and the British were welcomed and assisted by Yap Tek Loy, head of the local branch of the Thian Ti Society, and himself a Hakka. In Perak in 1871 the Thian Ti, locally known as Hai San, had a victory and drove their rivals from the tin mines. The Ghee Hin counter-attacked and tried to blockade the coast, being backed by the Chinese merchants of the Straits Settlements. This chaotic situation now began to ruin the trade of all concerned; the Chinese coastal merchants were alarmed for their investments, and pressed the British to intervene. Sir Andrew Clarke, Governor of the Straits Settlements, persuaded a rather reluctant Whitehall to permit him to take action, and he then called a conference of all the warring claimants and rival societies at the island of Pangkor, off the west coast. Both Ghee Hin

G

and Thian Ti agreed to submit their cases to British arbitration, and the rival Sultans also accepted the same mediation. From this conference emerged the famous formula, by which the sultans concerned agreed to accept British Residents at their courts "whose advice must be asked for and acted upon in all matters except those touching Malay custom and religion". The terms so briefly stated, carried a very wide meaning, which in effect ended the real independence of these states and established British suzerainty and effective control. It was, however, more than five years before the terms could be fully implemented, and at the cost of the life of the first British Resident appointed.

No settlement could have been achieved, except with the use of large-scale military operations, had the rival Chinese secret societies not been ready to accept one. But they represented tin mining interests and tin must be marketed. The Chinese merchants of Penang, Malacca and Singapore were the agents through whom the tin was sold and who supplied the miners with many necessities. The Malay states at that time had few if any banking facilities, and money must be sent to the Straits Settlements for safety. So the interest both of the rival mining groups and the coastal merchants was similar, and the British were at that time the only power able to impose the peace and order which all groups desired. It is clear that the Chinese could not then look to China, and the possibility that some other European power might step in if the English feared to tread was a factor in inducing the government in London to sanction Sir Andrew Clarke's intervention. It is thus an important fact that British rule over Malaya was not the result of a conquest, as in Burma, but of an agreement to impose order upon a country which was unable to attain this state itself, and which was undergoing a process of very rapid and chaotic economic development and demographic change. The importance of winning the consent of the Chinese societies was illustrated in this early stage of British rule by the fact that in the new state council of Perak the chiefs of the recently victorious Hai San (Thian Ti) and defeated Ghee Hin were alike included as full members. Chinese secret societies were at this time recognised as important political entities which should be, if possible, enlisted on the side of government.

This attitude was to change: secret societies (secret only in the most formal sense that their ritual of initiation was secret) existed also in Singapore, and there, under direct British rule, their activity was less welcome to the authorities. In 1854 there had been a great riot between two rival societies, which had resulted in an estimated four hundred deaths and much destruction. It had taken the British governor by surprise, since neither he nor his officers had any close contact with the Chinese community nor knew the Chinese language. Until 1867 the civil servants were recruited from the Indian Civil Service, and knew very little of either Chinese or Malays. After the transfer of the Straits Settlements from the authority of the viceroy of India to the colonial office and its own appointed governor-general, in that year, the new civil servants thenceforward recruited with a view to the new commitments which the Pangkor settlement had imposed only four years later, were trained to be Malay scholars and to study Malay customs and law. Chinese was still disregarded, because the new generation of administrators tended to view them as transients, and not as natives of the land.

This attitude might have had some justification for the Chinese who were now pouring into the Malay states, but it certainly was quite unrealistic in respect of the Straits Settlements cities, which had been settled from the first by Chinese, and equally in the case of Malacca, where the Chinese had been present for nearly four hundred years. Yet until 1877 there was no officer of the Civil Service who could speak or read Chinese. Even then this branch of the service remained small, and never gained the influence which the Malay-trained members acquired. A result of this imbalance in the British administration was that the Chinese continued to be left very much to themselves, and to their secret societies. In 1889 the secret societies were forbidden and became illegal organisations. No one now believes that this meant their disappearance, nor the loss of their influence among the Chinese people; they merely became in fact, as in name, secret. On the other hand the British administration was perfectly well aware that the societies continued to exist and that various activities, some baneful, others not, must be attributed to their direction.

The political system remained, until after the First World War, entirely colonial and authoritarian. There were no elected assemblies, and no democratic institutions. At this time the Malay rulers, who had the ear of the British, did not want any such innovations, and the Chinese made no political impact upon the administration whatever. Chinese, as they prospered, and became an educated class, tended to take an increasing interest in the politics of the revolutionary movement in the home country which aimed at the overthrow of the Manchu dynasty, but they made no claim for political rights in Malaya nor in the Straits Settlements. Some eminent men were appointed to the Governor's Council, but none were elected to any office. In retrospect it would seem that it would have been wiser for the British to anticipate the tendencies which were already manifest in other parts of their Asian empire, and introduce some forms of democratic government, which could have led the two races, Malays and Chinese (and the smaller Indian minority) to learn to co-operate in political parties and institutions. This might have had the effect of diverting Chinese attention from exclusive reliance on the secret societies as the only organ of national protection outside the official world. It must now seem strange that the British brought into existence, for economic reasons, a multi-national country, but failed to make any provision for the problems which this ethnic character would certainly bring in the future. By the end of the nineteenth century, still more than fifty years before Britain conceded independence, the dual nature of the country, almost equally divided among Malays and Chinese, was clearly apparent. In so far as they acknowledged this fact the Malay-trained civil servants deplored it; they also tried, mentally at least, to ignore it.

Malaysia and Singapore, as the countries in which the Chinese population has won a measure of political power, and very strongly retained its ethnic character while forming the second largest community in a multi-racial nation (the majority in Singapore) have a different character from most of the other countries of South-East Asia, where the Chinese, although numerous, are a smaller minority and have no share of power. There is one exception, which in itself not a large nor very important country, should be considered with Malaysia, of which it is politically a part. Former British Borneo consisted of the protectorate of Brunei, under a Malay Sultan, Sarawak, the domain of the White Rajahs, the Brook family, and Sabah, formerly known as British North Borneo. In the latter two countries Chinese immigrant communities do form a large and economically powerful minority, and they have political rights. Brunei declined to join the Malaysian Federation when it was formed; it has only a very small population in which the Malays, 45,000, outnumber the 21,000 Chinese more than two to one. This state, the declined remnant of the once great state which ruled most of Borneo (and gave its name to the island) now survives in a small area rich in oil. As the former capital of the large state and the headquarters of the conquering Malays who founded it, the population remains still predominantly Malay. This is not the case in the other two territories, which is no doubt the underlying reason why the Malay sultans failed to retain them.

Sarawak had been in effect ceded to Charles Brook who was at first the Sultan's viceroy, but became before long an independent ruler who was able to add large areas to the original state. His descendants continued to rule Sarawak until the country was overrun by the Japanese invasion in the Second World War. After the Surrender of Japan the Rajah in exile, an old man, felt that the problems of reconstruction in a devastated country were beyond his powers, and ceded the country to Britain. In 1956 Sarawak was granted self-government and in 1963 joined the Malaysian Federation. The Brook régime had not discouraged Chinese immigration, in spite of various troubles, notably in 1875 when mis-understandings led to a Chinese revolt which was for a moment a real threat to the government. By the end of the régime the Chinese population had grown to 236,000 out of a total 750,000, which included several indigenous peoples, Dyaks, Dusuns and others, and was already a multi-racial community in which no race was predominant in numbers, although the Chinese were the most numerous.

The Chinese migrants came from a variety of regions and dialect groups in China: the Hakkas, some of whom had migrated from Dutch Borneo, were prominent, but Hokkien, Teochiu and Cantonese are also strongly represented. A peculiarity of Sarawak's Chinese community is the presence in the city of Sibu of a majority of people from Foochow, the capital of Fukien, who are not elsewhere anything but a very small migrant community. Sibu is so dominated by them that it has been nicknamed "New Foochow". The Chinese have a strong political party, Sarawak United Peoples' Party, and one wing of this has been under Communist influence. Their large numbers, not far from one-third of the population, led many Chinese to hope for complete independence and to oppose the country joining the Federation of Malaysia, which they feared would result in political and other discrimination against the Chinese. This apprehension has not wholly been allayed; it is the fact that Sarawak gains economically from membership of the Federation which induces the majority to accept, with some qualifications, the overriding authority of distant Kuala Lumpur. Virtually a "new country", only sparsely settled mainly by the local tribes before the middle of the nineteenth century, the Chinese can and do feel that Sarawak is as much their country as that of any other people. They are the mainstay of the economy, and they expect to play a larger rôle in the government in future. In Sarawak these expectations are in the long run likely to depend more upon the attitude which the native peoples of the country take as their political education advances than upon the wishes of the Chinese or the policies of mainland Malaya.

Sabah, the erstwhile British North Borneo, exhibits a similar pattern. The region was wild, inhabited by tribes in the interior, and on the coast by Malay pirates, who acknowledged in vague terms the suzerainty of the Sultan of Sulu in the southern Philippines. In 1877, after the British Navy had suppressed the main force of this piracy, an English merchant, A. Dent, secured from the Sultan of Sulu a concession over the region in the hope of developing its resources. The question of how far the Sultan had the right to concede anything, and whether this act amounted to a renunciation of sovereignty has lately been in dispute between Malaysia and the Philippines since the end of British rule. In 1881 the British government took over the country from the concessionaires and it became a Crown colony. The shortage of labour was acute and the government encouraged Chinese immigration which soon attained significant numbers. As in Sarawak, the native peoples were divided among several tribes, but of these the Dusun, with 145,000, are the largest ethnic group in the country. The Chinese with more than 100,000 are the second and the remainder of the population, about half (total 450,000), are divided among other tribes with a minority of Malays.

As in Sarawak, and many other countries of South-East Asia, the Chinese are the economic masters, and almost all trade, business and professional work is in their hands. Predominantly, although not exclusively, urban, they have, since self-rule in 1956, and adherence to the Malaysian Federation in 1963, become an active political force often in alliance with parties formed by the indigenous peoples. From the point of view of the migrant Chinese inhabitants Sabah and Sarawak are almost one country, and now that politically they form two states within a Federation, and make up more than one-third of the total population of the Borneo states of the Federation, it is obvious that their cohesion and economic domination in a country otherwise divided among several peoples, some still backward, will before long result in a political influence matching their economic power. The absence of a native people with a long tradition of independent authority and indigenous higher culture makes the situation of the Borneo countries more comparable to that of Yünnan in the Middle Ages than in any other country of South-East Asia. The Malays, who exercised a nominal authority over much of North Borneo, but were in practice only in control of the coastal settlements, were a minority, just as the Thai rulers of Nanchao were a minority exercising suzerainty of a kind over mountain tribes of very varying ethnic composition. It is therefore in the North Borneo states of the Federation of Malaysia that the continuity and relationship between the earlier land migration of the Chinese and the later seaborne migration is most conspicuous.

This situation is very different from that of the Chinese in the Philippines, or in Indonesia, where their numbers may be large, but the proportion they bear to the whole population is small, and their political power either negligible or non-existent. In Indonesia the Chinese number about 2,500,000 out of a population of 95,000,000. Prior to the imposition of Dutch rule the Chinese population was very small, although it had been locally powerful in such places as Palembang in Sumatra from an early age. Dutch conquest was by no means swift nor continuous; as early as 1619 Batavia was founded, or rather renamed and occupied, and the Moluccas, the Spice Islands, taken from the Portuguese. No attempt was made for many years to expand beyond Java; it was not until the eighteenth century that Dutch authority began to be felt along the coasts of the southern part of Borneo and in Sumatra, and not until 1876 that most of the latter large island was brought under direct rule. Even then the fanatical Muslims of the north, Atchin, resisted with success until 1909. Only from that time can it be said that the Dutch were in full control of the whole archipelago which just forty years later they were to yield to the new independent Republic of Indonesia.

In Borneo the Dutch had destroyed the old Chinese trade with the island which had continued for centuries, largely by attacks upon Chinese merchant ships. In consequence by the end of the eighteenth century the migration of the Chinese to that island had sharply decreased, although the settlers already there established their "kongsis" or autonomous régimes under the toleration of the local sultans who still controlled the rivers and such parts of the jungle-covered interior as were settled at all. Early in the nineteenth century the Dutch decided to take control of the mining areas in Borneo, hitherto worked by the Chinese Kongsis, and this led to prolonged hostilities, lasting until 1854. The war ended in the destruction of the Kongsis, and the virtual cessation of all Chinese immigration, although a large population remained. Another consequence was for many years the economic ruin of the country since no other labour force was available, and the Dutch seizure of the mines meant that they could not be economically worked and ceased to produce. It was estimated that there were 150,000 Chinese in what was now to become Dutch Borneo, and many of these were descended from migrants who had come to the country up to a century earlier.

On the other hand the Dutch conquest of southern Sumatra in the first half of the nineteenth century led to massive Chinese immigration following the establishment of the plantation industries, sugar and tobacco. This influx began in 1864 and between 1888 and 1931 300,000 Chinese settled in the island. Settlement in the further islands, Amboyna and the Moluccas, had never been large and remained unimportant in numbers, although significant in economic life. In Java, where the Chinese did not work plantations, there being an ample supply of Javanese labour, the Chinese became merchants, middlemen and at a later date, professional men. In Sumatra they also occupied these positions, but there was a large majority of newcomers who were plantation workers. Thus, at the turn of the century, although Chinese settlement in much of Java was far earlier than in Sumatra (except Palembang and in Borneo, where the inland settlements were long established), the Chinese population of Java was only slightly larger than that of these so-called "Outer Islands", 277,000 for Java and 250,000 for the Outer Islands.

Dutch policy had always restricted the activities of the Chinese. They did not enjoy equality before the law until very modern times; they were restricted in their right to travel without permits until 1910, although

these restrictions were often evaded. The Chinese were more or less con
fined to certain activities, but some of these were not in the interests of th
country as a whole, nor ultimately in those of the Chinese themselve
The Dutch used the Chinese as tax farmers and from this there develope
a vicious system by which the local Sultan made over large estates to th
Chinese tax farmer, who having paid his rent to the overlord, was free t
take what he could get out of the people not only to pay Dutch taxes, bu
for his own profit. The Indonesian resentment against the Chines
undoubtedly stems from this system which continued into the earl
twentieth century. As a result some Java Chinese became very wealthy
and among them there emerged a cultured class clinging to the tradition
of Ming China. Largely derived from Fukien province, these élit
families lived in luxury, and treasured the arts and literature of the home
land which few of them, if any, had ever visited. Resentment against th
Manchus, strong in their province of origin, kept them apart from an
nationalist movement, but equally conservative of their culture. Thi
aspect of the wealthy Java Chinese is not one found in other oversea
communities, except to a much more limited extent among the Chines
of Malacca.

The Chinese of Indonesia were thus diverse communities, conditione
by the varying situations they found in the different islands, and th
varying dates at which the main bodies of the Chinese migration arrived
They remained in the country, but not of it; the Dutch permitted them
only a limited and circumscribed rôle, which tended to emphasise thei
separation from the Javanese and other Indonesian peoples. These in turn
being mainly Muslim, did not assimilate the Chinese, and for economi
causes, partly the result of Dutch policies, disliked the Chinese and saw
them as alien. Yet in hardly any other part of South-East Asia had th
Chinese been settled so long nor grown so prosperous before moderr
times. In 1931 all Chinese immigration was stopped, and for the last
forty years the community, still over two and a half million, has been ir
effect native born, thus tending to wipe out the distinction between old
settlers and new arrivals which was so significant until immigration
ceased. On the other hand it is doubtful whether this change has really
improved the lot of the Chinese under the rule of independent Indonesia
where old prejudices and long-standing dislikes have been translated into
policies of discrimination and even persecution.

The history of the Chinese in the Philippines follows in some ways a
similar pattern to that of the Indonesian communities. Spanish rule was
often harsh and Spanish fears of the Chinese exaggerated. Massacres
occurred, but the dependence of the economy on Chinese enterprise was
even more total than elsewhere since the native Filipino had no high level

of technical skills when the Spanish conquest occurred, and Spanish land policy kept the native peoples in almost serf-like subjection. The Chinese came to form the middle class, shop-keepers, craftsmen and later professional men and entrepreneurs. They were always a minority: 181,000 in 1960, out of a total population of 27,000,000. Neither in Indonesia nor in the Philippines did the Chinese have the numbers in proportion to the whole population to claim a share in political power, which in Malaya, although long ignored, had in time to be granted. This situation is the main and all-important difference between those countries, often with relatively small actual numbers of Chinese settlers, but where these form a very considerable minority of the whole nation, and those where although much more numerous they are still a small minority on the national scale. In political terms it is the difference between potential power and complete exclusion.

There are some countries of a slightly different pattern to these two main divisions among the Chinese of the Nanyang. In Burma, which is contiguous to Chinese Yünnan, the main body of Chinese, in 1931 already as high as 300,000, is found near Rangoon and the south coastal ports, not near the Chinese frontier. They are seaborne immigrants from the southern provinces, not land travellers from Yünnan. They are also only a small minority and have not had the economic power which they have attained elsewhere, since they had to face the competition of Indians under British rule in Burma. The population of Burma is probably nearer sixteen than fifteen millions, and the Chinese with at the outside half a million are thus not a significant challenge. Burma, moreover, a nation with a strong national identity, is unlikely to accept Chinese immigration in such numbers as could affect its ethnic character. Burma was beyond the limit of the main thrust of Chinese land expansion, mainly for the geographical reasons considered in Chapter Three; it is equally at the far limit of the Chinese expansion by sea, and local factors have also restricted the extent and the significance of that movement. The relations between Burma and China, whether more, or less, friendly, are not dependent upon the question of Chinese settlement, but upon the wider factors of national policies.

The situation of Chinese migrants to the former countries of French Indo-China, now Vietnam, Cambodia and Laos, is not unlike that of the settlers in Burma. In these countries there was an ancient land connection, but it was much more significant in political than in demographic terms. After French rule was imposed, and with it a growth in mining and plantation industry, Chinese immigration was for a time large, but was never so important as the migration of the Vietnamese both into the south of their own country and into Cambodia. It was estimated that in

North Vietnam there were not more than 60,000 Chinese in 1963, and about 800,000 in South Vietnam, mainly in Saigon, in 1962. Cambodia estimated 350,000 Chinese in 1961, but Laos only had a mere 30,000. In comparison with the native peoples, even of Cambodia, these figures are a small proportion of the total. As in Burma, the real relationship between China and these countries does not rest on numbers of ethnic Chinese who have settled there in the past century, but on the national status and policies of the countries themselves in the international sphere.

Thailand, however, does not quite fit this pattern. The number of Chinese, or of people of Chinese ancestry, is undoubtedly very large, but the number of those who have assimilated is also high. In 1960, the Thai government records only 400,000 Chinese nationals out of a total population of 26,000,000, but this figure excludes all Chinese of Thai nationality, and also, all persons who although descended from ethnic Chinese ancestors are now Thai in culture and speech. It has been estimated that the former category is no less than 2,300,000, but the latter category is one so elusive as to defy statistical treatment. Families are found in Thailand where one brother may bear a Chinese name and play a prominent part in a Chinese firm or organisation of trade and commerce; his sibling will have a Thai name and hold a public office under the Thai government. The relationship is acknowledged, but the classification of such people on cultural affinities becomes very difficult, and perhaps unreal. Many Thai nationals of Chinese descent take Thai names for business purposes, to avoid the discriminatory laws, but retain their Chinese names and family relationships. There is no question that there is a high proportion of Chinese blood in many Thai families among whom may be found some of the more extreme nationalists, anti-Chinese in word and deed, a feature not unknown in other countries of mixed ethnic origins.

Assimilation was for so long the normal development that it had come almost to blur the distinction between the two peoples, who are not so far apart in ethnic characteristics. Buddhism is the religion of Thailand, and it is no bar to assimilating the Chinese, who are, more or less, Buddhists also, even if of a different rite to the Theravada of Thailand. This distinction has never had the overtone of violence and intolerance which has sullied the Protestant and Catholic churches. For a long period assimilation was encouraged and accepted. It was probably the increased number of immigrants, brought about by the development of sea traffic between China and Thailand which gradually changed the toleration of the early nineteenth century into the discrimination and hostility which has developed since the beginning of the present century. From 1860 onwards the tide of immigration flowed strongly; whereas the earlier immigrants were often wholly assimilated by the third generation, partly because there were few women migrants, the second half of the century saw the growth of a new community strong enough to lead its own life, and indifferent to the attractions of assimilation which had included office under the royal government, titles and power, but which were now faced with the competition of great wealth easily acquired in an expanding economy.

From 1910 onwards the Thai government began to oppose assimilation and was in this policy largely inspired by the personal views of the King Rama VI, who feared that the Chinese would swamp the native race and destroy its identity. These fears were certainly much exaggerated, but in line with ideas which were then prevalent in many circles in the Far East. The difference in the case of Thailand was that as an independent country, local feeling against the Chinese on account of their economic dominance was not modified by the influence of a distant metropolitan power, which often considered that Chinese enterprise was developing a backward economy rather than swamping a native culture and people. Thai policy, already turning to animosity in place of earlier tolerance, was intensified after the *coup* of 1932 ended the Absolute Monarchy and installed the nationalist politicians who have subsequently dominated the royal government. The fall of the Manchu dynasty and the enthusiasm and nationalist fervour which this evoked among the overseas Chinese, including those of Thailand, was seen with fear and suspicion; China, rid of her effete dynasty, might now become a formidable power. The fear was premature in 1912, but history has caught up with it.

From this period the Thai government tended to rely more and more upon an educational policy which depressed and finally suppressed Chinese schools, and compelled all Chinese to study in Thai schools. This policy has been effective in making the Chinese bi-lingual, and probably has diminished the number of those who are, or who might have become literate in Chinese. It is not so certain that it can eradicate national feelings. The importance of language in this connection can be over-estimated; Irish and English today speak English; so do the Americans and West Indians. But this fact has not meant any diminution of the national feelings and sentiments of national identity felt by these different peoples.

Thai policy has thus not yet shown what the future of the Chinese community is to be; it may be that within a generation it will all speak Thai, and no longer be able to read Chinese. But if discrimination based on ethnic origin continues and forces people of Chinese ancestry to see themselves as differing from their neighbours, and under-privileged, the fact of common language will no more assuage bitterness and bring harmony than it did between Irish peasant and Anglo-Irish landlord.

The situation of the Chinese communities in the countries of the
Nanyang had thus reached a turning-point with the end of the colonial
empires and the almost contemporary rise of the Chinese Peoples'
Republic at the conclusion of the Second World War. The situation of
these communities today, and their relations with a newly strong, and
perhaps interested China must next be examined.

CHAPTER TEN

CHINA AND THE NANYANG COMMUNITIES TODAY

The disappearance of the colonial empires of the Western nations, and the subsequent steady decline of their influence and even of their trade with the newly independent former colonies has placed the Chinese settled in this region in an entirely new situation. It is not merely that politically the new régimes are the revived successors of the independent kingdoms of the sixteenth century; that situation, given the re-emergence of a strong rule in China, would perhaps fall sooner or later into the pattern set by the early Ming emperors. The other new factors are the great expansion of economic relations between the Chinese of the Nanyang and the peoples among whom they live, and the great change in the demographic strength of the Chinese communities. Yet another factor is the new, strong nationalism of the local peoples themselves, and the political attitudes which this feeling sustains and inspires. There are other elements also; the Nanyang Chinese are no longer communities of transients; they have ceased to obtain massive increases from immigration for nearly forty years, and the main body of these people are now born in the countries where they live, only the more elderly being direct immigrants from China. In less than twenty years the immigrants will have dwindled to a handful of aged people, and the locally born Chinese will be the overwhelming majority.

The new situation is therefore very dissimilar to that which prevailed under the colonial empires and which was brought about under their aegis. It does, however, in some respects resemble the second stage of Chinese penetration by land which has been considered in earlier chapters. Once more there is a large Chinese population established in an alien land, not under Chinese rule, as in Nanchao. Once more the rulers of this region are rather more hostile than friendly to the government of China, even if this stance has not yet led to wars between them. Again, the resident Chinese have developed the economy and brought a great increase of trade and prosperity. Also, as was the case in Yünnan, the majority of the immigrants have taken to urban life and occupations, leaving the ownership and occupation of the land to the natives. In most parts of Yünnan this is still the situation after more than six hundred years of incorporation with China. Lastly, the immigrant community, at first poor, unsophisticated and often illiterate, has, as in Yünnan, been culturally enriched both by its own growing prosperity and by the advent of a significant number of Chinese of the educated classes. In Yünnan these latter were more often political exiles sent to the remote province by the Chinese government of the day; in the Nanyang they are more likely to be exiles who have preferred to live abroad rather to remain in, or return to China under Communist rule. The difference is not really one of substance when considering the development of the Nanyang Chinese. Exiles of both kinds hoped that some change in the government of China might enable them to return to the capital; they were usually disappointed in the past, and will probably experience the same frustration in the present age. Effectively they will remain abroad and contribute profoundly to the cultural character of the Chinese migrant community.

Nanchao remained hostile until the more pacific Sung renounced any intention of establishing political control; but the infiltration of Chinese settlers and culture continued and increased until, when the Mongol conquerors appeared, the country succumbed to annexation to China without significant opposition. Vietnam rejected Chinese rule, but absorbed the culture. There is no certainty that any country of South-East Asia must follow one or other of these alternatives, and in many respects their situations are so diverse that differing experiences are more probable. Vietnamese nationalism which proved strong enough to expel Chinese political control seems to be at present more in tune with the sentiments of the local peoples than the later supine attitude of the kingdom of Tali, successor to Nanchao. Yet there is here also another significant difference; the Vietnamese are the vast majority in their own country, the Chinese community, small urban and mercantile, resembles more the earlier Chinese settlements in Sumatra and Java than the large diverse settlement in Yünnan. The existence of Chinese communities of almost equal numbers to the native peoples in some parts of South-East Asia, and the importance and strength of those who are in demographic terms only a minority in other lands, makes the situation in this respect more similar to Yünnan under Nanchao than to Vietnam in the tenth century A.D.

Under these circumstances much depends upon the policy which a new and powerful régime in China may pursue towards the countries of the south and the Chinese who live in them. In the period of land penetration, both in Vietnam and in Yünnan, the first policy of the Chinese dynasties, in the Han period, was conquest or imposition of suzerainty without significant immigration or settlement. China herself was not yet fully populated and the urge to move south could still be satisfied within her borders, in Kuangtung. The T'ang were more openly imperialist; they did seek to conquer Yünnan, and they held Vietnam as a province. The Sung renounced the aim of conquest in Yünnan and allowed Vietnam, under a nominal suzerainty, to become independent. It was the alien Mongol conquerors who brought Yünnan into the Chinese empire, and tried, but failed, to do the same in Vietnam. The present rulers of China have thus a choice of policies; they can seek to exert influence without direct political control, occupation or conquest. This is the modern equivalent of the old policy of suzerainty; the former kings acknowledged the Chinese emperor and sent tribute missions, for which they in return received very handsome presents and remuneration. They governed their kingdoms as they pleased, so long as they did not give aid and support to the emperor's enemies. The modern version would have the southern states acknowledge "co-existence" or co-operation with Communist China under régimes not hostile to China, but aloof to all Western power blocs. Attendance at Communist congresses, Chinese national days and other occasions would be expected if not positively required. One may observe these aspects of such a relationship in the cases of North Vietnam and North Korea, and Cambodia under Prince Sihanouk. But neither North Vietnam nor North Korea were, it seems, expected nor pressed to carry out "Cultural Revolutions"; that event being a matter of internal Chinese politics.

The second policy, that of the T'ang, is that which many Western observers fear and many South-East Asians also expect: that China, when fully armed and ready, will engage in policies aimed to bring the countries of South-East Asia, or at least some of them, under her direct political control, either by the creation of wholly subservient Communist governments, or by outright military occupation or conquest. This policy was attempted without success by the T'ang in Yünnan, and also failed ultimately under the successors of the T'ang in Vietnam. Only the alien Mongols finally incorporated Yünnan into the Chinese empire. The third policy was that of the Sung, which was in effect non-intervention, but no restriction placed upon the migration of Chinese to Yünnan and the penetration of the Chinese culture. In Vietnam a nominal suzerainty was all that was required. It is clear that the policy of the Sung was not primarily a policy for the south, but a reflection of the dynasty's preoccupation with the north. The Sung did not fully possess all north China; their enemies the Liao, later the Kin, held the vital passes through the Yin Shan mountains along which the Great Wall is built. They could at any time, and ultimately they did, invade the north China plain and wrest this great region from the Sung. When the Southern Sung had lost north China they became interested in the expansion of trade with the countries of the south, but they did not aspire to rule them.

The policy of a Chinese government is likely to be governed in the future, as in the past, by these unchanging circumstances. Once the intervention of overseas and geographically remote nations in South-East Asia diminishes or ceases, the Chinese will have nothing to fear from the native power of these countries; but they will continue to need to take into account the great power to their north, the U.S.S.R., just as the emperors of the past could never, unless at their peril, ignore the rise and power of some new nomad combination in the Mongolian steppe or the Manchurian plains. One major cause of the Ming abandonment of sea power and their southern policy was the increasing fear of Mongol resurgence and the northern-mindedness of the later Ming rulers. The government of the Peoples' Republic is also established in Peking, and it, too, has deteriorating relations with a great northern neighbour, Soviet Russia. This fact argues in favour of a "Sung" policy; but the intervention of a foreign power of great strength in the south, thus creating another menace, argues in favour of a "T'ang" or at least a "Han" or even a "Ming" policy in the Nanyang. In a less involved age the weight of Chinese friendship was regularly given to those kings of the south who opposed whichever power seemed likely to achieve domination in the region. The policy was an early version of the later "playing off one barbarian against another". On the whole it achieved the results expected: no single powerful kingdom was formed uniting the countries of the south.

American hegemony threatened to produce the modern equivalent of this danger; therefore the Chinese Communist government, in this matter not fundamentally at difference with their imperial predecessors, gave the weight of their support to those movements and states which opposed American domination; North Vietnam, the National Liberation Front of South Vietnam, and the Pathet Lao movement. Whether the reality of American domination is now diminishing, or whether it will be continued by other means than massive military intervention, will no doubt be a problem much under consideration in Peking, and policy towards the southern borderlands will be shaped in accordance with the assessment made. It is in this respect that the attitudes of the resident Chinese in the Nanyang, and of the régimes under which they live, are in the final analysis secondary to the rôle which the great powers, and especially in this context China, decide to play in their own interests, not in those of the peoples of the Nanyang of any race. There is also the consideration that the present clash of policies is in large part motivated by conflicting ideology, although as it continues, this aspect decreases in importance and gives way to the long-standing consideration of national interests. The suppression or the triumph of Communism in the Chinese borderlands is only one aspect of the struggle. No one now expects a clear-cut victory for either side; North Vietnam will not be conquered by its anti-Communist rival in Saigon, and it is improbable that anti-Communist Thailand will succumb to, or accept, a Communist revolution.

The nature of the conflict changes; the British have made it quite plain that the maintenance of the economic system in Malaysia and Singapore which suits their national investment in the area is the real motive for a continuing presence; Burma, which has a government whose internal policies are Left Socialist, tries to keep China at arm's length and is much more afraid of Chinese power than of Chinese economic and social theories. The fact, so long obscured, that it is the existence of China and her power when once more united and strong, which is the key to the future of the Nanyang, is now increasingly recognised: it is also now beginning to be seen that this factor is largely independent of whether China is ruled by this or that type of régime. The importance of the Communist system in the context of China's foreign relations with these countries lies in its use as a modern substitute, or successor, to the ancient system of tributary and suzerain relationship. Common allegiance to Communism (in the manner of Mao Tse-tung) can unite dominant and minor power; while sweetening the tang of a relationship which is in essentials that of strength and weakness. That was, at least, one purpose and function of a common respect for the Confucian system of political philosophy.

In the Nanyang the Chinese Peoples' Republic has inherited a situation which is historically familiar. A long-standing Chinese expansion, commercial, demographic and to a lesser extent cultural, has created in the countries of the south a community which is beyond the political control of the Chinese state, but bound to it by many ties. The Chinese government in the recent past (the last three centuries) did nothing to forward this movement, and often, at first, tried to oppose it. If China is now to be involved, under a new régime, it is involvement in a situation which no Chinese government actually strove to bring about. Previous experience gives precedents for varying policies, but history also records that once a massive Chinese penetration has taken place it is difficult for a Chinese government to ignore it, and that the involvement originally created by independent individuals and the undirected movement of large numbers of poor people seeking a better environment, has in the end brought the Chinese state into the situation where it must choose a policy to meet circumstances which cannot be reversed. The nature of the problem posed to China by the Nanyang Chinese, and the nature of the communities themselves in their new setting of established residents, no longer transients, nor recent immigrants, must be examined if the probable lines of future Chinese policy are to be usefully assessed.

The fact that the Peoples' Republic of China, the Communist-led régime, came to power almost in the same year as independence, or self-government, was won by the former colonies of the Western powers in South-East Asia meant that the situation of the Nanyang Chinese communities was changed in two ways simultaneously. Firstly they became subject to the new nationalist-minded governments of the countries in which they lived, unscreened by the relatively impartial and remote-controlled colonial authorities. In many countries they found that the long-standing dislike or suspicion which they had aroused in the native races was now translated into discriminatory legislation and denial of equal citizenship, not only for immigrants, but also for those born in the country. Secondly they were now under a new suspicion as kindred of the Chinese of China, who had clearly acquiesced in, if not actually warmly welcomed the coming of a Communist government to power. In the early years of the post-war period the belief in the non-Communist world in "monolithic communism" under the direct control of the Soviet Union was very widespread, and constantly fanned by the prevalence and official sanction given to this view in the U.S.A. Consequently since China was Communist, and Communism meant Russian domination, therefore Nanyang Chinese must be suspected of being, or in danger of becoming, a "fifth column" undermining the non-Communist régimes which ruled over them.

There was some slight support for such beliefs, in Malaya particularly, where the Communist Insurrection from 1948 until it faded away ten years later, was recruited overwhelmingly from the Chinese community, and its hard core were the Chinese guerrillas who had resisted the Japanese invasion in the jungles—at that time with Allied assistance and encouragement. But looked at objectively, the Emergency, as it was called, really proved that the danger of a Chinese-led Communist revolution was slight, even if the terrorist guerrillas could for some years create great insecurity and take a high toll of lives. But, in the very years during which the Communists in China were sweeping forward to final victory, the Malaya rebels were unable to establish or secure a single "liberated area"—a territory free from the intrusion, patrols and punitive raids of the government forces. The rebels remained on the run, moving from hideout to hideout, never able to rest for long, soon more and more preoccupied with their need to obtain supplies. The reason was clear; they did not win the support of the Malay peasantry who formed the great majority of the rural population. When the British removed from the fringes of the jungle the Chinese squatter farmers who had occupied these vacant lands to escape from Japanese oppression in the cities, the Communist guerrillas lost the one large group of acquiescent or intimidated peasantry on whom they had mainly relied for support, recruits and food. The true lesson of the Emergency was that a Communist movement led by Chinese in South-East Asia was counter-productive to real revolution; where Chinese led, others would not follow. It was, in fact the Chinese, not the South-East Asian governments, who first understood this truth and acted on it.

In other parts of the Nanyang the Chinese were never prominent in Communist Parties except, later, in Sarawak, where the local Chinese Communist faction attempted with little success to gain control of the Sarawak United Peoples' Party (S.U.P.P.), a party largely Chinese-supported, which emerged as one of the legal political parties after Sarawak obtained self-government in 1956. Local factors, the fear that the 30% Chinese minority would be subjected to discrimination by a combination of the other racial groups, none of which is a majority community, gave this attempt some support, but it is at least very doubtful whether this movement was directly aided or encouraged by Peking. The fears of political subversion that were entertained on somewhat scanty grounds, and the long-standing jealousy and envy of Chinese commercial prosperity and business acumen none the less combined to produce a climate of opinion very hostile to the Chinese communities in Indonesia, the Philippines, and to a lesser degree, in Thailand. In all these countries some of the local leadership had accepted, or supported the Japanese invaders, if only to gain a position of strength before the Allied cause triumphed and the colonial governments came back. But the Chinese had been the declared enemies of the Japanese, the community most persecuted by the occupiers, and the most active in organised clandestine resistance.

This was also true in Malaya and the Borneo possessions of Great Britain, but the British came back, for more than ten years; in that period they did, indeed, undertake a political reorganisation in Malaya which was not altogether popular with the Chinese, who had hoped for more equal treatment, but at least they gave no countenance to discrimination against Chinese business or commerce, and they insisted, as part of the basic terms to be established before they relinquished authority, that the Malay and Chinese communities should prove able and willing to work in harmony a democratic constitution. The Dutch could not, even if they had tried, obtain any such rights for their erstwhile Chinese subjects in Indonesia; Thailand was an independent kingdom where power soon fell to a group of military men rather well known for their collaboration with Japan in the war and their fervent anti-Communist policies in the post-war period. Under these régimes anti-Chinese legislation has been brought into effect, even if it often proves less efficient than might have been expected. The Philippines have continued as an independent state to enforce discriminatory laws against their Chinese minority.

Everywhere, except in Malaya and Singapore, the political situation of the Chinese in the Nanyang was worse after the war than under colonial rule; in matters of economic prosperity and opportunity, this was also true, again with the exception of the former British territories. No government in Malaysia has attempted, or even proposed to pass laws discriminating against Chinese business and commerce; the Malay ruling party, the dominant partner of the coalition which ruled Malaysia until 1969, was content to insist on various degrees of political and civil service privilege for Malays, and to ensure that the Malay wing of the alliance was predominant in government policy. The violent riots, with a strong anti-Chinese character, which broke out in the capital, Kuala Lumpur, in May 1969, after the Malay–Chinese Alliance Parties had met with a marked, but not catastrophic set-back in the general elections, seem to have seriously impaired a communal harmony which was never very deeply rooted. Malaysia is now ruled by an extra-parliamentary group, in which Malays hold the great majority of posts, as a temporary measure, until harmony is sufficiently restored to permit a return to parliamentary democracy. On the basis of experience elsewhere the interim may well be long.

Singapore was driven out of the Malaysian Federation, by pressure from the more nationalist Malays in the Alliance, in 1965; it became a separate nation state, and a republic, within the British Commonwealth, but in effect an independent city state of some two million inhabitants, 85% Chinese in ethnic origin. It has been described as a "Third China", which is a term the Singaporeans deplore. Yet it remains a name which does describe one important fact, that here alone in the Nanyang a Chinese populated area has attained national independence under a government which although by no means exclusively manned by Chinese, is dependent on Chinese votes. It is ruled by a government whose leaders are socialists by profession and long adherence, who were in British colonial days often suspected of being even more to the Left, and potential revolutionaries. Yet this régime has kept its Communist critics to the Left under strict watch and frequent detention, and uses methods which others have criticised as falling short of democratic freedoms. No one denies the great economic progress, and social progress also, which has been achieved since independence. The Singapore ruling party is not always well regarded by the very rich in its own state, but they have learned to live with it, and perhaps to accept that they are better off than they would be anywhere else in South-East Asia.

This then is the general condition of the Nanyang Chinese some twenty years after the fall of the colonial empires, and twenty years after the Chinese Communists came to power in Peking. It is a varying condition, changing with every decade. In the whole region the Chinese are no longer an immigrant people in the sense that they are constantly reinforced by new arrivals. They are stabilised communities which now increase only by their own natural reproduction. Immigration has ceased, mostly for a full forty years. In some countries this change, which has reversed the situation of the past two centuries, has meant that the level of the livelihood of the Chinese population has on an average risen. Cheap and indigent immigrant labour no longer competes to keep wages low. Men must be paid according to their skills, and the Chinese have never lacked skill or the ability to acquire it. Where economic discrimination has been less severe, or absent, the tendency, as in Thailand, is for the Chinese to move into the higher and more international range of business, formerly the monopoly of the Western residents, or, as in Malaya, and Indonesia, the foreign colonial masters. Chinese now engage in banking, export and import trade, insurance and shipping, occupations requiring large capital resources. The discrimination which in Thailand and elsewhere tended to drive them out of such occupations as tin mining, rice milling and small-scale commerce, has led to a movement upward in the economic scale rather than (as it may have been intended by the discriminators) downward. It is comparatively easy to force a Chinese out of control of a tin mine or a rice milling business, a lumbering firm or a large-scale shop; for these occupations others can be found who can make them a going, if not always such a profitable concern. But for the higher range of finance and big business much more is needed both in resources and in abilities. Both the resources and the abilities are still virtually Chinese monopolies in South-East Asia.

On the other hand the existence of discrimination in some degree in all the Nanyang except Singapore tends to make the Chinese, no longer "alien" nor "transient", into a peculiar people, a separate nation within the nation, which should not be what the ruling races desire, but which is the inevitable result of their policies. Even the strong pressure upon Chinese to abandon their own education system, receive education only in the language of the majority nation, and thus lose their distinctive cultural characteristics, is not so sure a method of denationalising the Chinese as these ruling peoples imagine. The examples of England and Ireland show how little identical language matters when two peoples are from political or religious causes separated and mutually antagonistic.

The example of America and England equally shows that the use of the same language in no way overturns the verdicts of history nor leads to reunion, even when relations are excellent between the two nations. Thai-speaking Chinese will, if not given the same legal and political status as Thais, remain just that—Thai-speaking Chinese: a new, minority people.

The same development will in time overtake the Indonesian Chinese, equally deprived of their own language for education and of the now suppressed Chinese Press. The Chinese in the Philippines will form another similar new minority nation. Only in Malaya and above all in Singapore (with Sarawak and Sabah as likely to develop the same way) will the Chinese, by virtue of their near equality in numbers be able to resist and reject this status. They will continue to strive for a truly multi-racial state system, based on equal justice and rights for all inhabitants. It has been shown, by the example of Switzerland, that this is not an impossible ideal; it has also been shown, by the example of many other nations, that it is a very difficult ideal to realise, and that such a realisation is impossible without goodwill from all the races concerned. Equality or near equality of strength and numbers is not necessarily a handicap in the search for just and fair multi-racial harmony. On the contrary, the situation where one race is in a conspicuously small minority is much more likely to cause unrest and difficulty. Malaysia, counting the North Borneo states, has no overwhelming predominant race. Malays are balanced by Chinese, and the addition of the 10% Indian population of the peninsula and the indigenous peoples of Sabah and Sarawak makes the total of the non-Malay population to exceed that of the Malays, but not by any great proportion.

China therefore has been confronted with a situation very different from that which the former Nationalist régime faced in the Nanyang. The Kuomintang relied heavily upon the loyalty to China of the over-seas Chinese. Reversing the Manchu indifference to their condition, it pushed forward an active policy of retaining and stimulating the nationalism of the Nanyang Chinese. China then adopted the *jus sanguinis*, the doctrine that claims that nationality goes by the ethnic descent through the patrilineal line. In popular terms, "once a Chinese, always a Chinese". If in fact many Indonesian Chinese were of non-Chinese descent on their mother's or grandmother's side, it did not matter; their fathers were "Chinese" in language, culture and custom. It was the business of the Nationalist government and its party branches overseas to sustain educa-tion in this language, spread the culture and maintain the customs. This policy met with a great deal of hostility from colonial rulers, and would certainly have encountered head-on collision with the policy of post-colonial independent states. At one period before the Second World War the British authorities in Malaya actually banned the Kuomintang as a subversive organisation. It was then the ruling party in the Chinese government, with which Britain was on friendly terms.

Chinese overseas were also encouraged and indeed pressured into making large financial contributions to the political causes of China itself. The revolution of 1911 had been greatly helped forward by overseas Chinese contributions; the opposition to the warlords by Dr Sun Yat-sen, the anti-Japanese campaigns and rearmament programmes, famine relief, "national reconstruction" and a host of other causes, some worthy, some tainted with political jobbery and plain corruption, were promoted to draw money from the Nanyang. The Chinese themselves in those countries were much more concerned with the politics of China than with those of the countries where they lived. There were no "politics" in colonial countries other than those of subversion, clandestine nationalist aspiration, or the routine service of the dominant power. It was never plain that the Nationalist Chinese, even in the further future, actually contemplated a day when, aided by their countrymen abroad, they would move south with political control or military force. Yet a policy which urged the youth of the Nanyang Chinese through the textbooks they read, and the teachers who instructed them, to think of China as their nation, and themselves as citizens of the Chinese Republic as well as subjects of a colonial empire, was obviously open to the charge of promoting ideas which could pave the way for Chinese rule. It was this aspect of Chinese cultural activity which most alarmed the native peoples, even before they recovered their independence.

Up until the years immediately before the Second World War Chinese immigration continued into the Nanyang in strong stream. It was being checked in some countries, ever since the depression of 1931–2, but in others it continued until the Japanese invasions. It was encouraged by the Nationalist régime in China, and they were thus suspected of building up the Chinese population for ulterior motives. Even if these had been no more than to increase the number of people who would remit part of their earnings to China to support their families at home, and thus bring in valuable foreign exchange, such encouragement was becoming unpopular with the rulers of the colonial empires: but many people, not least the King of Thailand, Rama VI, claimed that much more was at stake. They foresaw a steady swamping of the native by the Chinese immigrant; they possibly knew something of the history of Yünnan; in any case they feared a like outcome to constant Chinese influx.

When the war was over, and the shaky colonial régimes that were able to return soon showed that they had no permanence and would before long yield power to the natives of the land, all these fears revived. It was true that the Nationalist régime was collapsing as fast as the colonial empires themselves, or faster, but this did not allay fear. Its successor, the Communist régime, was very soon obviously much stronger, ruled a united China, which it at once began to modernise with an extensive and intensive plan for industrial revolution. If the Nationalists had professed and tried to practise somewhat ultra-Chinese nationalism in the Nanyang, the new rulers would use the same techniques to promote something much more dangerous—Communism. It was accepted as a matter of established fact that China would lead the Nanyang Chinese into a revolutionary conspiracy against the colonial empires that still remained, or against the anti-Communist successor governments elsewhere. The Malayan Emergency seemed to prove it.

Yet from the first months of the establishment of the Chinese Peoples' Republic the facts spoke otherwise, only very few were willing to take them into consideration, or to try to penetrate the mysteries of the new Chinese policy towards the outside world. Easy assumptions about "world-wide Communist conspiracy" were the soft alternative to hard thinking and careful analysis. When Britain recognised the new Chinese government in January 1950 the event was received with acute alarm by the colonial authorities in Malaya. The Emergency had been in progress for nearly two years; Communist guerrillas, still very active, and far from clearly losing the struggle, were daily taking their toll. But with recognition the Chinese Communist government had the right under international treaties to reopen in Malaya the consulates formerly maintained by the fallen Nationalist régime in Singapore, Penang, Kuala Lumpur and several smaller cities. These consulates had never been too popular with the colonial administrators. They had been foci of nationalist propaganda, fund-raising, and educational and cultural nationalist activities. Now, inevitably it seemed they were to become similar foci of Communist propaganda, secret assistance to the rebels, havens, hideouts and headquarters of subversion, terror and violence. There was no help for it; Britain, interested in trade with China—her abiding and sole national interest in that country—wanted to be able to reopen her consulates in China. This meant reciprocity. Malaya must accept the secret, immune centres of subversion in every major city.

Then a strange thing happened. The Nationalists departed, leaving the vacant premises for their rivals to take over, but China appointed no consuls to Malaya, neither then nor later. Foregoing this major advantage in the cold war she was credited with waging upon the colonial world, China simply made no consular appointments. Equally, she showed no willingness to permit the reopening of British consulates in China; very few were reopened, or continued from the Nationalist régime, and of these before long only one, Shanghai, remained until in the Cultural Revolution it too was violently occupied and closed by Red Guards. China, it seemed, was not interested in the kind of trade that consulates fostered; she preferred nation to nation bargains conducted by diplomatic level ministerial representatives. Whether the failure to open the Malayan consulates was a means of keeping the British consulates in China closed, or had some deeper purpose, was for many years obscure. Whatever the cause, it was a sharp contrast to the activity of the Nationalist government before the war, and in the brief years after the Japanese surrender. It was not taken on that account to portend any real change of policy, nor to diminish the danger and fear of Chinese Communist subversion. There was always the Emergency to testify to the reality of that threat.

Yet a study of that rather little known and rarely read medium, the Chinese Press as it appeared in China itself in the years when the Emergency was at its height, and of the Chinese Communists recently come to power after a triumphant civil war, could have revealed another very strange fact. The triumphant leaders of the revolutionary Chinese people were not acclaiming the heroic resistance of their Chinese compatriots in colonial oppressed Malaya. They were indeed deploring the brutal repression of popular and democratic forces in that benighted colony, but the heroic Communists fighting for freedom, and the oppressed peasantry uprooted from their homes by harsh British police measures, were never, on no account ever, described as Chinese. There was no mention of Chinese participation in the rebel ranks; no hint that the uprooted peasants were Chinese squatters from whom the Chinese Communist rebels obtained their supplies. No; these people, guerrillas or peasants were "Malayans". It may truly be said that when Malays and Nanyang Chinese were both unwilling to sink their communal identities, only the British and the Communist Chinese governments were giving currency to and trying to popularise the new term "Malayan". However there seems to have been very little analysis of why the Chinese should take this line.

It has needed the revelations which came through the operation of the Cultural Revolution in China from 1966 onward to provide the evidence for facts which even with it available, would have been unacceptable to Western Press and politicians fifteen years ago, and even now seem but partly understood. When Prime Minister Chou En-lai, at the Bandung Conference of Asian Nations in 1955 made an offer to all governments ruling Chinese minorities in South-East Asia, to conclude with them a new treaty embodying new principles, provided such governments would recognise the Peking government, or were in diplomatic relations with it, the offer was for the most part ignored, although taken up by Indonesia, but the resulting treaty not ratified for many years. Chou had none the less announced a complete change of policy on the part of China. The *jus sanguinis* doctrine was abandoned in favour of the alternative *jus solis*, the law of locality, which makes nationality depend on birthplace, not on descent. This meant that China no longer claimed "once a Chinese, always a Chinese" but on the contrary proclaimed that those Chinese born abroad ought to be citizens of the land of their birth, and those who had immigrated, if not accepted for naturalisation, must continue to be recognised as Chinese, but aliens abroad, and China herself would be willing to welcome them home. China needed skilled labour, Nanyang migrants had learned skills, let them return and put their abilities at the service of the people of China. China would be ready to negotiate arrangements by which the locally born should renounce Chinese citizenship, if they wished to, and obtain that of the land of their birth. It is known that in Burma, a year later (1956), Chou addressed an audience of overseas Chinese explaining the new policy, and urged his hearers to learn the language of the country where they lived, intermarry with the women of the land, obtain citizenship, abstain from activity in Chinese associations, and refrain from political activity in Burma. What was said of Burma was meant for every country of South-East Asia. China had reversed policy.

Even if this was believed, which on the whole it was not, it was un-explained and seemingly inexplicable. It ran counter to too many well-established prejudices and beliefs. If China did not wish to use nor influence her ethnic kin abroad, then how could she make them into a "fifth column"? If China did not want to promote Chinese education abroad, then how could the national identity of the Chinese be preserved, and was not China surely anxious to do that, to provide herself with instruments for subversion abroad? If China urged her overseas kin to withdraw from all political activity, then how could this fit into her well-known policy of promoting revolution everywhere and especially in South-East Asia? There was only one possible answer to these conundrums: Chou En-lai was trying to deceive his hearers, be they foreign diplomats and heads of state at Bandung, or Chinese businessmen in Rangoon. But why he was doing this; if it was a trick, how the trick was worked, was something which received no explanation. The explanation was in fact simple; it was not a trick, it was a policy.

Since the Cultural Revolution in China in 1966 the policy which lay behind the proposals made at Bandung, the restraint shown in the matter of the consulates in Malaya and the treatment of the Communist insur-rection in that country has been exposed, and violently criticised by the Red Guard tabloid press. The leading exponent and executant of that policy, Liao Ch'eng-chih, Chairman of the Overseas Chinese Affairs Commission, was the main target of attack; he was denounced as a revisionist, taking the capitalist road back to bourgeois society, and was driven out of office and public life. The fact that these same denounced policies were expounded by the Prime Minister, Chou En-lai, and must surely have then represented the agreed views of the inner leadership, has been ignored; Chou En-lai bears a charmed political life. The policies which he then propounded are now described as in effect counter-revolutionary; mass movements in favour of the Communists in the Nanyang were, it is shown, played down in so far as they concerned the Chinese residents. Chinese must be discouraged from open support of revolution, must be urged to obey the local laws and keep out of politics. They could, indeed, be encouraged to remit funds to their families in China, since this brought in useful foreign exchange. Equally, to make this more worth their while, the recipients at home were permitted to enjoy the use of the funds sent to them from overseas, and thus to live like bourgeois off their earnings from the capitalist world. Special rates, favourable to the overseas remitter, and banking facilities for the recipient were made available. This, said the Red Guards, was very plainly a revisionist policy. They were surely right in this assessment.

Why then was it the policy of the Chinese Government, as it equally surely was, during these first fifteen years of the Peoples' Republic? The answer is to be found in the fact that is so often overlooked; China may or may not be a danger in South-East Asia, but South-East Asia is most certainly a very difficult problem for China. The Nationalist Party was prevented by the then weakness of China in the international sphere from encountering the full measure of trouble which their policies were likely to provoke. Had they won the civil war and remained in power after the coming of independence to the former colonial countries, their policy would have come into direct collision with those adopted by the new states, who would have most strongly resisted the implications of the *jus sanguinis* ideal as applied to their resident Chinese. Relations between Kuomintang China and the new states in the south would have been very bad, possibly involving open conflict, certainly disastrous to the Nanyang Chinese. Situations comparable to the Middle Eastern conflict of Arab and Jew would have been more than possible, and the absence of Communism as an issue would have been no more of a palliative in South-East Asia than it has proved to be in Palestine. It is no accident that King Rama VI of Thailand and other sharp critics of the Chinese in the Nanyang had described them as "the Jews of the Far East". It is also perhaps no accident that the rulers of the new Republic of Singapore, when seeking instructors for its new armed forces, found Israelis to their liking.

These were the realities which the Chinese Communist régime faced in 1950, when it had won complete control of all China except the island of Taiwan. Mao Tse-tung, in his work "New Democracy" urges his followers to remember to take account of the "realities we see before us". The policy which he must then have sanctioned, but now permits to be denounced, did indeed do just that. From the point of view of Peking, that new northern-based régime which has inherited so many of the northern preoccupations of its imperial predecessors, the overseas Chinese were much more of a problem than an asset. They presented several unsatisfactory aspects; firstly they lived in distant countries beyond the control of China, and unlikely to come under that control in the foreseeable near future. Thus they could not be subjected to the policies of persuasion and propaganda to the same degree as the citizens of the Peoples' Republic. Secondly they were, to a large extent, capitalists and commercial entrepreneurs, classes inimical to Communist doctrines, and denounced by Communists as parasitical and socially undesirable. So they were not very useful material for Chinese Communists and might prove refractory. Thirdly the overseas Chinese poor, while much more inclined to the Left, and possible material for Communist movements and membership of clandestine parties, were also Chinese, and experience had long shown that Nanyang Chinese revolutionaries were not only suspect and disliked by the local authorities but unwelcome to revolutionary movements of native origin. The P.K.I., the Communist Party of Indonesia, the strongest, oldest and then most influential Communist Party in South-East Asia, was led by Indonesians and gave no warm welcome to Chinese members, whose numbers were minimal. Liao Ch'eng-chih in his directives, now published and denounced, made this point strongly; Chinese Communists in the southern lands were counter-productive, and must be described as natives of the land, not as Chinese. Hence the "Malayan" Communist Party in the Emergency.

Liao enunciated a policy of "Survival". The main objective was to avoid situations which would lead to the persecution of the Chinese communities, and thus place Peking in an embarrassing situation, which it had not the power to prevent nor to cure. If grounds were given for thinking that Peking was building a "fifth column", persecution and repression would be justified and intensified. If Chinese displayed the open pro-China ethnic enthusiasm which the Kuomintang had constantly stimulated, this, too, would rebound upon them, and cause further suspicion of Communist inclinations, for China was herself now Communist ruled. Those who favoured China would be deemed to favour Communism; the two were now inseparable. China could do little or nothing to ameliorate this situation. Most of the new states either did not recognise the Peoples' Republic (the Philippines and Thailand were very hostile to it) or, if they did, as in Indonesia, were swayed by strong anti-Chinese sentiment among the mass of the people. In Malaya the Emergency was a further complication; Britain recognised China, and had reopened trade, which was mutually advantageous, and has continued to grow despite varying political degrees of warmth or chill between the two countries. But the Emergency was a Chinese Communist-led and manned revolt against British colonial rule; in Korea, only one year later, British troops serving under the banner of the United Nations were to be engaged in battles with Chinese troops serving as "volunteers". These transparent disguises were valuable to diplomats and the high policy of governments; they were not so readily comprehended by ordinary people.

Moreover the Chinese of Malaya and Singapore were the largest proportional minority in any South-East Asian country; they were wealthy as a community, they had some political rights and hoped to win more, they suffered from no economic discrimination. There was every probability that when the British relinquished power, as it was soon evident they intended to do, the Chinese of Malaya, and still more certainly in Singapore, would win a rightful place in the new states, influence their policies and partake in their government.

Those who played this rôle would be mainly from the wealthy Chinese classes who were often more educated in British ways and the English language than in their ancestral culture. Even the left-wing socialist politicians of Singapore fell largely into this category. Neither Chinese Communism nor strident Chinese nationalism had a great appeal to these men. They saw their future as leaders of the Chinese communities in the multi-racial states which should succeed to the colonial system.

A policy of pro-Chinese chauvinism or a policy of promoting Communist allegiance among the Chinese overseas would be equally certain to provoke strong reactions, and equally unavailing, since China had not the power to mount overseas expeditions in support of either. Such policies would inherit all the faults and weakness of the Kuomintang policy, and compound them with the new identification with "communist subversion". The difficulty was that the prestige of China had risen tremendously with the restored unity of the country, its manifest embarkation on a sweeping policy of modernisation, social reform and industrialisation, and above all from the results of Chinese intervention in Korea, where for the first time a Chinese army had defeated a Western army, and an American army into the bargain. The battle along the Yalu had a traumatic effect on the minds of Chinese overseas, even in such unpolitical places as Hong Kong. The newsboys selling the first editions of evening papers bringing news of the retreat of General MacArthur's army from North Korea carried two posters; one, in English, read "Grave News from Korea"; the other, in Chinese, read "Glorious Victory of the Peoples' Liberation Army". Cheerful parties to celebrate China's first victory over a Western army since the intrusion of the Europeans one hundred years before were gaily attended by very many people who were themselves recent exiles from Communist China, or who had no intention or wish to return to that country. Peking could not escape these somewhat embarrassing consequences of its own new prestige. The youth of the overseas Chinese were swept by a wave of enthusiasm for the new China. Although, in the post-war world, education was often in need of funds and these could best be supplied by the American Foundations, who would have been more than willing to do so, it was held in Singapore, even some four years later, that no institution dared to accept American financial aid. This opinion was expressed independently by a very senior British official, by an eminent Chinese educator, who was a strong anti-Communist, and by a local Chinese millionaire. It was hardly necessary in these circumstances to enquire into the opinions of students and academic staff.

Liao Ch'eng-chih and the Overseas Chinese Affairs Commission had therefore to cope with some very real problems; on the one hand the suspicion, hostility and discrimination which was either practised or promised against the Chinese community; on the other, the force of ethnic sentiment and the appeal of the new régime in China itself. He and his Commission—by implication the whole Chinese government of that day—are now denounced for flouting ethnic sentiment and repressing revolutionary enthusiasm. In 1955, after the Korean War had been brought to a ceasefire and prolonged armistice, still unconsummated in a peace treaty, the Bandung Conference of Asian Nations, which was attended by Chou En-lai, Prime Minister of China, afforded a stage on which the real policy of China could be exhibited and support for it won. It was the policy of the Overseas Chinese Affairs Commission, the policy of "Survival". China wanted to disembarrass herself of the problem of the overseas Chinese; let those who could nationalise in the countries of their residence, and become true citizens of them, with if possible, equal rights with other citizens. China would not claim them. Let those who could not naturalise under the laws prevailing, accept their status as resident aliens, obey the laws, and wait in hope for better treatment; if they did not expect any, they would be welcome to come home to China, where use could be made of their talents and skills.

A year later, in Rangoon, Chou re-emphasised this policy to a gathering of Chinese businessmen in Burma. He was not then speaking to the heads of states in the presence of the world Press, as at Bandung; he was speaking to a group of influential Chinese resident in Burma, and it was his own

Press, not the Western papers, which gave his speech publicity. If it is argued that the Bandung policy was a trick, which China sought to play upon the Asian leaders, it is not easy to see how the same trick could have been expected to work upon Chinese residents in Burma. The policy which Chou En-lai announced would have been very sweet in the ears of colonial authorities had it been expounded by a Kuomintang Chinese Prime Minister in the years before (or just after) the Second World War. At Bandung it made very little impression. Derided as a trick by the Western Press, and virtually ignored by the South-East Asian states—some of which would on no account accept the only condition Chou made, i.e. the recognition of his government as the government of China—it was tepidly welcomed by Indonesia, the host country, but not ratified for several years until the political pressure of the parties opposed to any equal treatment for the Chinese minority had obtained new legislation which virtually invalidated the provisions of the treaty which were of any value to the resident Chinese. Now not only immigrant Chinese were forever debarred from Indonesian citizenship, but the children of first-generation immigrants were also excluded. Those who could still qualify were to be hedged about by legal discriminations which clearly placed them in a position of inferior status to other citizens.

The policy of repatriation fared no better. Only Indonesia expressed any desire to implement it; and then only with so much obstruction that the total result was perhaps much less than 100,000 persons—some estimates would make it much lower than this—and it failed to meet the problem of the 300,000 Chinese rural traders who were evicted from their shops and the villages in which they lived, driven into the cities in destitution, and often attacked physically, with not a few fatalities, during these procedures. Only a small minority of them were able to leave the country; the rest remain virtually as refugees. The Philippines, where repression and discrimination are comparable to the Indonesian policy, made no attempt to repatriate; her government would have nothing to do with that of China. There was equally no such repatriation from Thailand, and the colonial authorities still ruling in Malaya were not interested in raising so thorny a question. In any case the Chinese of Malaya did not suffer from economic discrimination, even if they did experience political discrimination, and there was no serious movement among them to leave the country of their birth or their adoption. Deportation to China was more of a threat against the revolutionary than a promise of deliverance for the trader.

The policy of Liao Ch'eng-chih, realistic although it must seem, was in fact a failure, and delivered no useful results; the suspicions of China and the fears of Communism were not allayed, since these attitudes are too useful to politicians both in South-East Asia and further west (and south) to be laid aside. The lot of the Nanyang Chinese was not improved, or if it was in some countries such as Malaya and Singapore, it was by their own wisdom and efforts, not by the action, or inaction of China. As the Red Guard critics now say (or rather said in 1966 when they were still powerful), the policy was revisionist, made concessions to capitalist ways and thinking, played down revolution, and deplored expressions of Chinese chauvinism. In a word, ignored the needs and aspirations of the Chinese people of the Nanyang. This, of course, is its cardinal sin. Not even its alleged financial advantages have proved durable; the flow of remittances from overseas Chinese to their families constantly diminishes; exchange controls, the erosion of close family ties by the passage of time and the death of aged people, the doubts which movements such as the Cultural Revolution itself (strongly opposed to this "bourgeois" practice) bred in the minds of the senders of funds, have made it plain that it is a fading asset, which will soon disappear. Vacillation, paralysis, indecision and ineffectiveness, are the verdicts which Red Guard and Cultural Revolutionary have recorded upon the policy of the Chinese government (for such it was) from 1949 to 1966. It is a picture wholly at variance with the accepted set of Western stereotypes of Chinese Communist policy; but it is extremely well documented by the revelations of the Cultural Revolution and cannot now be disproved.

This policy, which, had the non-Communist world been sufficiently free from its own prejudices to appreciate and assess, could have made a great contribution to the peace of South-East Asia, has now been denounced and rejected. What, then, is to be put in its place, or has been adopted already? The answer would seem to be, in short, nothing. The Overseas Chinese Affairs Commission, the organ through which the Chinese government conducted its previous policy, has been inactive since the Cultural Revolution, its staff dismissed, its Shanghai branch overrun by Red Guards in 1966, and it is not even certain that the institution still exists at all. From time to time the Ministry of Foreign Affairs, when occasion required, has issued anodyne statements to the effect that the government of China has always urged its overseas communities to obey the laws of the lands where they live, but these statements have avoided any definitions or more detailed descriptions of what groups of overseas Chinese they are intended to mean. Having formerly eschewed the strong policies which were expected of them, and now permitted the soft—or weak—policy which they actually followed to be criticised and denounced, it would seem that there is now no policy at all.

It must be remembered that the denunciation of Liao Ch'eng-chih and his policy by Red Guards must be seen as more a move in the internal

politics of China than a change in overseas policy. Liao was a party
hierarch, one of the men who owed their rank and careers to the denounced "top Party person taking the capitalist line"—Liu Shao-ch'i,
former Head of the Chinese State. The Party hierarchs, with the exception
of the few who were identified with the Cultural Revolution itself
(notably Chou En-lai) have been driven from power and disgraced. The
policies they followed must be condemned, and aspects of the policy
towards the Nanyang Chinese laid Liao and his followers wide open to
this attack; their policy had clearly failed, as much in Indonesia, with
which country the treaty was actually signed, as with the Philippines
which would have nothing to do with Peking, and in Malaya where the
Chinese as a whole were not interested in this solution to their problems.
It was also a policy which made manifest concessions to capitalism, and
played down revolutionary activity. All this was adequate ground for
denouncing and dismissing Liao. But if pressed further it could be very
awkward; Chou En-lai himself was, on the record, quite as clearly
identified with this policy as Liao Ch'eng-chih; but Chou was aligned
with Mao Tse-tung in the Cultural Revolution, even if he continued to
exercise an influence which was clearly one in support of moderation.
Furthermore the criticised policy had been, obviously, that of the government and Communist Party as a whole in the years from 1950 to 1966; and
during those years Mao Tse-tung was at first both head of the state and
leader of the party, and has retained the second, more significant post until
today.

Ideologically the critics might be right, but practically their implied
alternative would be as disastrous today as in 1950. To encourage revolutionary activity among the Nanyang Chinese, to promote Chinese
ethnic chauvinism, to urge the Nanyang Chinese to manifest their open
support of the "Thought of Mao Tse-tung" would—as it did in Burma in
1966—lead to anti-Chinese riots, the destruction of good relations with
the government concerned, and the spreading suspicion that all the old
fears were proving to be well founded; China was out for subversion, as a
prelude to conquest. Since the Cultural Revolution officially ended—in
triumph—with the Ninth Congress of the Chinese Communist Party in
April 1969, China has begun, with increasing momentum, a new foreign
policy initiative, designed as a first step to repair the damage done by the
extremists among the Red Guards (who have now been disbanded and
vanished from the Chinese political scene), and secondly to pursue some
further objective, still obscure, but very possibly a circuitous approach
to a *détente* with the Western nations which would enable China to con-
front Russia with more assurance. The negotiation of diplomatic recognition with Canada, and the prospect of similar negotiations, and a like

H

result, with Italy, Belgium and Austria; the indication of China's new interest in the seating of Peking's delegation at the United Nations in place of that of the Nationalists, invitations to prominent politicians and officials of Western nations to visit Peking—not presumably for sight-seeing—all these activities have been paralleled by a studious avoidance of involvement in the controversial affairs of South-East Asia, beyond the arena of the Vietnam War. China took no action, nor made any open comment upon the riots in Kuala Lumpur in 1969; one may conjecture what would have been the Kuomintang reaction to similar events in the pre-war period. The new government in Malaysia seems to have recog-nised the meaning of this, and made some indications of a wish for closer, or less uncompromisingly aloof relations, which may indicate an inten-tion to explore the possibilities of mutual recognition.

It is thus at least possible that a new policy is evolving, or has already been adopted, and that it is founded on a new basis. The affairs of the overseas Chinese will not now be the concern of any special organ, but in so far as China must take cognisance of them, will be a factor in her foreign policy towards the country concerned, managed by the Ministry of Foreign Affairs. The principle of "non-intervention in the internal affairs of other countries", frequently invoked ever since first announced at Bandung, will be the guideline. It will imply that the foreign country concerned reciprocates by refusing bases and military facilities to other foreign powers whom China regards as hostile or unfriendly. These are primarily the U.S.A. and Soviet Russia. The U.S.A. may be withdrawing from military commitments on the mainland of Asia; so far, so good; but it is not clear that any such withdrawal of sea power from the south-west Pacific is even under contemplation; and in China's relations with the Nanyang, as all history has proved, it is sea power which ultimately decides the issues. Russia is also deploying an increasing sea power in the Indian Ocean and Pacific; it is important to China that she too should not find easy access to new bases in the countries of South-East Asia. In these calculations, concerned with the vital interests of the Chinese State, the Nanyang Chinese are but marginal. They cannot be effectively helped by intransigent policy, they may be able to survive and prosper by a new, more normal Chinese foreign policy. It is not in the interests of the small or large South-East Asian countries to exacerbate China and create an issue which she could not ignore without loss of prestige.

The founder of the Northern Sung dynasty refrained from the pro-posed invasion and conquest of the declining kingdom of Nanchao in Yünnan, not because it was beyond his strength, but because he did not believe it to be in the true interests of his dynasty and empire, which had grave and unsolved dangers on its northern frontiers. For similar reasons he made no attempt to impose Chinese rule on Vietnam, which had only recently rejected it. T'ang policy had in the end failed; Nanchao remained unconquered, even if deeply penetrated by Chinese culture; Vietnam had rebelled and driven out the long-established Chinese authority although here, too, Chinese culture remained a major force in society. Mao Tse-tung is a keen and deeply read student of Chinese history, which, if he interprets it in accordance with his own ideology, yet has many useful lessons for the statesman in power. It may be that for a time at least, China must adopt the Sung policy, which did result in great expansion of trade and influence in the further countries of China's southern borderlands, and left the Sung a freer hand to meet their northern problems. China remains the most powerful country concerned; in the future a very great super-power; no present accommodation, however conciliatory or restrained, need, or can alter those facts.

What has also remained is the fact of a massive Chinese settlement in the Nanyang; it will not disappear, even if its character and its peoples' aspirations alter. The Chinese are there to stay; on what terms, with what future, will be the concern of the governments under which they live, and may vary from state to state. But it will also inevitably be the concern of China also, sooner or later. Because the South-East Asian countries dislike the presence of large or smaller Chinese communities, and their economic and financial power, they will not at present face the policies necessary to accommodate a phenomenon which they cannot remove; because the Chinese government finds this problem very difficult, and ideologically unsatisfactory, it has failed so far to find a policy adequate to cope with it, and has at times seemed anxious to forget that it existed. A new initiative designed to bring the problem into the focus of diplomatic activity and international relationships rather than ideological or chauvinistic nationalist policies may perhaps in time reconcile the dislikes of the southern countries and the difficulties of the Chinese government, but whether to the advantage, or disadvantage of the Chinese of the Nanyang and their ultimate destiny, remains a matter worthy of some speculation.

CHAPTER ELEVEN

THE PROSPECTS FOR CHINA'S SOUTHERN EXPANSION

It has been shown that there is no certain correlation between the power of a strong Chinese central government and the rate or force of Chinese expansion to the south; under some dynasties, when China was strong and unified, such as the Han, expansion was vigorous, but under others, equally strong within the Chinese empire, such as the T'ang, expansion was halted and ultimately there was a retreat. The relatively powerful Northern Sung refrained from southern expansion, the much less powerful Southern Sung developed commercial and diplomatic contacts in the overseas region which laid the foundation for later Mongol and Ming sea power. The Ming began with a great involvement in the Nanyang; then abandoned it, and with it, Chinese sea power. The Manchu dynasty, one of the most powerful by land, never engaged in sea power politics and in its period of weakness and total disregard, none the less saw the largest expansion of Chinese settlement and economic power in the Nanyang in all history. On the other hand there is evidence that disorder in China stimulated migration, and that consequently periods of weak dynastic rule are sometimes also periods of active southern expansion. A factor which has at all times operated, and still probably does, is that strong central governments ruling all the country were always preoccupied with the danger of their northern frontier, much less so with enemies to the south. It seems therefore that any attempt to equate Chinese southern expansion with long-term objectives and calculated policies breaks down; the forces tending to expansion came from the people, not from their rulers. Now that the government of China claims to interpret the wishes of the people as paramount, it is possible that the policy of government may be harnessed to popular pressure for further expansion to the south.

It is clear that any such expansion must involve an overseas movement; the old areas of Chinese landward expansion are no longer significant. China long ago recognised that the colonisation or domination of Vietnam was unrewarding, and that another type of relationship with this erstwhile cultural colony was more viable. Yünnan is incorporated; Burma is populous and also not easily accessible by direct contact by land.

It is overseas that large Chinese settlements have been formed, and it is the overseas lands of the Nanyang that attract the Chinese migrant in modern times. The situation of those migrant communities today is not privileged, nor in most countries even ultimately tolerable; they are either persecuted, discriminated against, or threatened with such treatment. In some respects their position can be compared to that of the large numbers of Chinese either carried off to Nanchao in wars or conquered and incorporated in that kingdom. There are of course wide differences, but there are also significant similarities, and Yünnan and its history is in many ways a test case for assessing the character and development of Chinese expansion. The captive or conquered Chinese in Nanchao in the ninth century had no political power, nor were they at first able to develop much economic strength either. But gradually, due to their cohesive character, their advanced culture and their membership of a great race in an adjoining strong nation, they gained both political ascendancy and economic domination. The later rulers of the Tali kingdom, successor to Nanchao, were of Chinese descent, although they were not inclined to submit to Chinese rule. The economic life of the country came to be controlled by Chinese settlers, profiting from their widespread connections with China and with each other, and from the diverse character and economic incapacity of the non-Chinese races, even those who had exercised political power. Literary culture became Chinese.

There are aspects of this story which have been repeated in the Nanyang. There, too, the early Chinese migrants had neither political nor real economic power; they were predominantly illiterate labourers, who arrived very poor. They first grew rich, then educated, and later in some of the countries where conditions were favourable, they have also acquired their share of political power. But neither in Nanchao nor in the Nanyang had the power or activity of the Chinese government any part to play in these developments. The Sung refrained from taking any interest in Yünnan; the Manchus abjured any concern with the migrants to the Nanyang. Ultimately the Mongols having conquered Yünnan, the Ming inherited it, and found that Chinese influence, settlement and culture provided a secure foundation for the permanent incorporation of the new province. It has been the fear of some leaders in South-East Asia—whether they were familiar with the history of Yünnan or not—that the course of future events would run on similar lines in their own countries. Since this apprehension lies at the root of much of the policy of these countries towards their Chinese residents and also towards China herself, it is necessary to examine what are the real prospects, so far as they can now be assessed, of further Chinese expansion into the region to the south of the Peoples' Republic.

Since any such expansion can only be enforced against the desire of the ruling peoples of the south, China must first develop power, that is sea power, now almost wholly lacking. The ease and finality with which all Chinese immigration into the Nanyang has been stopped for nearly forty years shows that without Chinese sea power to assure its progress and continuance there can be no real Chinese expansion, and certainly no political domination. The Chinese government today clearly recognises that it can by its own efforts do nothing to ensure that migration resumes, nor that existing migrants are justly treated, nor modify the persecutions which they suffer.

This is, however, a transitory, or at least a contingent situation. There is no reason why the Peoples' Republic should not devote some part of its resources to the creation of naval power or to those associated forms of modern air power which have become complementary and indispensable to naval power itself. All this could be accomplished in a few decades at the most, probably much more rapidly. There are even reasons why, if the new form of the northern menace is seen as Soviet Russia, a modern strong Chinese government concerned with this danger should not find it equally necessary to develop naval power as to maintain military power. The Russians are becoming interested and involved in sea power in the Indian Ocean. These reasons would be reinforced by a continued American withdrawal from Asia. The prospect of creating a significant counter force to U.S. naval power was remote; the need to build such power to challenge any Russian aspiration to succeed to America's position is quite another question, as is the risk that if America went, Japan might take her place. It cannot be assumed that by the end of the century China will still be insignificant as a sea power.

There is also the question, similar to that posed in earlier times by Chinese settlement beyond the frontiers, of whether China can in the long run avoid being drawn into the problems of her migrant ethnic kinsmen and the treatment they may receive from the host countries. Such questions are charged with tense emotions, and it is not always possible for governments to ignore popular sentiment. The fact that alleged slackness in caring for Chinese overseas was the brunt of the accusations brought by Red Guards against the former Director of the Overseas Chinese Commission, Liao Ch'eng-chih, and led to his elimination from political life, is a sign that, even if there were other reasons why his removal may have been desired by the men in power, sentiment on behalf of the overseas Chinese is a political factor which can be used, but cannot be ignored. At present China has, as in this example, denounced the former policy of quiescence without announcing any other; this, too, could be but a very temporary pause. It might be that China considers the risks and costs of a "forward" policy in South-East Asia too great, or not worth the return, or too premature, and that we now see an example of Sung restraint rather than late T'ang weakness. It could equally be that all present policies are still too fluid for precise appreciation. We are in the time of a "new dynasty" as it would have been seen in the past; what the new rulers may do, whether they will take up the policy of their predecessors, or devise another, was often obscure in the early years when power was being consolidated.

The policy of new rulers had none the less to take account of the facts, and the great fact which must govern Chinese relations with the Nanyang is that there is now a large group of Chinese communities established in these countries, already for much more than a century in almost all of them, and that these people will not disappear, and must exercise a continuing influence on the thinking of all Chinese in government in China. China may renounce the policy of the Kuomintang which treated all overseas Chinese as full citizens no matter where they were born, nor whether they had ever set foot in China itself. But this is an outside approach; it does not basically affect the existence nor the character of the Chinese communities themselves. They are no longer groups of poor migrant labourers, but predominantly better off economically and active intellectually; they present an alternative picture of the modern Chinese, not the picture of Mao's choice. In this way they are potentially, not so much a fifth column in South-East Asia, as a centre for possible subversion in China itself, just as they were in the days of the Manchu dynasty. As the Chinese of Singapore continue and progress in their purpose of creating a viable, wealthy, socially just and inevitably predominantly Chinese state, they not only set an uncomfortable precedent before the eyes of some of their South-East Asian neighbours, but they also unconsciously, or consciously, challenge the doctrines of Mao Tse-tung. China could in time find other reasons than the rescue of the Nanyang Chinese for seeking to assert her influence in those countries. The Chinese rulers of Nanchao and Tali may have been Chinese in culture and descent, but they were not disposed to submit to the rule of distant emperors in north China.

These considerations may now seem remote, but it is only much less than a lifetime since any idea of the Chinese of the Nanyang exercising any political power at all in the countries of their residence would have been seen as pure fantasy. It is also doubtful whether the policy of abstention from interference or even protection which China has applied in the recent past, the acceptance of policies designed to denationalise the Chinese, and the apparent willingness to disclaim any allegiance from them, are themselves likely to be effective in removing the issue from the political field. Much evidence from all parts of the world shows that discrimination and persecution strengthens rather than weakens ethnic identity. Deny a people the right to use their language, and if they are forced to use yours, they will become eloquent seditionists in the new medium. To teach people a nationalism in which they are accorded only an inferior status is to ensure that they will develop their own still more intransigent form. There is no certainty, indeed no probability, that by making overseas Chinese learn a foreign language and forego their own, while treating them as inferior citizens, Chinese ethnic identity will be weakened; on the contrary it will be merely transformed into a local manifestation.

Since the end of the colonial empires there has developed in South-East Asia an unstable situation, in the form of a power vacuum. No one local country can impose leadership on the others, and as the experience of Indonesia under Sukarno showed, any attempt to assume such an attitude meets immediate and firm opposition. U.S. power has been deployed in only part of the region, and it would seem probable that it will have been withdrawn before the end of the century. On the other hand there is as yet no certainty that some of the countries of the south, having a multiracial character, can survive as national states. The boundaries which now define their territories are often the result of colonial balance of power rather than historical or ethnic lines. Peninsula Malaya was always historically connected with Sumatra, and a high proportion of the Malays of the peninsula descend from immigrants from Sumatra. Japan proposed to join the two countries together after the war, had she won it; Malay leaders do not seem to have found this plan repellent to their own ideas. The union of all the islands of Indonesia in one state is a consequence of the relatively short period during which the Dutch had pacified and administered the entire archipelago; it has no other historical foundation and no ethnic unity in the outer islands. Thailand holds in its southern provinces a majority Malay Muslim population, not always well content with the rule of Bangkok. The balance between Chinese, Malays and Indians in Peninsula Malaya is very even; in the North Borneo states of the Malaysian Federation there is equally a multi-racial situation with no people predominant in numbers. Burma has its minorities, Karens, Kachins and Shan, who have at times resisted the centralising policy of Rangoon, and are peoples distinct in language from Burmese. Cambodia (which had a large Vietnamese population) and Vietnam itself, north or south, are the most homogeneous countries, even though both have hill tribe minorities traditionally hostile to the valley farmers.

The region which this racial pattern most resembles, and which its political situation, that of several medium-size to small nations recently freed from a long foreign domination, most recalls, is that of the Balkans in the period immediately before the First World War. An unhappy augury; the jealousies and nationalism of those new kingdoms provoked local wars and finally acted as the catalyst for the fatal encounter of the major European powers. It can hardly be ignored that this situation is one which could easily occur in the Nanyang. Indeed the main difference is, once more, the fact of large Chinese settlement in some of these countries. No such massive immigration of the nationals of any of the major European powers, Russia, Austria or Germany, had occurred in the Balkans; local rivalries could be ardently pursued with the hope of enlisting great power support, but not with the added risk of offending one such power by persecuting its migrants: but this risk is precisely the one which might bring about a major conflict in South-East Asia. The Chinese of the Nanyang are too numerous to be driven out, and too intelligent and economically strong to be reduced to serfdom; they must be accepted and brought into co-operation and partnership with the other peoples of these countries. It is a supremely difficult task, one which has only very seldom been carried out elsewhere—Switzerland being the outstanding example of success, and the old Austro-Hungarian Empire the conspicuous example of tragic failure. Yet the German-Swiss and Austrians, the majority peoples in both of these states, were of the same stock, used the same language and shared a common culture.

The outlook for stability is therefore clouded; the possibility that China, even if she continued to desire non-involvement, could escape the consequences of her size, her geographical location, her potential power and her demographic expansion into the Nanyang, and for ever avoid entanglement; or that her government could resist popular pressure if overseas Chinese were under continuing and intensifying persecution, is slight. However at present China could only intervene effectively by land and across frontiers accessible to her own territory. Apart from Vietnam and Laos, this condition applies to Burma, and with short intervening stretches of other territory, to Cambodia and to Thailand. As it happens these are not the countries in which large Chinese resident communities are under great pressure, with the possible exception of Thailand. The countries such as Indonesia and the Philippines, where the Chinese are oppressed, are across the seas, and moreover the Chinese minority, although numerous, is proportionately only a small part of the total population. In Malaysia, both continental and in Borneo, the distances to the one and the sea passage to the other make any direct intervention very difficult if not impossible, and at present there is not the local political situation which would provoke or justify a major operation.

From the Chinese point of view the danger is rather that where she cannot yet go, even if she wished to, others may be able to forestall her, and the consequences of their intervention could be contrary to Chinese national interests. China sees the U.S. military and naval presence in south-eastern as well as in eastern Asia in this light. If the Americans withdrew; and either Russia or Japan, or both, seemed likely to fill the gap, Chinese apprehensions would be even stronger. Japan could thus become once more the enemy; Russia, like the U.S.A., is far away; her presence could be transitory. Japan is there, and will remain, already a potential military power of first rank, with an economy far more developed than China as a whole can hope to achieve for perhaps more than half a century. Japan learned the hard lesson, which the English had learned from Joan of Arc five centuries earlier, that continental empire is an unwise venture for island states. The English, expelled from France, turned to the seas, and found their destiny; Japan could do the same, indeed tried to do so, but made the mistake of pursuing the two aims, continental and naval empire, at the same time, not realising that the two objectives are contradictory. If Japan became the naval power which protected or dominated the island countries of the Nanyang and the parts of the mainland most easily occupied on a limited scale by a sea power—the ports and bases, not the hinterlands—the absence of Chinese sea power would be a complete barrier to any Chinese intervention, and a severe limitation upon all Chinese political influence.

Yet such a situation, in which the Chinese came to fear that a new naval power was established in lands which were of strategic importance to the safety of the Chinese state, is the parallel form of the very cause which brought the Mongols into Yünnan, to outflank the Southern Sung empire, and which impelled the Ming to take Yünnan from the Mongols themselves when the Ming were reconquering China. Yünnan in alien hands could be a menace; independent, it was too weak to resist a conqueror. On the wider scale of the modern world this character can be applied to several of the states of South-East Asia. It has been shown that when China did intervene to impose her own direct rule it was in the interests of the security of the Chinese empire, not in the interests of any group of migrant Chinese. Non-intervention in their affairs, and unconcern over their present condition, would not extend to a situation in which one of the countries where they dwell became a potential base for a major hostile power. A clear understanding of this truth has been the foundation of Burma's neutral stance and careful cultivation of correct, if not always cordial, relations with China. It was also the inspiration of the policy of Prince Sihanouk when he ruled Cambodia.

If the precedents set by the history of Yünnan and Vietnam are seen as having any value for forecasting the future of the Nanyang countries, it has to be recognised that apart from the considerations of national security and strategic aspects, there was another process at work in both those countries, even though it did not have the same result. Chinese never settled in large numbers in Vietnam, for the country was heavily occupied from an early period by Vietnamese; but the Chinese culture and type of government, the religions and the literature, even the language, were introduced and remained as very powerful influences long after political control was terminated. Perhaps as one consequence of this cultural conquest, when Vietnam threw off Chinese rule the new independent rulers never made any attempt to invade, occupy or contest for power in China itself. There were no doubt other factors, but the cultural affinity seems to have acted as an inhibiting force on any Vietnamese ruler who might have been tempted to profit by the periodic weakness of dynastic control in the far south of China, to enlarge his domains by annexing imperial territory. On the other hand the Nanchao rulers of Yünnan had no sooner rejected Chinese suzerainty than they started a war, which endured for more than a century, during which they made repeated invasions of China, seized and annexed large areas inhabited by Han Chinese, and held them for several decades. The kings of Nanchao sought to increase their power by seizing parts of the empire; the kings of Vietnam turned on their non-Vietnamese neighbours to the south and despoiled them of their possessions. The result of the Nanchao policy was ultimately to undermine the distinct character of the state as a non-Chinese country, and prepare the way for full Chinese authority; the result of the Vietnamese policy was to advance the frontiers of Vietnam, bringing Chinese culture as the advance proceeded, and to create a situation where the Vietnamese people gained a national identity which made further Chinese intrusion improbable, rare, and finally wholly discontinued. Cultural penetration therefore produced opposite political results in the two countries.

The assimilation process was also unlike. The Chinese in Yünnan have to a large degree assimilated the non-Chinese population. The old languages have fallen to the standing of local dialects, never used in literature. Chinese surnames are universal, only Muslims retain any form of personal name not of Chinese origin. Yünnanese, although conscious of provincial particularisms, are certainly Chinese in thought, and would not accept any suggestion that they were not fully as Chinese as any other provincial population. But in Vietnam the Vietnamese do not think of themselves as some sort of Chinese, but cling strongly to their own identity; they used to read only Chinese literature and write only in Chinese ideographs; their old government, their way of life, and their religion were all close to Chinese models. But they never accepted direct

Chinese rule with goodwill, and finally ended it by armed revolt. If Chinese troops, stationed in the country, remained there after the political change, they became absorbed into and assimilated with the native race.

How do these conflicting precedents apply to any part of the Nanyang where Chinese are numerous enough to sway the ethnic balance, or influential enough to shape the culture of the future nation? There are probably only three countries where such possibilities are real; Thailand, peninsula and Borneo Malaysia. The Chinese minority in Indonesia has not the numbers: the same applies to the Philippines. In Burma the Chinese minority is quite small: but in Thailand there is no strong religious barrier, as with the Muslims of Malaya and Indonesia, to prevent assimilation, and indeed assimilation has occurred on a large scale in the past. The real number of Thais with Chinese ancestry, at least on the paternal side, remains unknown, but is certainly very large. On the other hand the number of people who now regard themselves as Chinese in Thailand, but who are in fact of Thai descent, is either extremely small, or non-existent. The assimilation model in Thailand works on the lines of Vietnam rather than on that of Nanchao, with the difference that the Thai people did not have the heavily preponderant numbers which marked the Vietnamese situation *vis-à-vis* the Chinese immigrants. Cultural relations show a less certain pattern. Until recent legislation impeded the use of Chinese in operations of commerce, Bangkok used to have the appearance of a Chinese city. Everywhere, everything was written in Chinese, except official notices and inscriptions. Shops, theatres, restaurants, company offices, banks—all commercial and financial institutions and activities appeared to be—and in fact largely were—transacted in Chinese both written and spoken. Much the same was once the case in Jakarta and even in Manila. It remains true in most parts of Malaysia and essentially so in Singapore. Here, then, the operation of the Yünnan model appears more prominent; the use of Chinese as the language of commerce and business in place of the language, or languages, of the native peoples.

In peninsula Malaya the Malays, although only about half the population, dominate politically. The Chinese are equally pre-eminent in all the non-political activities from commerce and business to the learned professions. Some possibility therefore exists of a Yünnan pattern developing over the century to come. The kingdom of Tali, ever more sinified in its institutions and culture, yet endured in independence, thanks to Sung restraint, for another three centuries. It could be argued that Singapore already exhibits the late Nanchao Tali dynasty pattern, a virtually Chinese state, ruled by Chinese, but unwilling to submit to Chinese imperial authority, and so far, enjoying the benefit of a Sung policy restraint on the part of China. In the Borneo states there are also more similarities with the Yünnan pattern than with that of Vietnam. Here there is no dominant race holding preponderant political power, as in peninsula Malaya and Thailand. The Chinese settlers are approximately one-third of the total population, which may well be a higher ratio than the Chinese in Yünnan bore to the natives in the period of Ming conquest. The non-Chinese, with the exception of a small Malay minority, were, and still are, culturally retarded, largely living under tribal systems. So were the non-Chinese peoples of Yünnan in the early fifteenth century, and many thousands of them still live in this way today. They do not form one people in Borneo, they are divided among several tribes and peoples speaking differing languages. So were and are, the non-Chinese peoples of Yünnan. Chinese have not only the predominance in economic life but in cultural and professional life also. So they did, and do, in Yünnan. Now the Chinese in Borneo have their share in the political government of the two states of Sarawak and Sabah, although not perhaps yet the share that some of them think is their due. In the late age of Nanchao Chinese scholars came to power and influence in the king's court; ultimately one of them usurped the throne, and the last dynasties of Yünnan, Tali and the Tuan, were of Chinese stock. On the whole the situation in the Borneo states of Malaysia seems to exhibit marked and strong characteristics of the Yünnan rather than the Vietnam model.

From these considerations of possible future developments in the relations of the Chinese state with the countries of the Nanyang, and with the Chinese migrant communities established in that region, there emerges the conclusion that while the present situation seems characterised by inactivity—a pause—there is very little reason to believe that it has reached a point of impasse which marks the end of Chinese expansion to the south. Such a conclusion would be very rash on such slight evidence, and on so short a period of experience. The Chinese movement southwards has continued, with pauses and spurts, for upward of two thousand five hundred years since it can first be discerned in the spread of Chinese culture, and later political control to the present Yangtze valley in what is now the heart of modern China. The pauses have been shorter than the periods of expansion, even if this movement was often undramatic, individualist, and unofficial. It reached what may have been the end of the direct landward expansion phase in the fifteenth century with the final incorporation of Yünnan and the acceptance of Vietnamese independence. Then the movement turned to the sea, was active in early Ming, went into long recession, when the Ming abandoned sea power, but revived on a very large scale when the colonial powers' need of labour brought massive Chinese emigration to the Nanyang despite the indifference and even outright opposition of the Manchu government. This migration ended just before and with the Second World War.

The southward movement has been one both of men as settlers and also of beliefs, practices and ideas—a cultural migration. In some regions like Vietnam the second characteristic enormously exceeds the first in importance; in others such as Yünnan the force of human migration and cultural colonisation has been approximately equal. In parts of the Nanyang the Chinese have built up large communities but exercise only slight influence on native thinking or custom, and none whatever in political life. The Philippines and Indonesia exhibit this aspect. In other countries proportionately large Chinese minorities are a factor great enough to sway the ethnic balance, and at the same time the influence of Chinese culture and civilisation pervades many aspects of life; such is the condition in peninsula and in Borneo Malaya. The Chinese migrant has both assimilated the native, when the latter was culturally retarded or few in numbers, and also himself become assimilated where the local situation made this easy and no racial or religious obstacle was conspicuous. South China and Yünnan are examples of Chinese assimilation of non-Chinese; Thailand and Cambodia, and to a lesser degree Vietnam, exhibit the assimilation of Chinese by host peoples who—as in Cambodia—are not always ethnically closely related.

The Chinese movement to the south has been, at all periods, a movement of men and ideas rather than of government policy and conquest. When government and military force were used it was either late, as in the final incorporation of Yünnan, or abortive as in the early relations with Nanchao and with Vietnam. The most impressive expansion of the Chinese to the south came at a period when the home government took no interest at all in any such development, and when China was so weak both by land and by sea that even the most concerned government could have done nothing to further the progress of the migration.

So long a process, so diverse in its operation and varying in its local results and consequences, has been shown to be an historical phenomenon in its own right, independent of the rise and fall of empires, the policies of expansive imperialism or cautious restriction. It has, too, been independent of government direction, indifferent to the policy of northern minded emperors, and beyond the control of local sovereigns. Some of these factors may change, temporarily, or permanently, or for a long period; but it seems very improbable that the fluctuating and unstable political situation of our own time is likely to reverse or to halt an operation which has continued for two millennia and more and has never been responsive to political direction, control or restriction.

BIBLIOGRAPHY

Chinese Sources—The Dynastic Histories

Hou Han Shu	C 116	LC 76	South-East Asian kingdoms; Yünnan
San Kuo Chih	Wei Shu C 30		
	Shu Han Shu C 35		Biography of Chu-ke Liang; Yünnan
Tsin Shu	C 96	LC 67	South-East Asia
Sung Shu	C 95	LC 55	South-East Asia
	C 97	LC 57	South-East Asia
Nan Ch'i Shu	C 58	LC 39	South-East Asia
	C 59	LC 40	South-East Asia
Liang Shu	C 54	LC 48	South-East Asia
Nan Shih	C 78	LC 68	South-East Asia
Sui Shu	C 82	LC 47	Vietnam; South-East Asia
Chiu T'ang Shu	C 197	LC 147	Southern Kingdoms
Hsin T'ang Shu	C 222 (three parts)	LC 147	Nanchao; Yünnan; South-East Asia
Sung Shih	C 488	LC 247	Yünnan; Vietnam
	C 489	LC 248	South-East Asia
	C 493	LC 252	South-west barbarians
	C 494	LC 253	South-west barbarians
	C 495	LC 254	South-west barbarians
	C 496	LC 255	South-west barbarians
Yüan Shih	C 209	LC 96	Vietnam
	C 210	LC 97	South-East Asia
Ming Shih	C 313	LC 201	Yünnan
	C 314	LC 202	Yünnan
	C 315	LC 203	Yünnan
	C 321	LC 209	Vietnam
	C 323	LC 211	South-East Asia
	C 324	LC 212	South-East Asia
	C 325	LC 213	South-East Asia
	C 326	LC 214	India; Indian Ocean
	C 304	LC 192	Biography of Cheng Ho

Other Chinese works

Ta Li Hsien Chih	Yünnan; Local Gazetteer of Tali district
Tai Ping Yu Lan	Yünnan; Nanchao
Ch'angan Shih Chi K'ao	Shanghai 1935
Ch'angan Chih	Gazeteer of Ch'angan

Chinese Sources of which
Western Translations are Extant

Tung Chien K'ang Mu, passim., translated into French as *Histoire Génerale De La Chine*, P. de Moyriac de Mailla. Paris, 1778. (Yünnan; Vietnam)

Fa Hsien, *Hsi Yu Chi*, translated as *The Travels of Fa Hsien*, H. A. Giles. Cambridge, 1923. (South-East Asia; India)

Chao Ju-kua, *Chu Fan Chih*, translated as *Chao Ju-kua*, F. Hirth and W. W. Rockhill. St. Petersburg, 1911. (South-East Asia; Indian Ocean)

Chou Ta-kuan, translated by G. Coedes. Bulletin de l'École Française d'Extreme Orient (BEFEO) ll and xvlll. (Cambodia; Angkor)

Chou Ta-kuan, translated as *Memoires Sur Les Coutumes du Cambodge*, P. Pelliot. Paris, 1902; with additional notes T'oung Pao, xxx, 1933.

Ma Huan (Ming Maritime expeditions)

Ma Huan Re-examined, J. J. L. Duyvendak. Amsterdam, 1933.

Ma Tuan-lin, translated by Marquis d'Hervey de Saint-Denys. Paris

SOUTH-EAST ASIA AND INDO-CHINA

Le Fou-nan, P. Pelliot. BEFEO III.

Deux Itineraires, P. Pelliot. BEFEO IV.

History of the Vietnamese Nation, J. Chesneaux. Sydney, 1966.

Les États Hindouisés d'Indo-chine, et d'Indonesie. G. Coedes. Paris, 1948. English edition, *General History of the Hinduized States of South-East Asia*.

History of South-East Asia, D. G. E. Hall. London, 1958.

Histoire Génerale de la Chine et de ses Relations avec Les Pays Etrangers, Henri Cordier. Paris, 1920, 4 vols.

Angkor, Henri Parmentier. Paris.

Cambodia, Indo-China, B. P. Groslier. Art of the World Series. English translation, Methuen, 1962.

YÜNNAN

China's March Towards the Tropics, H. J. Wiens. Yale, 1954.
The Tower of Five Glories (The Min Chia of Tali), C. P. FitzGerald. London, 1940.
The Book of Ser Marco Polo, Sir Henry Yule. London, 1903.

THE MING MARITIME EXPEDITIONS

Ma Huan Re-examined, J. J. L. Duyvendak. Amsterdam, 1933.
Ma Huan Ying-yai Sheng-lan, The Overall Survey of the Ocean's Shores (1433) Translated and edited by J. V. G. Mills Cambridge University Press for the Hakluyt Society 1970.
The True Dates of the Chinese Maritime Expeditions of the early fifteenth century, J. J. L. Duyvendak. T'oung Pao, xxxlv, 1938.
Science and Civilisation in China, vol lv, J. Needham. Cambridge, 1962.
Les Grandes voyages maritimes chinois au début du XVe siecle, P. Pelliot. T'oung Pao, xxx.
Le Relazione Della Cina Con L'Africa Nel Medio-evo, Teobaldo Filesi. Milano, 1962.
Studies in the Social History of China and S.E. Asia, Ed. Jerome Ch'en and N. Tarling. Cambridge, 1970.

THE CHINESE COMMUNITIES IN THE NANYANG

The Chinese in South-East Asia, Victor Purcell. 2nd edition, Oxford University Press, 1965.
Double Identity: The Chinese in Modern Thailand, R. J. Coughlin. Oxford University Press, 1960.
One Hundred Years of the Chinese in Singapore, Song Ong Siang. Revised edition, Oxford University Press, 1967.
History of Modern Malaya, K. G. Tregonning. London, 1964.
Malaya and its History, R. Winstedt. London, 1966.
The Chinese in Thailand, K. P. Landon. New York, 1941.
A History of Selangor, J. M. Gullick. Eastern Universities Press, Singapore, 1960.
Overseas Chinese and the Cultural Revolution. S. FitzGerald. China Quarterly, 1969.
China and the Overseas Chinese: Perceptions & Policies. S. FitzGerald. China Quarterly, 1970.
Communist China and the Education of Overseas Chinese Youth. S. FitzGerald. Canberra, 1970.

MAPS

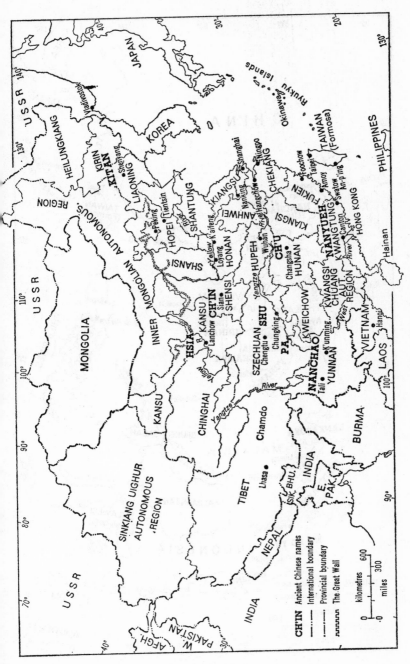

China

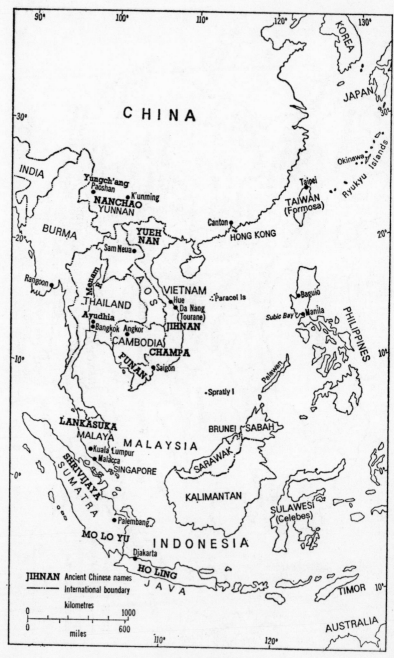

South-East Asia

Burma, Indo-China and The Malay Peninsula

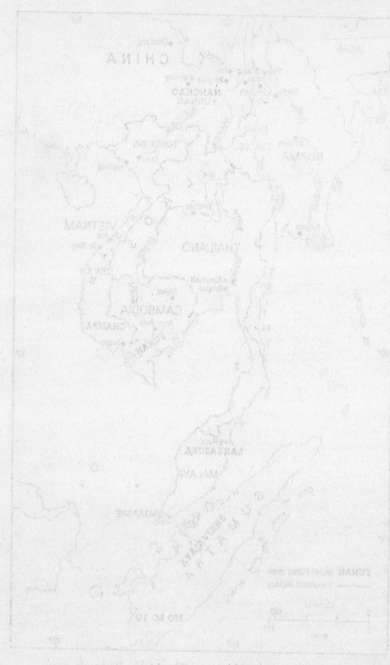

Burma, Indo-China and The Malay Peninsula

INDEX

Africa, 98
Alagakkonam, King, 96
Angkor Thom, 13, 18, 131 et seq.
Angkor Vat, 131 et seq.
Angkorian dynasty, 13
An Lu-shan, rebellion of, 53, 55, 56
Annam (An Nam), 14–16, 19, 24–5, 27, 56–7, 80, 82, 84, 145
Archaeological discoveries, xx, 43, 127
Architecture, Chinese and Cambodian, 123 et seq.

Bandung Conference, 195, 200
Bangkok, 137
Behaine, Pigneau de, 34–5, 36
Black Flags, 38
Borneo, 84, 119, 148, see also Sabah
Boxer outbreak, 159
British in S.E. Asia, 143 et seq., 167 et seq.
Bronze technique (Chinese), 43
Brook, Charles, 144, 174
Buddhism, xvi, 4, 6, 12, 17, 31, 35, 49, 95, 117, 119–20, 135
Burma, xv, xxi, 42, 45 et seq., 65, 68, 77, 80–1, 85, 117, 139, 142, 144, 155 et seq., 162, 179, 187, 210, 211

Cambodia (see also Funan, Chen La), xiv–vi, 2, 3, 9, 12–13, 30, 49, 80 et seq., 117, 118, 139, 157–9, 179–80, 211
Cambodian architecture, 123 et seq.
Caravan routes, 40, 45, 67
Ceylon, 6, 49, 96
Champa, 1–4, 9–11, 14–17, 19, 24, 28–30, 57, 80, 82, 84

Chams. See Champa
Chao Ju-kua, 16–17
Chao Wu, Emperor, 69
Chekiang province, 1, 20–1
Ch'en dynasty, 11, 24, 49
Chen La, 11–12, see also Cambodia
Cheng Ch'eng-kung, 111–12, 154
Cheng Ho, 89, 91–2, 94–8, 101–2, 120, 151
Ch'eng Hua, Emperor, 105
Cheng T'ung, Emperor, 100, 104–5
Ch'ien Lung, Emperor, 33–4
Chien Nan, province, 52
Ch'ien T'ang River, 20
Chien Wen, Emperor, 94
Ch'in dynasty, 1
Ch'in, Kingdom of, 44
Chinese Newspapers in S.E. Asia, 164
Cholon (Saigon), 30
Chou dynasty, xiii, 69
Chou En-lai, 23, 195, 197, 200–1
Chou Ta-Kuan, 83, 133–5
Chou Ying, 8, 9
Christianity, 31–3
Ch'u, Kingdom of, 42–3
Chu Fan Chih, 16
Chu-ko Liang, 47–8
Chu Yuan-chang (Hung Wu), 86, 91–2
Chuang Ch'iao, 43–4
Cinggis. See Genghiz Khan
Clarke, Sir Andrew, 143, 171–2
Compass, maritime, 8, 17, 86, 89
Conference of Asian Nations, Bandung, 195, 200
Confucianism, 122–3
Cultural revolution, 195 et seq.

227

KMT OSC poby — 192-3